INSIDE MACINTOSH

Memory

Addison-Wesley Publishing Company

Reading, Massachusetts Menlo Park, California New York
Don Mills, Ontario Wokingham, England Amsterdam Bonn
Sydney Singapore Tokyo Madrid San Juan
Paris Seoul Milan Mexico City Taipei

Apple Computer, Inc.
20525 Mariani Avenue
Cupertino, CA 95014-6299
408-996-1010

Simultaneously published in the United States and Canada.

The paper used in this book meets the EPA standards for recycled fiber.

ISBN 0-201-63240-3
1 2 3 4 5 6 7 8 9-MU-9695949392
First Printing, August 1992

Contents

Chapter 2 Memory Manager 2-1

Chapter 3 Virtual Memory Manager 3-1

Chapter 4 Memory Management Utilities 4-1

Figures, Tables, and Listings

About This Book

This book, *Inside Macintosh: Memory,* describes the parts of the Macintosh Operating System that allow you to allocate memory directly, release it, or otherwise manipulate it. The book includes introductory material about managing memory on Macintosh computers as well as a complete technical reference to the Memory Manager, the Virtual Memory Manager, and other memory-related services provided by the system software.

If you are new to programming on the Macintosh Operating System, you should begin with the chapter "Introduction to Memory Management." This chapter provides a general introduction to memory management on Macintosh computers. It describes how the Operating System organizes and manages the available memory, and it shows how you can use the services provided by the Memory Manager and other system software components to manage the memory in your application partition effectively. Because this chapter is designed to be largely self-contained, the reference and summary sections in this chapter are subsets of the corresponding sections from the other chapters in this book.

Once you are familiar with basic memory management on Macintosh computers, you should look at the chapter "Memory Manager." It describes how to allocate memory outside your application partition and how to perform more advanced memory operations than are described in the introductory chapter.

The chapter "Virtual Memory Manager" describes the operation of virtual memory and describes the routines that you can use to intervene in the otherwise automatic operations of the Virtual Memory Manager. Most applications are not affected by the operation of virtual memory and do not need to use the routines provided by the Virtual Memory Manager. If your application sends memory addresses to some NuBus™ master hardware, however, you should read the discussion of mapping virtual to physical addresses in that chapter.

The final chapter in this book, "Memory Management Utilities," describes a number of utility routines provided by the system software. You need to read this chapter primarily if you install routines that are executed by system software routines or in response to an interrupt, or if you need to change the addressing mode. You also need to read this chapter if your application might be affected by the normal operation of the processor's instruction or data caches.

Format of a Typical Chapter

Almost all chapters in this book follow a standard structure. For example, the Memory Manager chapter contains these sections:

- "About the Memory Manager." This section provides an overview of the features provided by the Memory Manager.
- "Using the Memory Manager." This section describes the tasks you can accomplish using the Memory Manager. It describes how to use the most common routines, gives related user interface information, provides code samples, and supplies additional information.
- "Memory Manager Reference." This section provides a complete reference to the Memory Manager by describing the data structures, routines, and resources that it uses. Each routine description also follows a standard format, which gives the routine declaration and description of every parameter of the routine. Some routine descriptions also give additional descriptive information, such as assembly-language information or result codes.
- "Summary of the Memory Manager." This section provides the Memory Manager's Pascal interface, as well as the C interface, for the constants, data structures, routines, and result codes associated with the Memory Manager. It also includes relevant assembly-language interface information.

Some chapters also contain additional main sections that provide more detailed discussions of certain topics. For example, the Memory Manager chapter contains the section "Organization of Memory" that describes how the Memory Manager organizes zones and blocks in RAM.

Conventions Used in This Book

Inside Macintosh uses various conventions to present information. Words that require special treatment appear in specific fonts or font styles. Certain information, such as parameter blocks, use special formats so that you can scan them quickly.

Special Fonts

All code listings, reserved words, and the names of actual data structures, constants, fields, parameters, and routines are shown in Courier (`this is Courier`).

Words that appear in **boldface** are key terms or concepts and are defined in the Glossary.

Types of Notes

There are several types of notes used in this book.

Note
A note like this contains information that is interesting but possibly not essential to an understanding of the main text. (An example appears on page 1-8.) ◆

IMPORTANT
A note like this contains information that is essential for an understanding of the main text. (An example appears on page 2-7.) ▲

▲ **WARNING**
Warnings like this indicate potential problems that you should be aware of as you design your application. Failure to heed these warnings could result in system crashes or loss of data. (An example appears on page 1-16.) ▲

Assembly-Language Information

Inside Macintosh provides information about the registers for specific routines like this:

Registers on entry

A0 Contents of register A0 on entry

Registers on exit

D0 Contents of register D0 on exit

In addition, *Inside Macintosh* presents information about the fields of a parameter block in this format:

Parameter block

↔	`inAndOut`	`Integer`	Input/output parameter.
←	`output1`	`Ptr`	Output parameter.
→	`input1`	`Ptr`	Input parameter.

The arrow in the far left column indicates whether the field is an input parameter, output parameter, or both. You must supply values for all input parameters and input/output parameters. The routine returns values in output parameters and input/output parameters.

The second column shows the field name as defined in the MPW Pascal interface files; the third column indicates the Pascal data type of that field. The fourth column provides a brief description of the use of the field. For a complete description of each field, see the discussion that follows the parameter block or the description of the parameter block in the reference section of the chapter.

Development Environment

The system software routines described in this book are available using Pascal, C, or assembly-language interfaces. How you access these routines depends on the development environment you are using. This book shows system software routines in their Pascal interface using the Macintosh Programmer's Workshop (MPW).

All code listings in this book are shown in Pascal. They show methods of using various routines and illustrate techniques for accomplishing particular tasks. All code listings have been compiled and, in most cases, tested. However, Apple Computer does not intend that you use these code samples in your application.

APDA, Apple's source for developer tools, offers worldwide access to a broad range of programming products, resources, and information for anyone developing on Apple platforms. You'll find the most current versions of Apple and third-party development tools, debuggers, compilers, languages, and technical references for all Apple platforms. To establish an APDA account, obtain additional ordering information, or find out about site licensing and developer training programs, contact

APDA
Apple Computer, Inc.
20525 Mariani Avenue, M/S 33-G
Cupertino, CA 95014-6299

Telephone:	800-282-2732 (United States) 800-637-0029 (Canada) 800-562-3910 (elsewhere in the world)
Fax:	408-562-3971
Telex:	171-576

If you provide commercial products and services, call 408-974-4897 for information on the developer support programs available from Apple.

For information on registering signatures, file types, Apple events, and other technical information, contact

Macintosh Developer Technical Support
Apple Computer, Inc.
20525 Mariani Avenue, M/S 75-3T
Cupertino, CA 95014-6299

Introduction to Memory Management

Contents

This chapter is a general introduction to memory management on Macintosh computers. It describes how the Operating System organizes and manages the available memory, and it shows how you can use the services provided by the Memory Manager and other system software components to manage the memory in your application partition effectively.

You should read this chapter if your application or other software allocates memory dynamically during its execution. This chapter describes how to

- set up your application partition at launch time
- determine the amount of free memory in your application heap
- allocate and dispose of blocks of memory in your application heap
- minimize fragmentation in your application heap caused by blocks of memory that cannot move
- implement a scheme to avoid low-memory conditions

You should be able to accomplish most of your application's memory allocation and management by following the instructions given in this chapter. If, however, your application needs to allocate memory outside its own partition (for instance, in the system heap), you need to read the chapter "Memory Manager" in this book. If your application has timing-critical requirements or installs procedures that execute at interrupt time, you need to read the chapter "Virtual Memory Manager" in this book. If your application's executable code is divided into multiple segments, you might also want to look at the chapter "Segment Manager" in *Inside Macintosh: Processes* for guidelines on how to divide your code into segments. If your application uses resources, you need to read the chapter "Resource Manager" in *Inside Macintosh: More Macintosh Toolbox* for information on managing memory allocated to resources.

This chapter begins with a description of how the Macintosh Operating System organizes the available physical random-access memory (RAM) in a Macintosh computer and how it allocates memory to open applications. Then this chapter describes in detail how the Memory Manager allocates blocks of memory in your application's heap and how to use the routines provided by the Memory Manager to perform the memory-management tasks listed above.

This chapter ends with descriptions of the routines used to perform these tasks. The "Memory Management Reference" and "Summary of Memory Management" sections in this chapter are subsets of the corresponding sections in the remaining chapters in this book.

About Memory

A Macintosh computer's available RAM is used by the Operating System, applications, and other software components, such as device drivers and system extensions. This section describes both the general organization of memory by the Operating System and the organization of the memory partition allocated to your application when it is launched. This section also provides a preliminary description of three related memory topics:

- temporary memory
- virtual memory
- 24- and 32-bit addressing

For more complete information on these three topics, you need to read the remaining chapters in this book.

Organization of Memory by the Operating System

When the Macintosh Operating System starts up, it divides the available RAM into two broad sections. It reserves for itself a zone or **partition** of memory known as the **system partition.** The system partition always begins at the lowest addressable byte of memory (memory address 0) and extends upward. The system partition contains a system heap and a set of global variables, described in the next two sections.

All memory outside the system partition is available for allocation to applications or other software components. In system software version 7.0 and later (or when MultiFinder is running in system software versions 5.0 and 6.0), the user can have multiple applications open at once. When an application is launched, the Operating System assigns it a section of memory known as its **application partition.** In general, an application uses only the memory contained in its own application partition.

Figure 1-1 illustrates the organization of memory when several applications are open at the same time. The system partition occupies the lowest position in memory. Application partitions occupy part of the remaining space. Note that application partitions are loaded into the top part of memory first.

Figure 1-1 Memory organization with several applications open

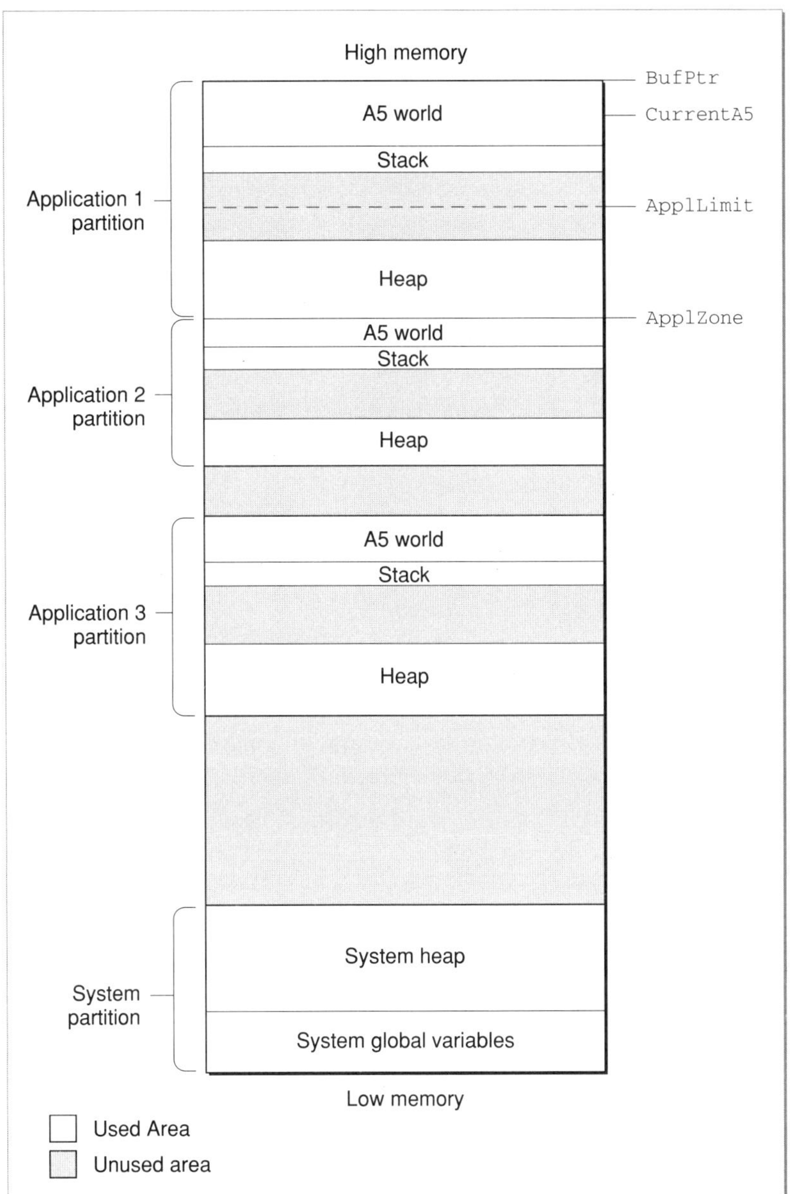

In Figure 1-1, three applications are open, each with its own application partition. The application labeled Application 1 is the active application. (The labels on the right side of the figure are system global variables, explained in "The System Global Variables" on page 1-6.)

The System Heap

The main part of the system partition is an area of memory known as the **system heap.** In general, the system heap is reserved for exclusive use by the Operating System and other system software components, which load into it various items such as system resources, system code segments, and system data structures. All system buffers and queues, for example, are allocated in the system heap.

The system heap is also used for code and other resources that do not belong to specific applications, such as code resources that add features to the Operating System or that provide control of special-purpose peripheral equipment. System patches and system extensions (stored as code resources of type `'INIT'`) are loaded into the system heap during the system startup process. Hardware device drivers (stored as code resources of type `'DRVR'`) are loaded into the system heap when the driver is opened.

Most applications don't need to load anything into the system heap. In certain cases, however, you might need to load resources or code segments into the system heap. For example, if you want a vertical retrace task to continue to execute even when your application is in the background, you need to load the task and any data associated with it into the system heap. Otherwise, the Vertical Retrace Manager ignores the task when your application is in the background.

The System Global Variables

The lowest part of memory is occupied by a collection of global variables called **system global variables** (or **low-memory system global variables**). The Operating System uses these variables to maintain different kinds of information about the operating environment. For example, the `Ticks` global variable contains the number of ticks (sixtieths of a second) that have elapsed since the system was most recently started up. Similar variables contain, for example, the height of the menu bar (`MBarHeight`) and pointers to the heads of various operating-system queues (`DTQueue`, `FSQHdr`, `VBLQueue`, and so forth). Most low-memory global variables are of this variety: they contain information that is generally useful only to the Operating System or other system software components.

Other low-memory global variables contain information about the current application. For example, the `ApplZone` global variable contains the address of the first byte of the active application's partition. The `ApplLimit` global variable contains the address of the last byte the active application's heap can expand to include. The `CurrentA5` global variable contains the address of the boundary between the active application's global variables and its application parameters. Because these global variables contain information about the active application, the Operating System changes the values of these variables whenever a context switch occurs.

In general, it is best to avoid reading or writing low-memory system global variables. Most of these variables are undocumented, and the results of changing their values can be unpredictable. Usually, when the value of a low-memory global variable is likely to be useful to applications, the system software provides a routine that you can use to read or write that value. For example, you can get the current value of the `Ticks` global variable by calling the `TickCount` function.

In rare instances, there is no routine that reads or writes the value of a documented global variable. In those cases, you might need to read or write that value directly. See the chapter "Memory Manager" in this book for instructions on reading and writing the values of low-memory global variables from a high-level language.

Organization of Memory in an Application Partition

When your application is launched, the Operating System allocates for it a partition of memory called its **application partition.** That partition contains required segments of the application's code as well as other data associated with the application. Figure 1-2 illustrates the general organization of an application partition.

Figure 1-2 Organization of an application partition

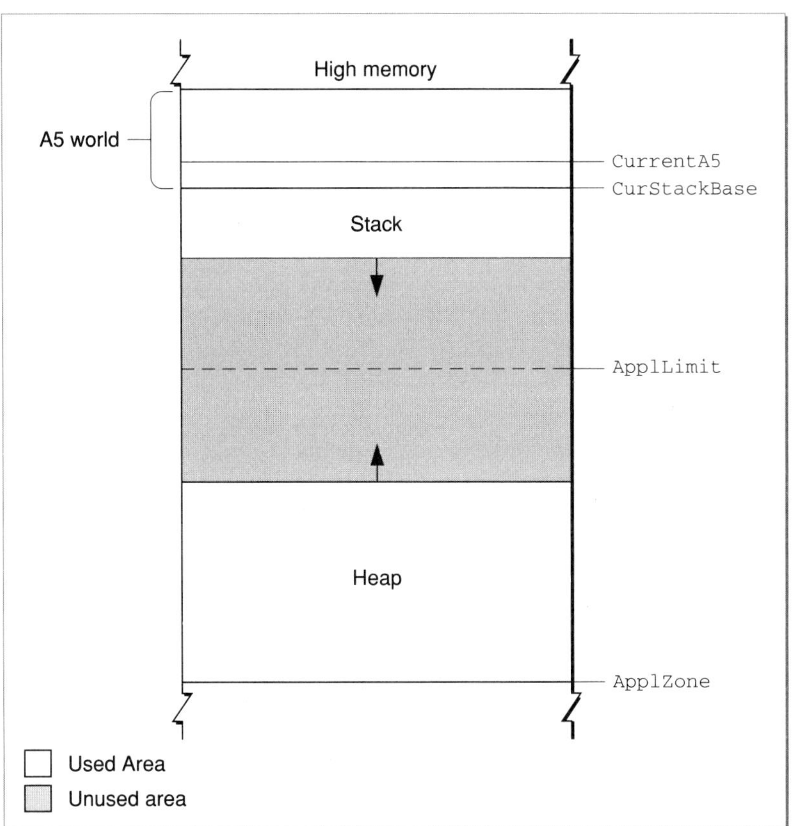

Your application partition is divided into three major parts:

- the application stack
- the application heap
- the application global variables and A5 world

The heap is located at the low-memory end of your application partition and always expands (when necessary) toward high memory. The A5 world is located at the high-memory end of your application partition and is of fixed size. The stack begins at the low-memory end of the A5 world and expands downward, toward the top of the heap.

As you can see in Figure 1-2, there is usually an unused area of memory between the stack and the heap. This unused area provides space for the stack to grow without encroaching upon the space assigned to the application heap. In some cases, however, the stack might grow into space reserved for the application heap. If this happens, it is very likely that data in the heap will become corrupted.

The `ApplLimit` global variable marks the upper limit to which your heap can grow. If you call the `MaxApplZone` procedure at the beginning of your program, the heap immediately extends all the way up to this limit. If you were to use all of the heap's free space, the Memory Manager would not allow you to allocate additional blocks above `ApplLimit`. If you do not call `MaxApplZone`, the heap grows toward `ApplLimit` whenever the Memory Manager finds that there is not enough memory in the heap to fill a request. However, once the heap grows up to `ApplLimit`, it can grow no further. Thus, whether you maximize your application heap or not, you can use only the space between the bottom of the heap and `ApplLimit`.

Unlike the heap, the stack is not bounded by `ApplLimit`. If your application uses heavily nested procedures with many local variables or uses extensive recursion, the stack could grow downward beyond `ApplLimit`. Because you do not use Memory Manager routines to allocate memory on the stack, the Memory Manager cannot stop your stack from growing beyond `ApplLimit` and possibly encroaching upon space reserved for the heap. However, a vertical retrace task checks approximately 60 times each second to see if the stack has moved into the heap. If it has, the task, known as the "stack sniffer," generates a system error. This system error alerts you that you have allowed the stack to grow too far, so that you can make adjustments. See "Changing the Size of the Stack" on page 1-39 for instructions on how to change the size of your application stack.

Note
To ensure during debugging that your application generates this system error if the stack extends beyond `ApplLimit`, you should call `MaxApplZone` at the beginning of your program to expand the heap to `ApplLimit`. For more information on expanding the heap, see "Setting Up the Application Heap" beginning on page 1-38. ◆

The Application Stack

The **stack** is an area of memory in your application partition that can grow or shrink at one end while the other end remains fixed. This means that space on the stack is always allocated and released in LIFO (last-in, first-out) order. The last item allocated is always the first to be released. It also means that the allocated area of the stack is always contiguous. Space is released only at the top of the stack, never in the middle, so there can never be any unallocated "holes" in the stack.

By convention, the stack grows from high memory toward low memory addresses. The end of the stack that grows or shrinks is usually referred to as the "top" of the stack, even though it's actually at the lower end of memory occupied by the stack.

Because of its LIFO nature, the stack is especially useful for memory allocation connected with the execution of functions or procedures. When your application calls a routine, space is automatically allocated on the stack for a stack frame. A **stack frame** contains the routine's parameters, local variables, and return address. Figure 1-3 illustrates how the stack expands and shrinks during a function call. The leftmost diagram shows the stack just before the function is called. The middle diagram shows the stack expanded to hold the stack frame. Once the function is executed, the local variables and function parameters are popped off the stack. If the function is a Pascal function, all that remains is the previous stack with the function result on top.

Figure 1-3 The application stack

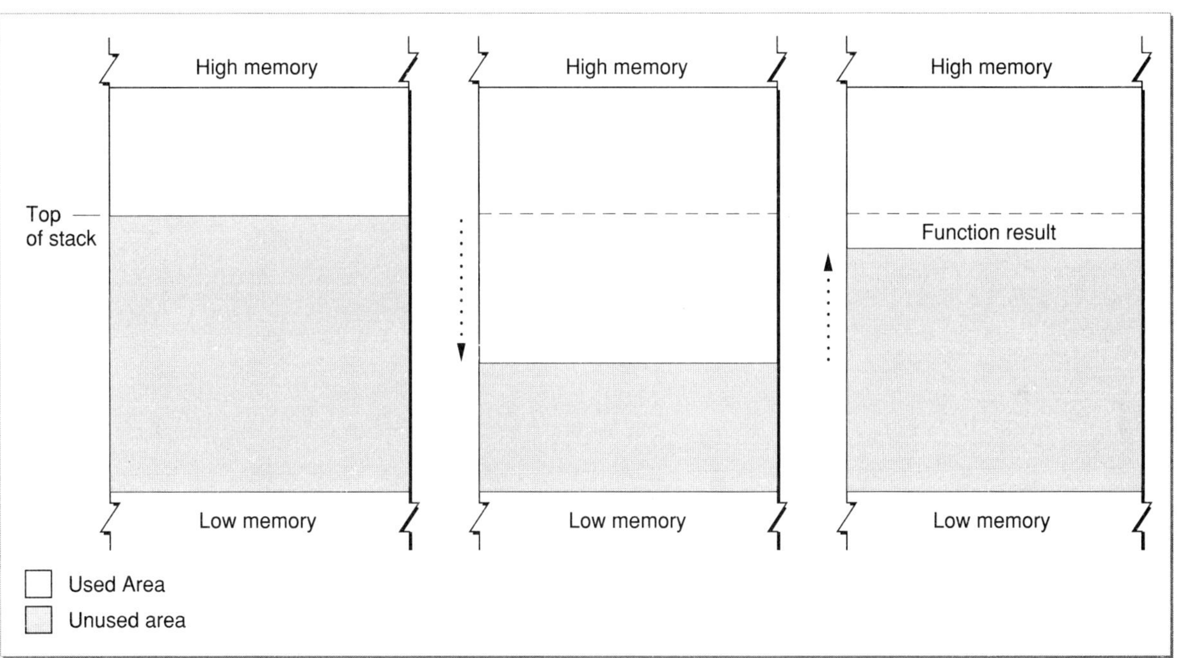

Note

Dynamic memory allocation on the stack is usually handled automatically if you are using a high-level development language such as Pascal. The compiler generates the code that creates and deletes stack frames for each function or procedure call. ◆

The Application Heap

An **application heap** is the area of memory in your application partition in which space is dynamically allocated and released on demand. The heap begins at the low-memory end of your application partition and extends upward in memory. The heap contains virtually all items that are not allocated on the stack. For instance, your application heap contains the application's code segments and resources that are currently loaded into memory. The heap also contains other dynamically allocated items such as window records, dialog records, document data, and so forth.

You allocate space within your application's heap by making calls to the Memory Manager, either directly (for instance, using the `NewHandle` function) or indirectly (for instance, using a routine such as `NewWindow`, which calls Memory Manager routines). Space in the heap is allocated in **blocks,** which can be of any size needed for a particular object.

The Memory Manager does all the necessary housekeeping to keep track of blocks in the heap as they are allocated and released. Because these operations can occur in any order, the heap doesn't usually grow and shrink in an orderly way, as the stack does. Instead, after your application has been running for a while, the heap can tend to become fragmented into a patchwork of allocated and free blocks, as shown in Figure 1-4. This fragmentation is known as **heap fragmentation.**

Figure 1-4 A fragmented heap

One result of heap fragmentation is that the Memory Manager might not be able to satisfy your application's request to allocate a block of a particular size. Even though there is enough free space available, the space is broken up into blocks smaller than the requested size. When this happens, the Memory Manager tries to create the needed space by moving allocated blocks together, thus collecting the free space in a single larger block. This operation is known as **heap compaction.** Figure 1-5 shows the results of compacting the fragmented heap shown in Figure 1-4.

Figure 1-5 A compacted heap

Heap fragmentation is generally not a problem as long as the blocks of memory you allocate are free to move during heap compaction. There are, however, two situations in which a block is not free to move: when it is a nonrelocatable block, and when it is a locked, relocatable block. To minimize heap fragmentation, you should use nonrelocatable blocks sparingly, and you should lock relocatable blocks only when absolutely necessary. See "Relocatable and Nonrelocatable Blocks" starting on page 1-16 for a description of relocatable and nonrelocatable blocks, and "Heap Fragmentation" on page 1-24 for a description of how best to avoid fragmenting your heap.

The Application Global Variables and A5 World

Your application's global variables are stored in an area of memory near the top of your application partition known as the application **A5 world.** The A5 world contains four kinds of data:

- application global variables
- application QuickDraw global variables
- application parameters
- the application's jump table

Each of these items is of fixed size, although the sizes of the global variables and of the jump table may vary from application to application. Figure 1-6 shows the standard organization of the A5 world.

Figure 1-6 Organization of an application's A5 world

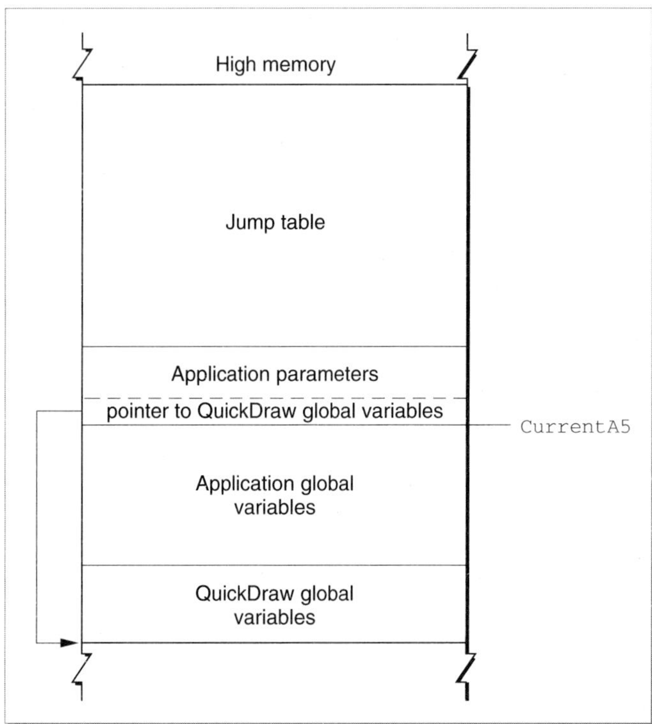

Note
An application's global variables may appear either above or below the QuickDraw global variables. The relative locations of these two items are determined by your development system's linker. In addition, part of the jump table might appear below the boundary pointed to by `CurrentA5`. ◆

The system global variable `CurrentA5` points to the boundary between the current application's global variables and its application parameters. For this reason, the application's global variables are found as negative offsets from the value of `CurrentA5`. This boundary is important because the Operating System uses it to access the following information from your application: its global variables, its QuickDraw global variables, the application parameters, and the jump table. This information is known collectively as the A5 world because the Operating System uses the microprocessor's A5 register to point to that boundary.

Your application's **QuickDraw global variables** contain information about its drawing environment. For example, among these variables is a pointer to the current graphics port.

Your application's **jump table** contains an entry for each of your application's routines that is called by code in another segment. The Segment Manager uses the jump table to determine the address of any externally referenced routines called by a code segment. For more information on jump tables, see the chapter "Segment Manager" in *Inside Macintosh: Processes*.

The **application parameters** are 32 bytes of memory located above the application global variables; they're reserved for use by the Operating System. The first long word of those parameters is a pointer to your application's QuickDraw global variables.

Temporary Memory

In the Macintosh multitasking environment, each application is limited to a particular memory partition (whose size is determined by information in the `'SIZE'` resource of that application). The size of your application's partition places certain limits on the size of your application heap and hence on the sizes of the buffers and other data structures that your application uses. In general, you specify an application partition size that is large enough to hold all the buffers, resources, and other data that your application is likely to need during its execution.

If for some reason you need more memory than is currently available in your application heap, you can ask the Operating System to let you use any available memory that is not yet allocated to any other application. This memory, known as **temporary memory,** is allocated from the available unused RAM; usually, that memory is not contiguous with the memory in your application's zone. Figure 1-7 shows an application using some temporary memory.

Figure 1-7 Using temporary memory allocated from unused RAM

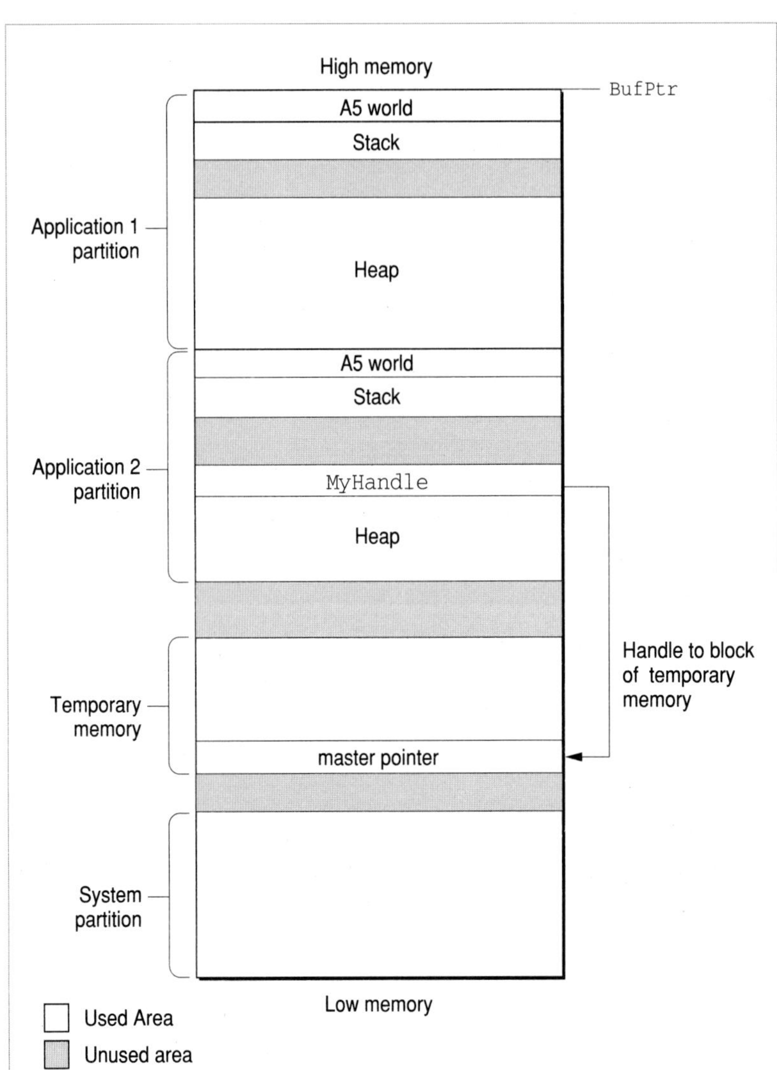

In Figure 1-7, Application 1 has almost exhausted its application heap. As a result, it has requested and received a large block of temporary memory, extending from the top of Application 2's partition to the top of the allocatable space. Application 1 can use the temporary memory in whatever manner it desires.

Your application should use temporary memory only for occasional short-term purposes that could be accomplished in less space, though perhaps less efficiently. For example, if you want to copy a large file, you might try to allocate a fairly large buffer of temporary memory. If you receive the temporary memory, you can copy data from the source file into the destination file using the large buffer. If, however, the request for temporary memory fails, you can instead use a smaller buffer within your application heap.

Although using the smaller buffer might prolong the copying operation, the file is nonetheless copied.

One good reason for using temporary memory only occasionally is that you cannot assume that you will always receive the temporary memory you request. For example, in Figure 1-7, all the available memory is allocated to the two open applications; any further requests by either one for some temporary memory would fail. For complete details on using temporary memory, see the chapter "Memory Manager" in this book.

Virtual Memory

In system software version 7.0 and later, suitably equipped Macintosh computers can take advantage of a feature of the Operating System known as **virtual memory,** by which the machines have a logical address space that extends beyond the limits of the available physical memory. Because of virtual memory, a user can load more programs and data into the logical address space than would fit in the computer's physical RAM.

The Operating System extends the address space by using part of the available secondary storage (that is, part of a hard disk) to hold portions of applications and data that are not currently needed in RAM. When some of those portions of memory are needed, the Operating System swaps out unneeded parts of applications or data to the secondary storage, thereby making room for the parts that are needed.

It is important to realize that virtual memory operates transparently to most applications. Unless your application has time-critical needs that might be adversely affected by the operation of virtual memory or installs routines that execute at interrupt time, you do not need to know whether virtual memory is operating. For complete details on virtual memory, see the chapter "Virtual Memory Manager" later in this book.

Addressing Modes

On suitably equipped Macintosh computers, the Operating System supports **32-bit addressing,** that is, the ability to use 32 bits to determine memory addresses. Earlier versions of system software use 24-bit addressing, where the upper 8 bits of memory addresses are ignored or used as flag bits. In a 24-bit addressing scheme, the logical address space has a size of 16 MB. Because 8 MB of this total are reserved for I/O space, ROM, and slot space, the largest contiguous program address space is 8 MB. When 32-bit addressing is in operation, the maximum program address space is 1 GB.

The ability to operate with 32-bit addressing is available only on certain Macintosh models, namely those with systems that contain a 32-bit Memory Manager. (For compatibility reasons, these systems also contain a 24-bit Memory Manager.) In order for your application to work when the machine is using 32-bit addressing, it must be **32-bit clean,** that is, able to run in an environment where all 32 bits of a memory address are significant. Fortunately, writing applications that are 32-bit clean is relatively easy if you follow the guidelines in *Inside Macintosh.* In general, applications are not 32-bit clean because they manipulate flag bits in master pointers directly (for instance, to mark the associated memory blocks as locked or purgeable) instead of using Memory Manager routines to achieve the desired result. See "Relocatable and Nonrelocatable Blocks" on page 1-16 for a description of master pointers.

▲ **WARNING**
You should never make assumptions about the contents of Memory Manager data structures, including master pointers and zone headers. These structures have changed in the past and they are likely to change again in the future. ▲

Occasionally, an application running when 24-bit addressing is enabled might need to modify memory addresses to make them compatible with the 24-bit Memory Manager. In addition, drivers or other code might need to use 32-bit addresses, even when running in 24-bit mode. See the descriptions of the routines `StripAddress` and `Translate24to32` in the chapter "Memory Management Utilities" for details.

Heap Management

Applications allocate and manipulate memory primarily in their application heap. As you have seen, space in the application heap is allocated and released on demand. When the blocks in your heap are free to move, the Memory Manager can often reorganize the heap to free space when necessary to fulfill a memory-allocation request. In some cases, however, blocks in your heap cannot move. In these cases, you need to pay close attention to memory allocation and management to avoid fragmenting your heap and running out of memory.

This section provides a general description of how to manage blocks of memory in your application heap. It describes

- relocatable and nonrelocatable blocks
- properties of relocatable blocks
- heap purging and compaction
- heap fragmentation
- dangling pointers
- low-memory conditions

For examples of specific techniques you can use to implement the strategies discussed in this section, see "Using Memory" beginning on page 1-38.

Relocatable and Nonrelocatable Blocks

You can use the Memory Manager to allocate two different types of blocks in your heap: nonrelocatable blocks and relocatable blocks. A **nonrelocatable block** is a block of memory whose location in the heap is fixed. In contrast, a **relocatable block** is a block of memory that can be moved within the heap (perhaps during heap compaction).

The Memory Manager sometimes moves relocatable blocks during memory operations so that it can use the space in the heap optimally.

The Memory Manager provides data types that reference both relocatable and nonrelocatable blocks. It also provides routines that allow you to allocate and release blocks of both types.

To reference a nonrelocatable block, you can use a **pointer** variable, defined by the `Ptr` data type.

```
TYPE
    SignedByte      = -128..127;
    Ptr             = ^SignedByte;
```

A pointer is simply the address of an arbitrary byte in memory, and a pointer to a nonrelocatable block of memory is simply the address of the first byte in the block, as illustrated in Figure 1-8. After you allocate a nonrelocatable block, you can make copies of the pointer variable. Because a pointer is the address of a block of memory that cannot be moved, all copies of the pointer correctly reference the block as long as you don't dispose of it.

Figure 1-8 A pointer to a nonrelocatable block

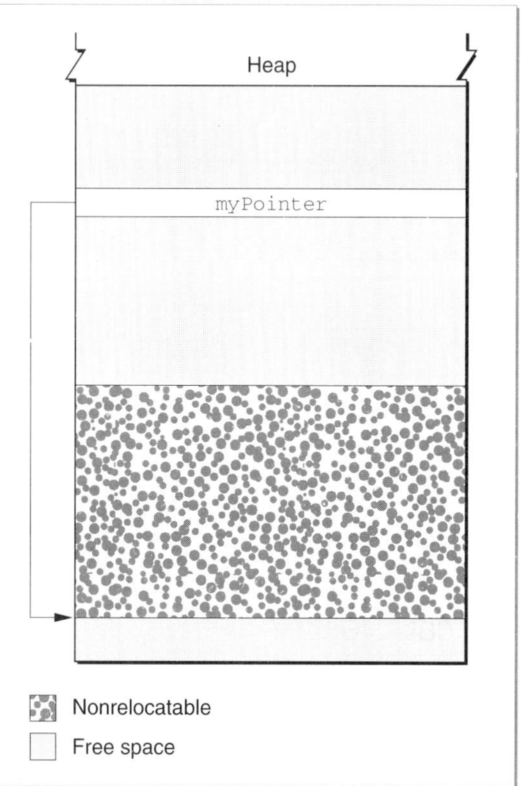

The pointer variable itself occupies 4 bytes of space in your application partition. Often the pointer variable is a global variable and is therefore contained in your application's A5 world. But the pointer can also be allocated on the stack or in the heap itself.

To reference relocatable blocks, the Memory Manager uses a scheme known as **double indirection.** The Memory Manager keeps track of a relocatable block internally with a **master pointer,** which itself is part of a nonrelocatable **master pointer block** in your application heap and can never move.

Note
The Memory Manager allocates one master pointer block (containing 64 master pointers) for your application at launch time, and you can call the `MoreMasters` procedure to request that additional master pointer blocks be allocated. See "Setting Up the Application Heap" beginning on page 1-38 for instructions on allocating master pointer blocks. ◆

When the Memory Manager moves a relocatable block, it updates the master pointer so that it always contains the address of the relocatable block. You reference the block with a **handle,** defined by the `Handle` data type.

```
TYPE
   Handle          = ^Ptr;
```

A handle contains the address of a master pointer. The left side of Figure 1-9 shows a handle to a relocatable block of memory located in the middle of the application heap. If necessary (perhaps to make room for another block of memory), the Memory Manager can move that block down in the heap, as shown in the right side of Figure 1-9.

Figure 1-9 A handle to a relocatable block

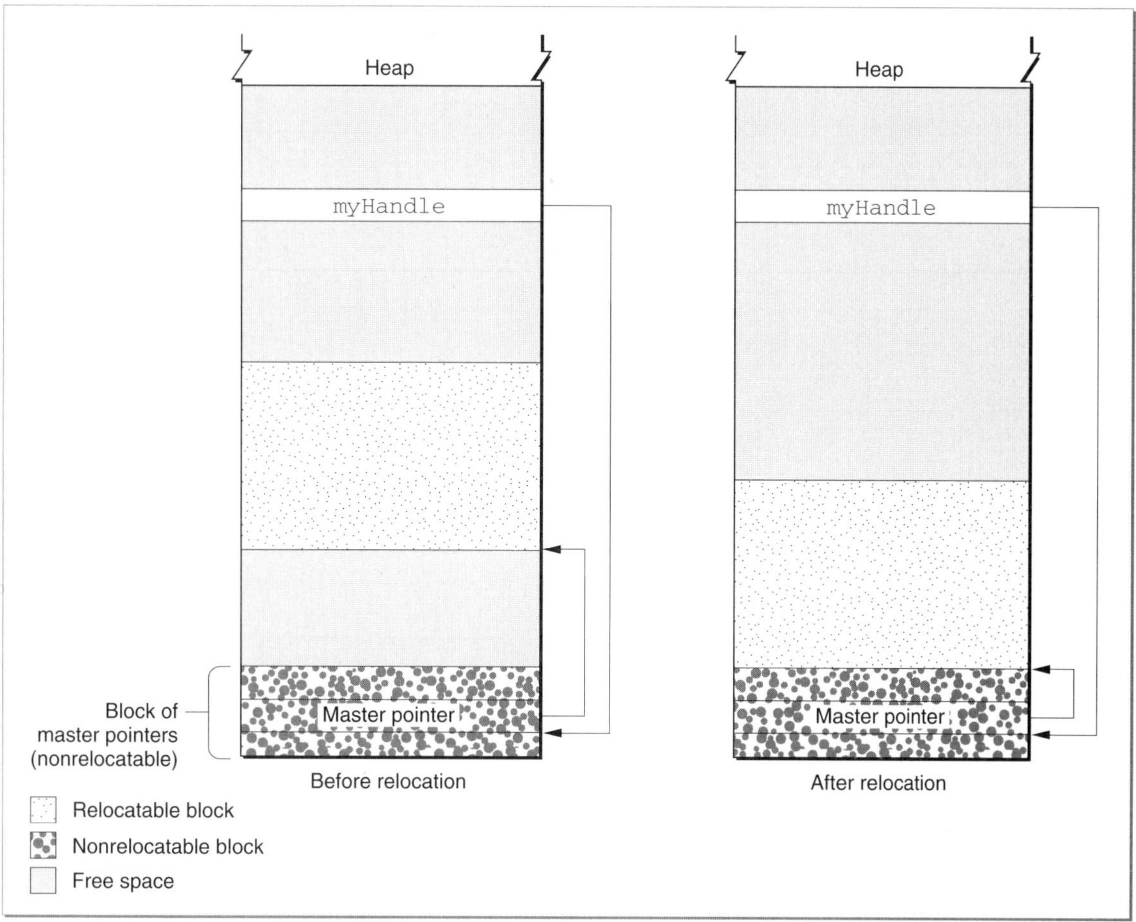

Master pointers for relocatable objects in your heap are always allocated in your application heap. Because the blocks of masters pointers are nonrelocatable, it is best to allocate them as low in your heap as possible. You can do this by calling the `MoreMasters` procedure when your application starts up.

Whenever possible, you should allocate memory in relocatable blocks. This gives the Memory Manager the greatest freedom when rearranging the blocks in your application heap to create a new block of free memory. In some cases, however, you may be forced to allocate a nonrelocatable block of memory. When you call the Window Manager function `NewWindow`, for example, the Window Manager internally calls the `NewPtr` function to allocate a new nonrelocatable block in your application partition. You need to exercise care when calling Toolbox routines that allocate such blocks, lest your application heap become overly fragmented. See "Allocating Blocks of Memory" on page 1-44 for specific guidelines on allocating nonrelocatable blocks.

Using relocatable blocks makes the Memory Manager more efficient at managing available space, but it does carry some overhead. As you have seen, the Memory Manager must allocate extra memory to hold master pointers for relocatable blocks. It groups these master pointers into nonrelocatable blocks. For large relocatable blocks, this extra space is negligible, but if you allocate many very small relocatable blocks, the cost can be considerable. For this reason, you should avoid allocating a very large number of handles to small blocks; instead, allocate a single large block and use it as an array to hold the data you need.

Properties of Relocatable Blocks

As you have seen, a heap block can be either relocatable or nonrelocatable. The designation of a block as relocatable or nonrelocatable is a permanent property of that block. If relocatable, a block can be either locked or unlocked; if it's unlocked, a block can be either purgeable or unpurgeable. These attributes of relocatable blocks can be set and changed as necessary. The following sections explain how to lock and unlock blocks, and how to mark them as purgeable or unpurgeable.

Locking and Unlocking Relocatable Blocks

Occasionally, you might need a relocatable block of memory to stay in one place. To prevent a block from moving, you can **lock** it, using the `HLock` procedure. Once you have locked a block, it won't move. Later, you can **unlock** it, using the `HUnlock` procedure, allowing it to move again.

In general, you need to lock a relocatable block only if there is some danger that it might be moved during the time that you read or write the data in that block. This might happen, for instance, if you dereference a handle to obtain a pointer to the data and (for increased speed) use the pointer within a loop that calls routines that might cause memory to be moved. If, within the loop, the block whose data you are accessing is in fact moved, then the pointer no longer points to that data; this pointer is said to dangle.

Note
Locking a block is only one way to prevent a dangling pointer. See "Dangling Pointers" on page 1-29 for a complete discussion of how to avoid dangling pointers. ◆

Using locked relocatable blocks can, however, slow the Memory Manager down as much as using nonrelocatable blocks. The Memory Manager can't move locked blocks. In addition, except when you allocate memory and resize relocatable blocks, it can't move relocatable blocks around locked relocatable blocks (just as it can't move them around nonrelocatable blocks). Thus, locking a block in the middle of the heap for long periods of time can increase heap fragmentation.

Locking and unlocking blocks every time you want to prevent a block from moving can become troublesome. Fortunately, the Memory Manager moves unlocked, relocatable blocks only at well-defined, predictable times. In general, each routine description in *Inside Macintosh* indicates whether the routine could move or purge memory. If you do not call any of those routines in a section of code, you can rely on all blocks to remain stationary while that code executes. Note that the Segment Manager might move memory if you call a routine located in a segment that is not currently resident in memory. See "Loading Code Segments" on page 1-31 for details.

Purging and Reallocating Relocatable Blocks

One advantage of relocatable blocks is that you can use them to store information that you would like to keep in memory to make your application more efficient, but that you don't really need if available memory space becomes low. For example, your application might, at the beginning of its execution, load user preferences from a preferences file into a relocatable block. As long as the block remains in memory, your application can access information from the preferences file without actually reopening the file. However, reopening the file probably wouldn't take enough time to justify keeping the block in memory if memory space were scarce.

By making a relocatable block **purgeable,** you allow the Memory Manager to free the space it occupies if necessary. If you later want to prohibit the Memory Manager from freeing the space occupied by a relocatable block, you can make the block **unpurgeable.** You can use the `HPurge` and `HNoPurge` procedures to change back and forth between these two states. A block you create by calling `NewHandle` is initially unpurgeable.

Once you make a relocatable block purgeable, you should subsequently check handles to that block before using them if you call any of the routines that could move or purge memory. If a handle's master pointer is set to `NIL`, then the Operating System has purged its block. To use the information formerly in the block, you must reallocate space for it (perhaps by calling the `ReallocateHandle` procedure) and then reconstruct its contents (for example, by rereading the preferences file).

Figure 1-10 illustrates the purging and reallocating of a relocatable block. When the block is purged, its master pointer is set to `NIL`. When it is reallocated, the handle correctly references a new block, but that block's contents are initially undefined.

Figure 1-10 Purging and reallocating a relocatable block

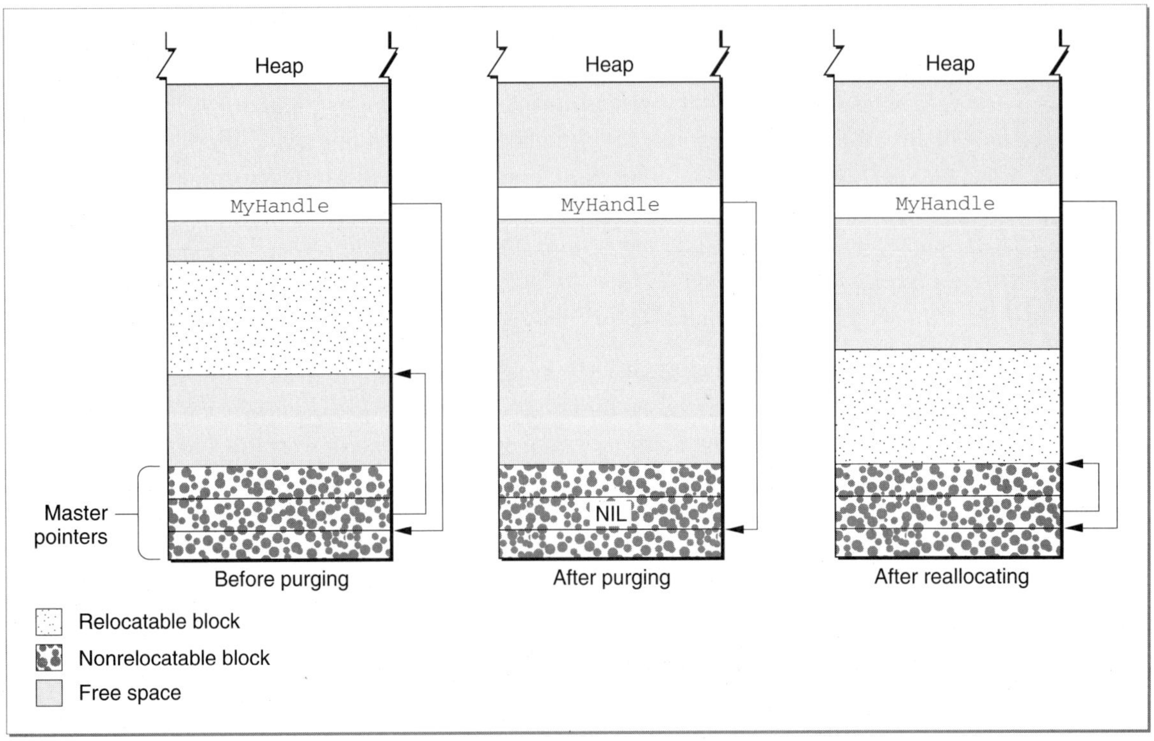

Memory Reservation

The Memory Manager does its best to prevent situations in which nonrelocatable blocks in the middle of the heap trap relocatable blocks. When it allocates new nonrelocatable blocks, it attempts to **reserve** memory for them as low in the heap as possible. The Memory Manager reserves memory for a nonrelocatable block by moving unlocked relocatable blocks upward until it has created a space large enough for the new block. When the Memory Manager can successfully pack all nonrelocatable blocks into the bottom of the heap, no nonrelocatable block can trap a relocatable block, and it has successfully prevented heap fragmentation.

Figure 1-11 illustrates how the Memory Manager allocates nonrelocatable blocks. Although it could place a block of the requested size at the top of the heap, it instead reserves space for the block as close to the bottom of the heap as possible and then puts the block into that reserved space. During this process, the Memory Manager might even move a relocatable block over a nonrelocatable block to make room for another nonrelocatable block.

Figure 1-11 Allocating a nonrelocatable block

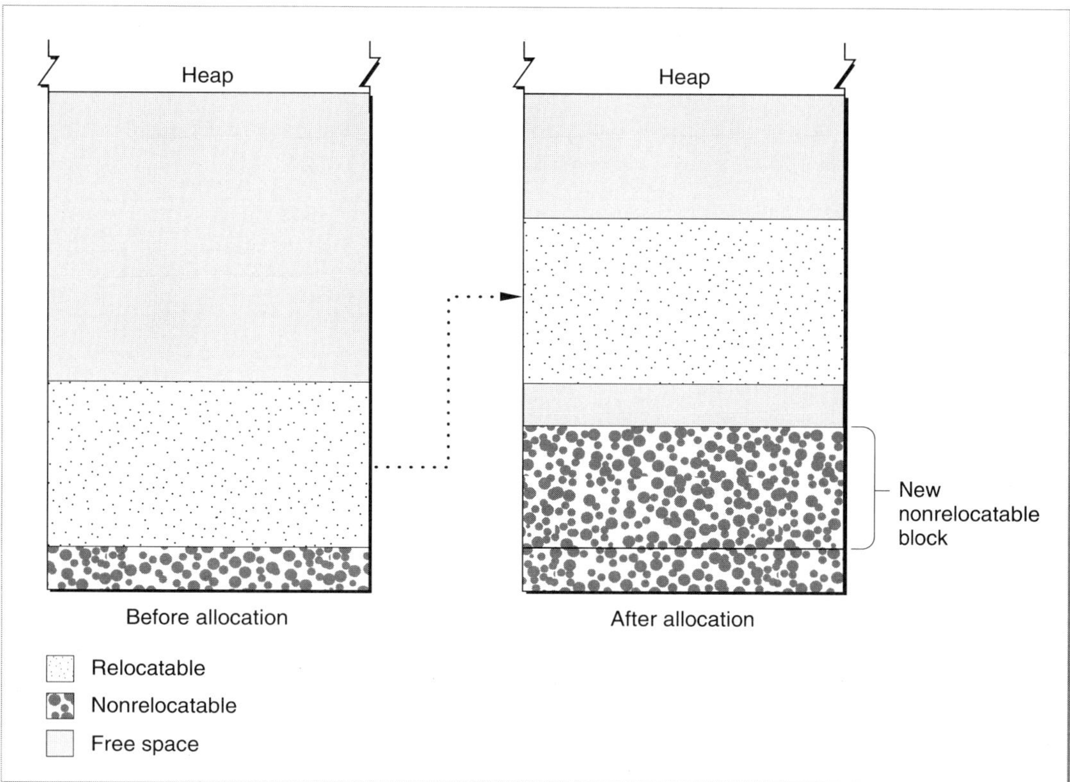

When allocating a new relocatable block, you can, if you want, manually reserve space for the block by calling the `ReserveMem` procedure. If you do not, the Memory Manager looks for space big enough for the block as low in the heap as possible, but it does not create space near the bottom of the heap for the block if there is already enough space higher in the heap.

Heap Purging and Compaction

When your application attempts to allocate memory (for example, by calling either the `NewPtr` or `NewHandle` function), the Memory Manager might need to **compact** or **purge** the heap to free memory and to fuse many small free blocks into fewer large free blocks. The Memory Manager first tries to obtain the requested amount of space by compacting the heap; if compaction fails to free the required amount of space, the Memory Manager then purges the heap.

When compacting the heap, the Memory Manager moves unlocked, relocatable blocks down until they reach nonrelocatable blocks or locked, relocatable blocks. You can compact the heap manually, by calling either the `CompactMem` function or the `MaxMem` function.

In a purge of the heap, the Memory Manager sequentially purges unlocked, purgeable relocatable blocks until it has freed enough memory or until it has purged all such blocks. It purges a block by deallocating it and setting its master pointer to `NIL`.

If you want, you can manually purge a few blocks or an entire heap in anticipation of a memory shortage. To purge an individual block manually, call the `EmptyHandle` procedure. To purge your entire heap manually, call the `PurgeMem` procedure or the `MaxMem` function.

Note
In general, you should let the Memory Manager purge and compact your heap, instead of performing these operations yourself. ◆

Heap Fragmentation

Heap fragmentation can slow your application by forcing the Memory Manager to compact or purge your heap to satisfy a memory-allocation request. In the worst cases, when your heap is severely fragmented by locked or nonrelocatable blocks, it might be impossible for the Memory Manager to find the requested amount of contiguous free space, even though that much space is actually free in your heap. This can have disastrous consequences for your application. For example, if the Memory Manager cannot find enough room to load a required code segment, your application will crash.

Obviously, it is best to minimize the amount of fragmentation that occurs in your application heap. It might be tempting to think that because the Memory Manager controls the movement of blocks in the heap, there is little that you can do to prevent heap fragmentation. In reality, however, fragmentation does not strike your application's heap by chance. Once you understand the major causes of heap fragmentation, you can follow a few simple rules to minimize it.

The primary causes of heap fragmentation are indiscriminate use of nonrelocatable blocks and indiscriminate locking of relocatable blocks. Each of these creates immovable blocks in your heap, thus creating "roadblocks" for the Memory Manager when it rearranges the heap to maximize the amount of contiguous free space. You can significantly reduce heap fragmentation simply by exercising care when you allocate nonrelocatable blocks and when you lock relocatable blocks.

Throughout this section, you should keep in mind the following rule: the Memory Manager can move a relocatable block around a nonrelocatable block (or a locked relocatable block) at these times only:

- When the Memory Manager reserves memory for a nonrelocatable block (or when you manually reserve memory before allocating a block), it can move unlocked, relocatable blocks upward over nonrelocatable blocks to make room for the new block as low in the heap as possible.
- When you attempt to resize a relocatable block, the Memory Manager can move that block around other blocks if necessary.

In contrast, the Memory Manager cannot move relocatable blocks over nonrelocatable blocks during compaction of the heap.

Deallocating Nonrelocatable Blocks

One of the most common causes of heap fragmentation is also one of the most difficult to avoid. The problem occurs when you dispose of a nonrelocatable block in the middle of the pile of nonrelocatable blocks at the bottom of the heap. Unless you immediately allocate another nonrelocatable block of the same size, you create a gap where the nonrelocatable block used to be. If you later allocate a slightly smaller, nonrelocatable block, that gap shrinks. However, small gaps are inefficient because of the small likelihood that future memory allocations will create blocks small enough to occupy the gaps.

It would not matter if the first block you allocated after deleting the nonrelocatable block were relocatable. The Memory Manager would place the block in the gap if possible. If you were later to allocate a nonrelocatable block as large as or smaller than the gap, the new block would take the place of the relocatable block, which would join other relocatable blocks in the middle of the heap, as desired. However, the new nonrelocatable block might be smaller than the original nonrelocatable block, leaving a small gap.

Whenever you dispose of a nonrelocatable block that you have allocated, you create small gaps, unless the next nonrelocatable block you allocate happens to be the same size as the disposed block. These small gaps can lead to heavy fragmentation over the course of your application's execution. Thus, you should try to avoid disposing of and then reallocating nonrelocatable blocks during program execution.

Reserving Memory

Another cause of heap fragmentation ironically occurs because of a limitation of memory reservation, a process designed to prevent it. Memory reservation never makes fragmentation worse than it would be if there were no memory reservation. Ordinarily, memory reservation ensures that allocating nonrelocatable blocks in the middle of your application's execution causes no problems. Occasionally, however, memory reservation can cause fragmentation, either when it succeeds but leaves small gaps in the reserved space, or when it fails and causes a nonrelocatable block to be allocated in the middle of the heap.

The Memory Manager uses memory reservation to create space for nonrelocatable blocks as low as possible in the heap. (You can also manually reserve memory for relocatable blocks, but you rarely need to do so.) However, when the Memory Manager moves a block up during memory reservation, that block cannot overlap its previous location. As a result, the Memory Manager might need to move the relocatable block up more than is necessary to contain the new nonrelocatable block, thereby creating a gap between the top of the new block and the bottom of the relocated block. (See Figure 1-11 on page 1-23.)

Memory reservation can also fragment the heap if there is not enough space in the heap to move the relocatable block up. In this case, the Memory Manager allocates the new nonrelocatable block above the relocatable block. The relocatable block cannot then move over the nonrelocatable block, except during the times described previously.

Locking Relocatable Blocks

Locked relocatable blocks present a special problem. When relocatable blocks are locked, they can cause as much heap fragmentation as nonrelocatable blocks. One solution is to reserve memory for all relocatable blocks that might at some point need to be locked, and to leave them locked for as long as they are allocated. This solution has drawbacks, however, because then the blocks would lose any flexibility that being relocatable otherwise gives them. Deleting a locked relocatable block can create a gap, just as deleting a nonrelocatable block can.

An alternative partial solution is to move relocatable blocks to the top of the heap before locking them. The `MoveHHi` procedure allows you to move a relocatable block upward until it reaches the top of the heap, a nonrelocatable block, or a locked relocatable block. This has the effect of partitioning the heap into four areas, as illustrated in Figure 1-12. At the bottom of the heap are the nonrelocatable blocks. Above those blocks are the unlocked relocatable blocks. At the top of the heap are locked relocatable blocks. Between the locked relocatable blocks and the unlocked relocatable blocks is an area of free space. The principal idea behind moving relocatable blocks to the top of the heap and locking them there is to keep the contiguous free space as large as possible.

Figure 1-12 An effectively partitioned heap

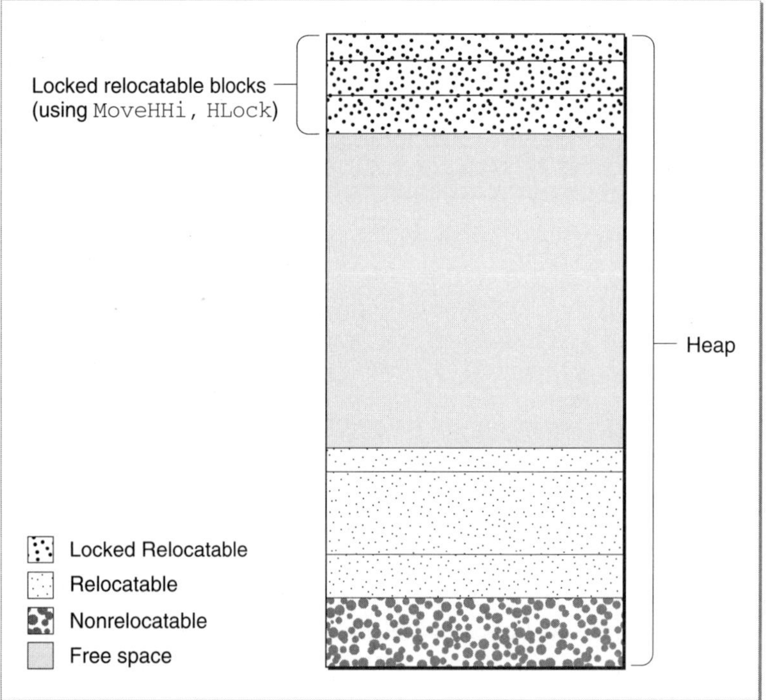

Using `MoveHHi` is, however, not always a perfect solution to handling relocatable blocks that need to be locked. The `MoveHHi` procedure moves a block upward only until it reaches either a nonrelocatable block or a locked relocatable block. Unlike `NewPtr` and `ReserveMem`, `MoveHHi` does not currently move a relocatable block around one that is not relocatable.

Even if `MoveHHi` succeeds in moving a block to the top area of the heap, unlocking or deleting locked blocks can cause fragmentation if you don't unlock or delete those blocks beginning with the lowest locked block. A relocatable block that is locked at the top area of the heap for a long period of time could trap other relocatable blocks that were locked for short periods of time but then unlocked.

This suggests that you need to treat relocatable blocks locked for a long period of time differently from those locked for a short period of time. If you plan to lock a relocatable block for a long period of time, you should reserve memory for it at the bottom of the heap before allocating it, then lock it for the duration of your application's execution (or as long as the block remains allocated). Do not reserve memory for relocatable blocks you plan to allocate for only short periods of time. Instead, move them to the top of the heap (by calling `MoveHHi`) and then lock them.

Note
You should call `MoveHHi` only on blocks located in your application heap. Don't call `MoveHHi` on relocatable blocks in the system heap. Desk accessories should not call `MoveHHi`. ◆

In practice, you apply the same rules to relocatable blocks that you reserve space for and leave permanently locked as you apply to nonrelocatable blocks: Try not to allocate such blocks in the middle of your application's execution, and don't dispose of and reallocate such blocks in the middle of your application's execution.

After you lock relocatable blocks temporarily, you don't need to move them manually back into the middle area when you unlock them. Whenever the Memory Manager compacts the heap or moves another relocatable block to the top heap area, it brings all unlocked relocatable blocks at the bottom of that partition back into the middle area. When moving a block to the top area, be sure to call `MoveHHi` on the block and then lock the block, in that order.

Allocating Nonrelocatable Blocks

As you have seen, there are two reasons for not allocating nonrelocatable blocks during the middle of your application's execution. First, if you also dispose of nonrelocatable blocks in the middle of your application's execution, then allocation of new nonrelocatable blocks is likely to create small gaps, as discussed earlier. Second, even if you never dispose of nonrelocatable blocks until your application terminates, memory reservation is an imperfect process, and the Memory Manager could occasionally place new nonrelocatable blocks above relocatable blocks.

There is, however, an exception to the rule that you should not allocate nonrelocatable blocks in the middle of your application's execution. Sometimes you need to allocate a nonrelocatable block only temporarily. If between the times that you allocate and dispose of a nonrelocatable block, you allocate no additional nonrelocatable blocks and do not attempt to compact the heap, then you have done no harm. The temporary block cannot create a new gap because the Memory Manager places no other block over the temporary block.

Summary of Preventing Fragmentation

Avoiding heap fragmentation is not difficult. It simply requires that you follow a few rules as closely as possible. Remember that allocation of even a small nonrelocatable block in the middle of your heap can ruin a scheme to prevent fragmentation of the heap, because the Memory Manager does not move relocatable blocks around nonrelocatable blocks when you call `MoveHHi` or when it attempts to compact the heap.

If you adhere to the following rules, you are likely to avoid significant heap fragmentation:

- At the beginning of your application's execution, call the `MaxApplZone` procedure once and the `MoreMasters` procedure enough times so that the Memory Manager never needs to call it for you.
- Try to anticipate the maximum number of nonrelocatable blocks you will need and allocate them at the beginning of your application's execution.
- Avoid disposing of and then reallocating nonrelocatable blocks during your application's execution.
- When allocating relocatable blocks that you need to lock for long periods of time, use the `ReserveMem` procedure to reserve memory for them as close to the bottom of the heap as possible, and lock the blocks immediately after allocating them.
- If you plan to lock a relocatable block for a short period of time and allocate nonrelocatable blocks while it is locked, use the `MoveHHi` procedure to move the block to the top of the heap and then lock it. When the block no longer needs to be locked, unlock it.
- Remember that you need to lock a relocatable block only if you call a routine that could move or purge memory and you then use a dereferenced handle to the relocatable block, or if you want to use a dereferenced handle to the relocatable block at interrupt time.

Perhaps the most difficult restriction is to avoid disposing of and then reallocating nonrelocatable blocks in the middle of your application's execution. Some Toolbox routines require you to use nonrelocatable blocks, and it is not always easy to anticipate how many such blocks you will need. If you must allocate and dispose of blocks in the middle of your program's execution, you might want to place used blocks into a linked list of free blocks instead of disposing of them. If you know how many nonrelocatable blocks of a certain size your application is likely to need, you can add that many to the beginning of the list at the beginning of your application's execution. If you need a nonrelocatable block later, you can check the linked list for a block of the exact size instead of simply calling the `NewPtr` function.

Dangling Pointers

Accessing a relocatable block by double indirection, through its handle instead of through its master pointer, requires an extra memory reference. For efficiency, you might sometimes want to **dereference** the handle—that is, make a copy of the block's master pointer—and then use that pointer to access the block by single indirection. When you do this, however, you need to be particularly careful. Any operation that allocates space from the heap might cause the relocatable block to be moved or purged. In that event, the block's master pointer is correctly updated, but your copy of the master pointer is not. As a result, your copy of the master pointer is a **dangling pointer.**

Dangling pointers are likely to make your application crash or produce garbled output. Unfortunately, it is often easy during debugging to overlook situations that could leave pointers dangling, because pointers dangle only if the relocatable blocks that they reference actually move. Routines that can move or purge memory do not necessarily do so unless memory space is tight. Thus, if you improperly dereference a handle in a section of code, that code might still work properly most of the time. If, however, a dangling pointer does cause errors, they can be very difficult to trace.

This section describes a number of situations that can cause dangling pointers and suggests some ways to avoid them.

Compiler Dereferencing

Some of the most difficult dangling pointers to isolate are not caused by any explicit dereferencing on your part, but by implicit dereferencing on the part of the compiler. For example, suppose you use a handle called `myHandle` to access the fields of a record in a relocatable block. You might use Pascal's `WITH` statement to do so, as follows:

```
WITH myHandle^^ DO
   BEGIN
      ...
   END;
```

A compiler is likely to dereference `myHandle` so that it can access the fields of the record without double indirection. However, if the code between the `BEGIN` and `END` statements causes the Memory Manager to move or purge memory, you are likely to end up with a dangling pointer.

The easiest way to prevent dangling pointers is simply to lock the relocatable block whose data you want to read or write. Because the block is locked and cannot move, the master pointer is guaranteed always to point to the beginning of the block's data. Listing 1-1 illustrates one way to avoid dangling pointers by locking a relocatable block.

Listing 1-1 Locking a block to avoid dangling pointers

```
VAR
   origState:  SignedByte;     {original attributes of handle}

origState := HGetState(Handle(myData));{get handle attributes}
MoveHHi(Handle(myData));              {move the handle high}
HLock(Handle(myData));                {lock the handle}
WITH myData^^ DO                      {fill in window data}
   BEGIN
      editRec := TENew(gDestRect, gViewRect);
      vScroll := GetNewControl(rVScroll, myWindow);
      hScroll := GetNewControl(rHScroll, myWindow);
      fileRefNum := 0;
      windowDirty := FALSE;
   END;
HSetState(origState);                 {reset handle attributes}
```

The handle `myData` needs to be locked before the `WITH` statement because the functions `TENew` and `GetNewControl` allocate memory and hence might move the block whose handle is `myData`.

You should be careful to lock blocks only when necessary, because locked relocatable blocks can increase heap fragmentation and slow down your application unnecessarily. You should lock a handle only if you dereference it, directly or indirectly, and then use a copy of the original master pointer after calling a routine that could move or purge memory. When you no longer need to reference the block with the master pointer, you should unlock the handle. In Listing 1-1, the handle `myData` is never explicitly unlocked. Instead, the original attributes of the handle are saved by calling `HGetState` and later are restored by calling `HSetState`. This strategy is preferable to just calling `HLock` and `HUnlock`.

A compiler can generate hidden dereferencing, and hence potential dangling pointers, in other ways, for instance, by assigning the result of a function that might move or purge blocks to a field in a record referenced by a handle. Such problems are particularly common in code that manipulates linked data structures. For example, you might use this code to allocate a new element of a linked list:

```
myHandle^^.nextHandle := NewHandle(sizeof(myLinkedElement));
```

This can cause problems because your compiler could dereference `myHandle` before calling `NewHandle`. Therefore, you should either lock `myHandle` before performing the allocation, or use a temporary variable to allocate the new handle, as in the following code:

```
tempHandle := NewHandle(sizeof(myLinkedElement));
myHandle^^.nextHandle := tempHandle;
```

Passing fields of records as arguments to routines that might move or purge memory can cause similar problems, if the records are in relocatable blocks referred to with handles. Problems arise only when you pass a field by reference rather than by value. Pascal conventions call for all arguments larger than 4 bytes to be passed by reference. In Pascal, a variable is also passed by reference when the routine called requests a variable parameter. Both of the following lines of code could leave a pointer dangling:

```
TEUpdate(hTE^^.viewRect, hTE);
InvalRect(theControl^^.contrlRect);
```

These problems occur because a compiler may dereference a handle before calling the routine to which you pass the handle. Then, that routine may move memory before it uses the dereferenced handle, which might then be invalid. As before, you can solve these problems by locking the handles or using temporary variables.

Loading Code Segments

If you call an application-defined routine located in a code segment that is not currently in RAM, the Segment Manager might need to move memory when loading that code segment, thus jeopardizing any dereferenced handles you might be using. For example, suppose you call an application-defined procedure `ManipulateData`, which manipulates some data at an address passed to it in a variable parameter.

```
PROCEDURE MyRoutine;
BEGIN
   ...
   ManipulateData(myHandle^);
   ...
END;
```

You can create a dangling pointer if `ManipulateData` and `MyRoutine` are in different segments, and the segment containing `ManipulateData` is not loaded when `MyRoutine` is executed. You can do this because you've passed a dereferenced copy of `myHandle` as an argument to `ManipulateData`. If the Segment Manager must allocate a new relocatable block for the segment containing `ManipulateData`, it might move `myHandle` to do so. If so, the dereferenced handle would dangle. A similar problem can occur if you assign the result of a function in a nonresident code segment to a field in a record referred to by a handle.

You need to be careful even when passing a field in a record referenced by a handle to a routine in the same code segment as the caller, or when assigning the result of a function in the same code segment to such a field. If that routine could call a Toolbox routine that might move or purge memory, or call a routine in a different, nonresident code segment, then you could indirectly cause a pointer to dangle.

Callback Routines

Code segmentation can also lead to a different type of dangling-pointer problem when you use callback routines. The problem rarely arises, but it is difficult to debug. Some Toolbox routines require that you pass a pointer to a procedure in a variable of type `ProcPtr`. Ordinarily, it does not matter whether the procedure you pass in such a variable is in the same code segment as the routine that calls it or in a different code segment. For example, suppose you call `TrackControl` as follows:

```
myPart := TrackControl(myControl, myEvent.where, @MyCallBack);
```

If `MyCallBack` were in the same code segment as this line of code, then a compiler would pass to `TrackControl` the absolute address of the `MyCallBack` procedure. If it were in a different code segment, then the compiler would take the address from the jump table entry for `MyCallBack`. Either way, `TrackControl` should call `MyCallBack` correctly.

Occasionally, you might use a variable of type `ProcPtr` to hold the address of a callback procedure and then pass that address to a routine. Here is an example:

```
myProc := @MyCallBack;
...
myPart := TrackControl(myControl, myEvent.where, myProc);
```

As long as these lines of code are in the same code segment and the segment is not unloaded between the execution of those lines, the preceding code should work perfectly. Suppose, however, that `myProc` is a global variable, and the first line of the code is in a different segment from the call to `TrackControl`. Suppose, further, that the `MyCallBack` procedure is in the same segment as the first line of the code (which is in a different segment from the call to `TrackControl`). Then, the compiler might place the absolute address of the `MyCallBack` routine into the variable `myProc`. The compiler cannot realize that you plan to use the variable in a different code segment from the one that holds both the routine you are referencing and the routine you are using to initialize the `myProc` variable. Because `MyCallBack` and the call to `TrackControl` are in different code segments, the `TrackControl` procedure requires that you pass an address in the jump table, not an absolute address. Thus, in this hypothetical situation, `myProc` would reference `MyCallBack` incorrectly.

To avoid this problem, make sure to place in the same segment any code in which you assign a value to a variable of type `ProcPtr` and any code in which you use that variable. If you must put them in different code segments, then be sure that you place the callback routine in a code segment different from the one that initializes the variable.

Note
Some development systems allow you to specify compiler options that force jump table references to be generated for routine addresses. If you specify those options, the problems described in this section cannot arise. ◆

Invalid Handles

An invalid handle refers to the wrong area of memory, just as a dangling pointer does. There are three types of invalid handles: empty handles, disposed handles, and fake handles. You must avoid empty, disposed, or fake handles as carefully as dangling pointers. Fortunately, it is generally easier to detect, and thus to avoid, invalid handles.

Disposed Handles

A **disposed handle** is a handle whose associated relocatable block has been disposed of. When you dispose of a relocatable block (perhaps by calling the procedure `DisposeHandle`), the Memory Manager does not change the value of any handle variables that previously referenced that block. Instead, those variables still hold the address of what once was the relocatable block's master pointer. Because the block has been disposed of, however, the contents of the master pointer are no longer defined. (The master pointer might belong to a subsequently allocated relocatable block, or it could become part of a linked list of unused master pointers maintained by the Memory Manager.)

If you accidentally use a handle to a block you have already disposed of, you can obtain unexpected results. In the best cases, your application will crash. In the worst cases, you will get garbled data. It might, however, be difficult to trace the cause of the garbled data, because your application can continue to run for quite a while before the problem begins to manifest itself.

You can avoid these problems quite easily by assigning the value `NIL` to the handle variable after you dispose of its associated block. By doing so, you indicate that the handle does not point anywhere in particular. If you subsequently attempt to operate on such a block, the Memory Manager will probably generate a `nilHandleErr` result code. If you want to make certain that a handle is not disposed of before operating on a relocatable block, you can test whether the value of the handle is `NIL`, as follows:

```
IF myHandle <> NIL THEN
   ...;             {handle is valid, so we can operate on it here}
```

Note
This test is useful only if you manually assign the value `NIL` to all disposed handles. The Memory Manager does not do that automatically. ◆

Empty Handles

An **empty handle** is a handle whose master pointer has the value `NIL`. When the Memory Manager purges a relocatable block, for example, it sets the block's master pointer to `NIL`. The space occupied by the master pointer itself remains allocated, and handles to the purged block continue to point to the master pointer. This is useful, because if you later reallocate space for the block by calling `ReallocateHandle`, the master pointer will be updated and all existing handles will correctly access the reallocated block.

Note
Don't confuse empty handles with **0-length handles,** which are handles whose associated block has a size of 0 bytes. A 0-length handle has a non-`NIL` master pointer and a block header. ◆

Once again, however, inadvertently using an empty handle can give unexpected results or lead to a system crash. In the Macintosh Operating System, `NIL` technically refers to memory location 0. But this memory location holds a value. If you doubly dereference an empty handle, you reference whatever data is found at that location, and you could obtain unexpected results that are difficult to trace.

You can check for empty handles much as you check for disposed handles. Assuming you set handles to `NIL` when you dispose of them, you can use the following code to determine whether a handle both points to a valid master pointer and references a nonempty relocatable block:

```
IF myHandle <> NIL THEN
   IF myHandle^ <> NIL THEN
      ...         {we can operate on the relocatable block here}
```

Note that because Pascal evaluates expressions completely, you need two `IF-THEN` statements rather than one compound statement in case the value of the handle itself is `NIL`. Most compilers, however, allow you to use "short-circuit" Boolean operators to minimize the evaluation of expressions. For example, if your compiler uses the operator `&` as a short-circuit operator for `AND`, you could rewrite the preceding code like this:

```
IF (myHandle <> NIL) & (myHandle^ <> NIL) THEN
   ...            {we can operate on the relocatable block here}
```

In this case, the second expression is evaluated only if the first expression evaluates to `TRUE`.

Note
The availability and syntax of short-circuit Boolean operators are compiler dependent. Check the documentation for your development system to see whether you can use such operators. ◆

It is useful during debugging to set memory location 0 to an odd number, such as $50FFC001. This causes the Operating System to crash immediately if you attempt to dereference an empty handle. This is useful, because you can immediately fix problems that might otherwise require extensive debugging.

Fake Handles

A **fake handle** is a handle that was not created by the Memory Manager. Normally, you create handles by either directly or indirectly calling the Memory Manager function `NewHandle` (or one of its variants, such as `NewHandleClear`). You create a fake handle—usually inadvertently—by directly assigning a value to a variable of type `Handle`, as illustrated in Listing 1-2.

Listing 1-2 Creating a fake handle

```
FUNCTION MakeFakeHandle: Handle;      {DON'T USE THIS FUNCTION!}
CONST
   kMemoryLoc = $100;                 {a random memory location}
VAR
   myHandle:   Handle;
   myPointer:  Ptr;
BEGIN
   myPointer := Ptr(kMemoryLoc);      {the address of some memory}
   myHandle := @myPointer;            {the address of a pointer}
   MakeFakeHandle := myHandle;
END;
```

▲ **WARNING**
The technique for creating a fake handle shown in Listing 1-2 is included for illustrative purposes only. Your application should never create fake handles. ▲

Remember that a real handle contains the address of a master pointer. The fake handle manufactured by the function `MakeFakeHandle` in Listing 1-2 contains an address that may or may not be the address of a master pointer. If it isn't the address of a master pointer, then you virtually guarantee chaotic results if you pass the fake handle to a system software routine that expects a real handle.

For example, suppose you pass a fake handle to the `MoveHHi` procedure. After allocating a new relocatable block high in the heap, `MoveHHi` is likely to copy the data from the original block to the new block by dereferencing the handle and using, supposedly, a master pointer. Because, however, the value of a fake handle probably isn't the address of a master pointer, `MoveHHi` copies invalid data. (Actually, it's unlikely that `MoveHHi` would ever get that far; probably it would run into problems when attempting to determine the size of the original block from the block header.)

Not all fake handles are as easy to spot as those created by the `MakeFakeHandle` function defined in Listing 1-2. You might, for instance, attempt to copy the data in an existing record (`myRecord`) into a new handle, as follows:

```
myHandle := NewHandle(SizeOf(myRecord));  {create a new handle}
myHandle^ := @myRecord;                   {DON'T DO THIS!}
```

The second line of code does *not* make `myHandle` a handle to the beginning of the `myRecord` record. Instead, it overwrites the master pointer with the address of that record, making `myHandle` a fake handle.

▲ **WARNING**
Never assign a value directly to a master pointer. ▲

A correct way to create a new handle to some existing data is to make a copy of the data using the `PtrToHand` function, as follows:

```
myErr := PtrToHand(@myRecord, myHandle, SizeOf(myRecord));
```

The Memory Manager provides a set of pointer- and handle-manipulation routines that can help you avoid creating fake handles. See the chapter "Memory Manager" in this book for details on those routines.

Low-Memory Conditions

It is particularly important to make sure that the amount of free space in your application heap never gets too low. For example, you should never deplete the available heap memory to the point that it becomes impossible to load required code segments. As you have seen, your application will crash if the Segment Manager is called to load a required code segment and there is not enough contiguous free memory to allocate a block of the appropriate size.

You can take several steps to help maximize the amount of free space in your heap. For example, you can mark as purgeable any relocatable blocks whose contents could easily be reconstructed. By making a block purgeable, you give the Memory Manager the freedom to release that space if heap memory becomes low. You can also help maximize the available heap memory by intelligently segmenting your application's executable code and by periodically unloading any unneeded segments. The standard way to do this is to unload every nonessential segment at the end of your application's main event loop. (See the chapter "Segment Manager" in *Inside Macintosh: Processes* for a complete discussion of code-segmentation techniques.)

Memory Cushions

These two measures—making blocks purgeable and unloading segments—help you only by releasing blocks that have already been allocated. It is even more important to make sure, *before* you attempt to allocate memory directly, that you don't deplete the available heap memory. Before you call `NewHandle` or `NewPtr`, you should check that, if the requested amount of memory were in fact allocated, the remaining amount of space free in the heap would not fall below a certain threshold. The free memory defined by that threshold is your **memory cushion.** You should not simply inspect the handle or pointer returned to you and make sure that its value isn't `NIL`, because you might have succeeded in allocating the space you requested but left the amount of free space dangerously low.

You also need to make sure that indirect memory allocation doesn't cut into the memory cushion. When, for example, you call `GetNewDialog`, the Dialog Manager might need to allocate space for a dialog record; it also needs to allocate heap space for the dialog item list and any other custom items in the dialog. Before calling `GetNewDialog`, therefore, you need to make sure that the amount of space left free after the call is greater than your memory cushion.

The execution of some system software routines requires significant amounts of memory in your heap. For example, some QuickDraw operations on regions can temporarily allocate fairly large amounts of space in your heap. Some of these system software routines, however, do little or no checking to see that your heap contains the required amount of free space. They either assume that they will get whatever memory they need or they simply issue a system error when they don't get the needed memory. In either case, the result is usually a system crash.

You can avoid these problems by making sure that there is always enough space in your heap to handle these hidden memory allocations. Experience has shown that 40 KB is a reasonably safe size for this memory cushion. If you can consistently maintain that amount of space free in your heap, you can be reasonably certain that system software routines will get the memory they need to operate. You also generally need a larger cushion (about 70 KB) when printing.

Memory Reserves

Unfortunately, there are times when you might need to use some of the memory in the cushion yourself. It is better, for instance, to dip into the memory cushion, if necessary, to save a user's document than to reject the request to save the document. Some actions your application performs should not be rejectable simply because they require it to reduce the amount of free space below a desired minimum.

Instead of relying on just the free memory of a memory cushion, you can allocate a **memory reserve,** some additional emergency storage that you release when free memory becomes low. The important difference between this memory reserve and the memory cushion is that the memory reserve is a block of allocated memory, which you release whenever you detect that essential tasks have dipped into the memory cushion.

That emergency memory reserve might provide enough memory to compensate for any essential tasks that you fail to anticipate. Because you allow essential tasks to dip into the memory cushion, the release itself of the memory reserve should not be a cause for alarm. Using this scheme, your application releases the memory reserve as a precautionary measure during ordinary operation. Ideally, however, the application should never actually deplete the memory cushion and use the memory reserve.

Grow-Zone Functions

The Memory Manager provides a particularly easy way for you to make sure that the emergency memory reserve is released when necessary. You can define a **grow-zone function** that is associated with your application heap. The Memory Manager calls your heap's grow-zone function only after other techniques of freeing memory to satisfy a memory request fail (that is, after compacting and purging the heap and extending the heap zone to its maximum size). The grow-zone function can then take appropriate steps to free additional memory.

A grow-zone function might dispose of some blocks or make some unpurgeable blocks purgeable. When the function returns, the Memory Manager once again purges and compacts the heap and tries to reallocate memory. If there is still insufficient memory, the Memory Manager calls the grow-zone function again (but only if the function returned a nonzero value the previous time it was called). This mechanism allows your grow-zone function to release just a little bit of memory at a time. If the amount it releases at any time is not enough, the Memory Manager calls it again and gives it the opportunity to take more drastic measures. As the most drastic step to freeing memory in your heap, you can release the emergency reserve.

Using Memory

This section describes how you can use the Memory Manager to perform the most typical memory management tasks. In particular, this section shows how you can

- set up your application heap at application launch time
- determine how much free space is available in your application heap
- allocate and release blocks of memory in your heap
- define and install a grow-zone function

The techniques described in this section are designed to minimize fragmentation of your application heap and to ensure that your application always has sufficient memory to complete any essential operations. Many of these techniques incorporate the heap memory cushion and emergency memory reserve discussed in "Low-Memory Conditions," beginning on page 1-36.

Note
This section describes relatively simple memory-management techniques. Depending on the requirements of your application, you might want to manage your heap memory differently. ◆

Setting Up the Application Heap

When the Process Manager launches your application, it calls the Memory Manager to create and initialize a memory partition for your application. The Process Manager then loads code segments into memory and sets up the stack, heap, and A5 world (including the jump table) for your application.

To help prevent heap fragmentation, you should also perform some setup of your own early in your application's execution. Depending on the needs of your application, you might want to

- change the size of your application's stack
- expand the heap to the heap limit
- allocate additional master pointer blocks

The following sections describe in detail how and when to perform these operations.

Changing the Size of the Stack

Most applications allocate space on their stack in a predictable way and do not need to monitor stack space during their execution. For these applications, stack usage usually reaches a maximum in some heavily nested routine. If the stack in your application can never grow beyond a certain size, then to avoid collisions between your stack and heap you simply need to ensure that your stack is large enough to accommodate that size. If you never encounter system error 28 (generated by the stack sniffer when it detects a collision between the stack and the heap) during application testing, then you probably do not need to increase the size of your stack.

Some applications, however, rely heavily on recursive programming techniques, in which one routine repeatedly calls itself or a small group of routines repeatedly call each other. In these applications, even routines with just a few local variables can cause stack overflow, because each time a routine calls itself, a new copy of that routine's parameters and variables is appended to the stack. The problem can become particularly acute if one or more of the local variables is a string, which can require up to 256 bytes of stack space.

You can help prevent your application from crashing because of insufficient stack space by expanding the size of your stack. If your application does not depend on recursion, you should do this only if you encounter system error 28 during testing. If your application does depend on recursion, you might consider expanding the stack so that your application can perform deeply nested recursive computations. In addition, some object-oriented languages (for example, C++) allocate space for objects on the stack. If you are using one of these languages, you might need to expand your stack.

Note

If you are programming in LISP or another language that depends extensively on recursion, your development system might allocate memory for local variables in the heap rather than on the stack. If so, expanding the size of the stack is not helpful. Consult your development system's documentation for details on how it allocates memory. ◆

To increase the size of your stack, you simply reduce the size of your heap. Because the heap cannot grow above the boundary contained in the `ApplLimit` global variable, you can lower the value of `ApplLimit` to limit the heap's growth. By lowering `ApplLimit`, technically you are not making the stack bigger; you are just preventing collisions between it and the heap.

By default, the stack can grow to 8 KB on Macintosh computers without Color QuickDraw and to 32 KB on computers with Color QuickDraw. (The size of the stack for a faceless background process is always 8 KB, whether Color QuickDraw is present or not.) You should never decrease the size of the stack, because future versions of system software might increase the default amount of space allocated for the stack. For the same reason, you should not set the stack to a predetermined absolute size or calculate a new absolute size for the stack based on the microprocessor's type. If you must modify the size of the stack, you should increase the stack size only by some relative amount that is sufficient to meet the increased stack requirements of your application. There is no maximum size to which the stack can grow.

Listing 1-3 defines a procedure that increases the stack size by a given value. It does so by determining the current heap limit, subtracting the value of the `extraBytes` parameter from that value, and then setting the application limit to the difference.

Listing 1-3 Increasing the amount of space allocated for the stack

```
PROCEDURE IncreaseStackSize (extraBytes: Size);
BEGIN
   SetApplLimit(Ptr(ORD4(GetApplLimit) - extraBytes));
END;
```

You should call this procedure at the beginning of your application, before you call the `MaxApplZone` procedure (as described in the next section). If you call `IncreaseStackSize` after you call `MaxApplZone`, it has no effect, because the `SetApplLimit` procedure cannot change the `ApplLimit` global variable to a value lower than the current top of the heap.

Note
Some compilers add to the beginning of your application some default initialization code that automatically calls `MaxApplZone`. You might need to specify a compiler directive that turns off such default initialization if you want to increase the size of the stack. Consult your development system's documentation for details. ◆

Expanding the Heap

Near the beginning of your application's execution, before you allocate any memory, you should call the `MaxApplZone` procedure to expand the application heap immediately to the application heap limit. If you do not do this, the Memory Manager gradually expands your heap as memory needs require. This gradual expansion can result in significant heap fragmentation if you have previously moved relocatable blocks to the top of the heap (by calling `MoveHHi`) and locked them (by calling `HLock`). When the heap grows beyond those locked blocks, they are no longer at the top of the heap. Your heap then remains fragmented for as long as those blocks remain locked.

Another advantage to calling MaxApplZone is that doing so is likely to reduce the number of relocatable blocks that are purged by the Memory Manager. The Memory Manager expands your heap to fulfill a memory request only after it has exhausted other methods of obtaining the required amount of space, including compacting the heap and purging blocks marked as purgeable. By expanding the heap to its limit, you can prevent the Memory Manager from purging blocks that it otherwise would purge. This, together with the fact that your heap is expanded only once, can make memory allocation significantly faster.

Note
As indicated in the previous section, you should call MaxApplZone only after you have expanded the stack, if necessary. ◆

Allocating Master Pointer Blocks

After calling MaxApplZone, you should call the MoreMasters procedure to allocate as many new nonrelocatable blocks of master pointers as your application is likely to need during its execution. Each block of master pointers in your application heap contains 64 master pointers. The Operating System allocates one block of master pointers as your application is loaded into memory, and every relocatable block you allocate needs one master pointer to reference it.

If, when you allocate a relocatable block, there are no unused master pointers in your application heap, the Memory Manager automatically allocates a new block of master pointers. For several reasons, however, you should try to prevent the Memory Manager from calling MoreMasters for you. First, MoreMasters executes more slowly if it has to move relocatable blocks up in the heap to make room for the new nonrelocatable block of master pointers. When your application first starts running, there are no such blocks that might have to be moved. Second, the new nonrelocatable block of master pointers is likely to fragment your application heap. At any time the Memory Manager is forced to call MoreMasters for you, there are already at least 64 relocatable blocks allocated in your heap. Unless all or most of those blocks are locked high in the heap (an unlikely situation), the new nonrelocatable block of master pointers might be allocated above existing relocatable blocks. This increases heap fragmentation.

To prevent this fragmentation, you should call MoreMasters at the beginning of your application enough times to ensure that the Memory Manager never needs to call it for you. For example, if your application never allocates more than 300 relocatable blocks in its heap, then five calls to the MoreMasters should be enough. It's better to call MoreMasters too many times than too few, so if your application usually allocates about 100 relocatable blocks but sometimes might allocate 1000 in a particularly busy session, you should call MoreMasters enough times at the beginning of the program to cover the larger figure.

You can determine empirically how many times to call MoreMasters by using a low-level debugger. First, remove all the calls to MoreMasters from your code and then give your application a rigorous workout, opening and closing windows, dialog boxes, and desk accessories as much as any user would. Then, find out from your debugger how many times the system called MoreMasters. To do so, count the nonrelocatable blocks of size $100 bytes (decimal 256, or 64 × 4). Because of Memory Manager size corrections, you should also count any nonrelocatable blocks of size $108, $10C, or $110 bytes. (You should also check to make sure that your application doesn't allocate other nonrelocatable blocks of those sizes. If it does, subtract the number it allocates from the total.) Finally, call `MoreMasters` at least that many times at the beginning of your application.

Listing 1-4 illustrates a typical sequence of steps to configure your application heap and stack. The `DoSetUpHeap` procedure defined there increases the size of the stack by 32 KB, expands the application heap to its new limit, and allocates five additional blocks of master pointers.

Listing 1-4 Setting up your application heap and stack

```
PROCEDURE DoSetUpHeap;
CONST
   kExtraStackSpace = $8000;              {32 KB}
   kMoreMasterCalls = 5;                  {for 320 master ptrs}
VAR
   count:   Integer;
BEGIN
   IncreaseStackSize(kExtraStackSpace);   {increase stack size}
   MaxApplZone;                           {extend heap to limit}
   FOR count := 1 TO kMoreMasterCalls DO
      MoreMasters;                        {64 more master ptrs}
END;
```

To reduce heap fragmentation, you should call `DoSetUpHeap` in a code segment that you never unload (possibly the main segment) rather than in a special initialization code segment. This is because `MoreMasters` allocates a nonrelocatable block. If you call `MoreMasters` from a code segment that is later purged, the new master pointer block is located above the purged space, thereby increasing fragmentation.

Determining the Amount of Free Memory

Because space in your heap is limited, you cannot usually honor every user request that would require your application to allocate memory. For example, every time the user opens a new window, you probably need to allocate a new window record and other associated data structures. If you allow the user to open windows endlessly, you risk running out of memory. This might adversely affect your application's ability to perform important operations such as saving existing data in a window.

It is important, therefore, to implement some scheme that prevents your application from using too much of its own heap. One way to do this is to maintain a memory cushion that can be used only to satisfy essential memory requests. Before allocating memory for any nonessential task, you need to ensure that the amount of memory that remains free after the allocation exceeds the size of your memory cushion. You can do this by calling the function IsMemoryAvailable defined in Listing 1-5.

Listing 1-5 Determining whether allocating memory would deplete the memory cushion

```
FUNCTION IsMemoryAvailable (memRequest: LongInt): Boolean;
VAR
   total:    LongInt;     {total free memory if heap purged}
   contig:   LongInt;     {largest contiguous block if heap purged}
BEGIN
   PurgeSpace(total, contig);
   IsMemoryAvailable := ((memRequest + kMemCushion) < contig);
END;
```

The IsMemoryAvailable function calls the Memory Manager's PurgeSpace procedure to determine the size of the largest contiguous block that would be available if the application heap were purged; that size is returned in the contig parameter. If the size of the potential memory request together with the size of the memory cushion is less than the value returned in contig, IsMemoryAvailable is set to TRUE, indicating that it is safe to allocate the specified amount of memory; otherwise, IsMemoryAvailable returns FALSE.

Notice that the IsMemoryAvailable function does not itself cause the heap to be purged or compacted; the Memory Manager does so automatically when you actually attempt to allocate the memory.

Usually, the easiest way to determine how big to make your application's memory cushion is to experiment with various values. You should attempt to find the lowest value that allows your application to execute successfully no matter how hard you try to allocate memory to make the application crash. As an extra guarantee against your application's crashing, you might want to add some memory to this value. As indicated earlier in this chapter, 40 KB is a reasonable size for most applications.

```
CONST
   kMemCushion =  40 * 1024;           {size of memory cushion}
```

You should call the IsMemoryAvailable function before all nonessential memory requests, no matter how small. For example, suppose your application allocates a new, small relocatable block each time a user types a new line of text. That block might be small, but thousands of such blocks could take up a considerable amount of space. Therefore, you should check to see if there is sufficient memory available before allocating each one. (See Listing 1-6 on page 1-44 for an example of how to call IsMemoryAvailable.)

You should never, however, call the IsMemoryAvailable function before an essential memory request. When deciding how big to make the memory cushion for your application, you must make sure that essential requests can never deplete all of the cushion. Note that when you call the IsMemoryAvailable function for a nonessential request, essential requests might have already dipped into the memory cushion. In that case, IsMemoryAvailable returns FALSE no matter how small the nonessential request is.

Some actions should never be rejectable. For example, you should guarantee that there is always enough memory free to save open documents, and to perform typical maintenance tasks such as updating windows. Other user actions are likely to be always rejectable. For example, because you cannot allow the user to create an endless number of documents, you should make the New Document and Open Document menu commands rejectable.

Although the decisions of which actions to make rejectable are usually obvious, modal and modeless boxes present special problems. If you want to make such dialog boxes available at all costs, you must ensure that you allocate a large enough memory cushion to handle the maximum number of these dialog boxes that the user could open at once. If you consider a certain dialog box (for instance, a spelling checker) nonessential, you must be prepared to inform the user that there is not enough memory to open it if memory space become low.

Allocating Blocks of Memory

As you have seen, a key element of the memory-management scheme presented in this chapter is to disallow any nonessential memory allocation requests that would deplete the memory cushion. In practice, this means that, before calling NewHandle, NewPtr, or another function that allocates memory, you should check that the amount of space remaining after the allocation, if successful, exceeds the size of the memory cushion.

An easy way to do this is never to allocate memory for nonessential tasks by calling NewHandle or NewPtr directly. Instead call a function such as NewHandleCushion, defined in Listing 1-6, or NewPtrCushion, defined in Listing 1-7.

Listing 1-6 Allocating relocatable blocks

```
FUNCTION NewHandleCushion (logicalSize: Size): Handle;
BEGIN
   IF NOT IsMemoryAvailable(logicalSize) THEN
      NewHandleCushion := NIL
   ELSE
      BEGIN
         SetGrowZone(NIL);           {remove grow-zone function}
         NewHandleCushion := NewHandleClear(logicalSize);
         SetGrowZone(@MyGrowZone);   {install grow-zone function}
      END;
END;
```

The NewHandleCushion function first calls IsMemoryAvailable to determine whether allocating the requested number of bytes would deplete the memory cushion.

If so, NewHandleCushion returns NIL to indicate that the request has failed. Otherwise, if there is indeed sufficient space for the new block, NewHandleCushion calls NewHandleClear to allocate the relocatable block. Before calling NewHandleClear, however, NewHandleCushion disables the grow-zone function for the application heap. This prevents the grow-zone function from releasing any emergency memory reserve your application might be maintaining. See "Defining a Grow-Zone Function" on page 1-48 for details on grow-zone functions.

You can define a function NewPtrCushion to handle allocation of nonrelocatable blocks, as shown in Listing 1-7.

Listing 1-7 Allocating nonrelocatable blocks

```
FUNCTION NewPtrCushion (logicalSize: Size): Handle;
BEGIN
   IF NOT IsMemoryAvailable(logicalSize) THEN
      NewPtrCushion := NIL
   ELSE
      BEGIN
         SetGrowZone(NIL);          {remove grow-zone function}
         NewPtrCushion := NewPtrClear(logicalSize);
         SetGrowZone(@MyGrowZone);  {install grow-zone function}
      END;
END;
```

Note
The functions NewHandleCushion and NewPtrCushion allocate prezeroed blocks in your application heap. You can easily modify those functions if you do not want the blocks prezeroed. ◆

Listing 1-8 illustrates a typical way to call NewPtrCushion.

Listing 1-8 Allocating a dialog record

```
FUNCTION GetDialog (dialogID: Integer): DialogPtr;
VAR
   myPtr: Ptr;                {storage for the dialog record}
BEGIN
   myPtr := NewPtrCushion(SizeOf(DialogRecord));
   IF MemError = noErr THEN
      GetDialog := GetNewDialog(dialogID, myPtr, WindowPtr(-1))
   ELSE
      GetDialog := NIL;       {can't get memory}
END;
```

When you allocate memory directly, you can later release it by calling the `DisposeHandle` and `DisposePtr` procedures. When you allocate memory indirectly by calling a Toolbox routine, there is always a corresponding Toolbox routine to release that memory. For example, the `DisposeWindow` procedure releases memory allocated with the `NewWindow` function. Be sure to use these special Toolbox routines instead of the generic Memory Manager routines when applicable.

Maintaining a Memory Reserve

A simple way to help ensure that your application always has enough memory available for essential operations is to maintain an emergency memory reserve. This **memory reserve** is a block of memory that your application uses only for essential operations and only when all other heap space has been allocated. This section illustrates one way to implement a memory reserve in your application.

To create and maintain an emergency memory reserve, you follow three distinct steps:

- When your application starts up, you need to allocate a block of reserve memory. Because you allocate the block, it is no longer free in the heap and does not enter into the free-space determination done by `IsMemoryAvailable`.
- When your application needs to fulfill an essential memory request and there isn't enough space in your heap to satisfy the request, you can release the reserve. This effectively ensures that you always have the memory you request, at least for essential operations. You can use a grow-zone function to release the reserve when necessary; see "Defining a Grow-Zone Function" on page 1-48 for details.
- Each time through your main event loop, you should check whether the reserve has been released. If it has, you should attempt to recover the reserve. If you cannot recover the reserve, you should warn the user that memory is critically short.

To refer to the emergency reserve, you can declare a global variable of type `Handle`.

```
VAR
   gEmergencyMemory: Handle;   {handle to emergency memory reserve}
```

Listing 1-9 defines a function that you can call early in your application's execution (before entering your main event loop) to create an emergency memory reserve. This function also installs the application-defined grow-zone procedure. See "Defining a Grow-Zone Function" on page 1-48 for a description of the grow-zone function.

Listing 1-9 Creating an emergency memory reserve

```
PROCEDURE InitializeEmergencyMemory;
BEGIN
   gEmergencyMemory := NewHandle(kEmergencyMemorySize);
   SetGrowZone(@MyGrowZone);
END;
```

The `InitializeEmergencyMemory` procedure defined in Listing 1-9 simply allocates a relocatable block of a predefined size. That block is the emergency memory reserve. A reasonable size for the memory reserve is whatever size you use for the memory cushion. Once again, 40 KB is a good size for many applications.

```
CONST
   kEmergencyMemorySize =  40 * 1024;  {size of memory reserve}
```

When using a memory reserve, you need to change the `IsMemoryAvailable` function defined earlier in Listing 1-5. You need to make sure, when determining whether a nonessential memory allocation request should be honored, that the memory reserve has not been released. To check that the memory reserve is intact, use the function `IsEmergencyMemory` defined in Listing 1-10.

Listing 1-10 Checking the emergency memory reserve

```
FUNCTION IsEmergencyMemory: Boolean;
BEGIN
   IsEmergencyMemory :=
      (gEmergencyMemory <> NIL) & (gEmergencyMemory^ <> NIL);
END;
```

Then, you can replace the function `IsMemoryAvailable` defined in Listing 1-5 (page 1-43) by the version defined in Listing 1-11.

Listing 1-11 Determining whether allocating memory would deplete the memory cushion

```
FUNCTION IsMemoryAvailable (memRequest: LongInt): Boolean;
VAR
   total:   LongInt;     {total free memory if heap purged}
   contig:  LongInt;     {largest contiguous block if heap purged}
BEGIN
   IF NOT IsEmergencyMemory THEN {is emergency memory available?}
      IsMemoryAvailable := FALSE
   ELSE
   BEGIN
      PurgeSpace(total, contig);
      IsMemoryAvailable := ((memRequest + kMemCushion) < contig);
   END;
END;
```

As you can see, this is exactly like the earlier version except that it indicates that memory is not available if the memory reserve is not intact.

Once you have allocated the memory reserve early in your application's execution, it should be released only to honor essential memory requests when there is no other space available in your heap. You can install a simple grow-zone function that takes care of releasing the reserve at the proper moment. Each time through your main event loop, you can check whether the reserve is still intact; to do this, add these lines of code to your main event loop, before you make your event call:

```
IF NOT IsEmergencyMemory THEN
   RecoverEmergencyMemory;
```

The `RecoverEmergencyMemory` function, defined in Listing 1-12, simply attempts to reallocate the memory reserve.

Listing 1-12 Reallocating the emergency memory reserve

```
PROCEDURE RecoverEmergencyMemory;
BEGIN
   ReallocateHandle(gEmergencyMemory, kEmergencyMemorySize);
END;
```

If you are unable to reallocate the memory reserve, you might want to notify the user that because memory is in short supply, steps should be taken to save any important data and to free some memory.

Defining a Grow-Zone Function

The Memory Manager calls your heap's grow-zone function only after other attempts to obtain enough memory to satisfy a memory allocation request have failed. A grow-zone function should be of the following form:

```
FUNCTION MyGrowZone (cbNeeded: Size): LongInt;
```

The Memory Manager passes to your function (in the `cbNeeded` parameter) the number of bytes it needs. Your function can do whatever it likes to free that much space in the heap. For example, your grow-zone function might dispose of certain blocks or make some unpurgeable blocks purgeable. Your function should return the number of bytes, if any, it managed to free.

When the function returns, the Memory Manager once again purges and compacts the heap and tries again to allocate the requested amount of memory. If there is still insufficient memory, the Memory Manager calls your grow-zone function again, but only if the function returned a nonzero value when last called. This mechanism allows your grow-zone function to release memory gradually; if the amount it releases is not enough, the Memory Manager calls it again and gives it the opportunity to take more drastic measures.

Typically a grow-zone function frees space by calling the `EmptyHandle` procedure, which purges a relocatable block from the heap and sets the block's master pointer to `NIL`. This is preferable to disposing of the space (by calling the `DisposeHandle` procedure), because you are likely to want to reallocate the block.

The Memory Manager might designate a particular relocatable block in the heap as **protected;** your grow-zone function should not move or purge that block. You can determine which block, if any, the Memory Manager has protected by calling the `GZSaveHnd` function in your grow-zone function.

Listing 1-13 defines a very basic grow-zone function. The `MyGrowZone` function attempts to create space in the application heap simply by releasing the block of emergency memory. First, however, it checks that (1) the emergency memory hasn't already been released and (2) the emergency memory is not a protected block of memory (as it would be, for example, during an attempt to reallocate the emergency memory block). If either of these conditions isn't true, then `MyGrowZone` returns 0 to indicate that no memory was released.

Listing 1-13 A grow-zone function that releases emergency storage

```
FUNCTION MyGrowZone (cbNeeded: Size): LongInt;
VAR
   theA5:   LongInt;              {value of A5 when function is called}
BEGIN
   theA5 := SetCurrentA5;         {remember current value of A5; install ours}
   IF (gEmergencyMemory^ <> NIL) & (gEmergencyMemory <> GZSaveHnd) THEN
      BEGIN
         EmptyHandle(gEmergencyMemory);
         MyGrowZone := kEmergencyMemorySize;
      END
   ELSE
      MyGrowZone := 0;            {no more memory to release}
   theA5 := SetA5(theA5);         {restore previous value of A5}
END;
```

The function `MyGrowZone` defined in Listing 1-13 saves the current value of the A5 register when it begins and then restores the previous value before it exits. This is necessary because your grow-zone function might be called at a time when the system is attempting to allocate memory and value in the A5 register is not correct. See the chapter "Memory Management Utilities" in this book for more information about saving and restoring the A5 register.

Note

You need to save and restore the A5 register only if your grow-zone function accesses your A5 world. (In Listing 1-13, the grow-zone function uses the global variable `gEmergencyMemory`.) ◆

Memory Management Reference

This section describes the routines used to illustrate the memory-management techniques presented earlier in this chapter. In particular, it describes the routines that allow you to manipulate blocks of memory in your application heap.

Note
For a complete description of all Memory Manager data types and routines, see the chapter "Memory Manager" in this book. ◆

Memory Management Routines

This section describes the routines you can use to set up your application's heap, allocate and dispose of relocatable and nonrelocatable blocks, manipulate those blocks, assess the availability of memory in your application's heap, free memory from the heap, and install a grow-zone function for your heap.

Note
The result codes listed for Memory Manager routines are usually not directly returned to your application. You need to call the `MemError` function (or, from assembly language, inspect the `MemErr` global variable) to get a routine's result code. ◆

You cannot call most Memory Manager routines at interrupt time for several reasons. You cannot allocate memory at interrupt time because the Memory Manager might already be handling a memory-allocation request and the heap might be in an inconsistent state. More generally, you cannot call at interrupt time any Memory Manager routine that returns its result code via the `MemError` function, even if that routine doesn't allocate or move memory. Resetting the `MemErr` global variable at interrupt time can lead to unexpected results if the interrupted code depends on the value of `MemErr`. Note that Memory Manager routines like `HLock` return their results via `MemError` and therefore should not be called in interrupt code.

Setting Up the Application Heap

The Operating System automatically initializes your application's heap when your application is launched. To help prevent heap fragmentation, you should call the procedures in this section before you allocate any blocks of memory in your heap.

Use the `MaxApplZone` procedure to extend the application heap zone to the application heap limit so that the Memory Manager does not do so gradually as memory requests require. Use the `MoreMasters` procedure to preallocate enough blocks of master pointers so that the Memory Manager never needs to allocate new master pointer blocks for you.

MaxApplZone

To help ensure that you can use as much of the application heap zone as possible, call the `MaxApplZone` procedure. Call this once near the beginning of your program, after you have expanded your stack.

```
PROCEDURE MaxApplZone;
```

DESCRIPTION

The `MaxApplZone` procedure expands the application heap zone to the application heap limit. If you do not call `MaxApplZone`, the application heap zone grows as necessary to fulfill memory requests. The `MaxApplZone` procedure does not purge any blocks currently in the zone. If the zone already extends to the limit, `MaxApplZone` does nothing.

It is a good idea to call `MaxApplZone` once at the beginning of your program if you intend to maintain an effectively partitioned heap. If you do not call `MaxApplZone` and then call `MoveHHi` to move relocatable blocks to the top of the heap zone before locking them, the heap zone could later grow beyond these locked blocks to fulfill a memory request. If the Memory Manager were to allocate a nonrelocatable block in this new space, your heap would be fragmented.

ASSEMBLY-LANGUAGE INFORMATION

The registers on exit for `MaxApplZone` are

Registers on exit

D0 Result code

RESULT CODES

`noErr`	0	No error

MoreMasters

Call the `MoreMasters` procedure several times at the beginning of your program to prevent the Memory Manager from running out of master pointers in the middle of application execution. If it does run out, it allocates more, possibly causing heap fragmentation.

```
PROCEDURE MoreMasters;
```

DESCRIPTION

The `MoreMasters` procedure allocates another block of master pointers in the current heap zone. In the application heap, a block of master pointers consists of 64 master pointers, and in the system heap, a block consists of 32 master pointers. (These values, however, might change in future versions of system software.) When you initialize additional heap zones, you can specify the number of master pointers you want to have in a block of master pointers.

The Memory Manager automatically calls `MoreMasters` once for every new heap zone, including the application heap zone.

You should call `MoreMasters` at the beginning of your program enough times to ensure that the Memory Manager never needs to call it for you. For example, if your application never allocates more than 300 relocatable blocks in its heap zone, then five calls to the `MoreMasters` should be enough. It's better to call `MoreMasters` too many times than too few. For instance, if your application usually allocates about 100 relocatable blocks but might allocate 1000 in a particularly busy session, call `MoreMasters` enough times at the beginning of the program to accommodate times of greater memory use.

If you are forced to call `MoreMasters` so many times that it causes a significant slowdown, you could change the `moreMast` field of the zone header to the total number of master pointers you need and then call `MoreMasters` just once. Afterward, be sure to restore the `moreMast` field to its original value.

SPECIAL CONSIDERATIONS

Because `MoreMasters` allocates memory, you should not call it at interrupt time.

The calls to `MoreMasters` at the beginning of your application should be in the main code segment of your application or in a segment that the main segment never unloads.

ASSEMBLY-LANGUAGE INFORMATION

The registers on exit for `MoreMasters` are

Registers on exit

D0	Result code

RESULT CODES

`noErr`	0	No error
`memFullErr`	–108	Not enough memory

GetApplLimit

Use the `GetApplLimit` function to get the application heap limit, beyond which the application heap cannot expand.

```
FUNCTION GetApplLimit: Ptr;
```

DESCRIPTION

The `GetApplLimit` function returns the current application heap limit. The Memory Manager expands the application heap only up to the byte preceding this limit.

Nothing prevents the stack from growing below the application limit. If the Operating System detects that the stack has crashed into the heap, it generates a system error. To avoid this, use `GetApplLimit` and the `SetApplLimit` procedure to set the application limit low enough so that a growing stack does not encounter the heap.

Note

The `GetApplLimit` function does not indicate the amount of memory available to your application. ◆

ASSEMBLY-LANGUAGE INFORMATION

The global variable `ApplLimit` contains the current application heap limit.

SetApplLimit

Use the `SetApplLimit` procedure to set the application heap limit, beyond which the application heap cannot expand.

```
PROCEDURE SetApplLimit (zoneLimit: Ptr);
```

`zoneLimit` A pointer to a byte in memory demarcating the upper boundary of the application heap zone. The zone can grow to include the byte preceding `zoneLimit` in memory, but no further.

DESCRIPTION

The `SetApplLimit` procedure sets the current application heap limit to `zoneLimit`. The Memory Manager then can expand the application heap only up to the byte preceding the application limit. If the zone already extends beyond the specified limit, the Memory Manager does not cut it back but does prevent it from growing further.

Note
The `zoneLimit` parameter is not a byte count, but an absolute byte in memory. Thus, you should use the `SetApplLimit` procedure only with a value obtained from the Memory Manager functions `GetApplLimit` or `ApplicationZone`. ◆

You cannot change the limit of zones other than the application heap zone.

ASSEMBLY-LANGUAGE INFORMATION

The registers on entry and exit for `SetApplLimit` are

Registers on entry

A0	Pointer to desired new zone limit

Registers on exit

D0	Result code

RESULT CODES

`noErr`	0	No error
`memFullErr`	–108	Not enough memory

SEE ALSO

To use `SetApplLimit` to expand the default size of the stack, see the discussion in "Changing the Size of the Stack" on page 1-39.

Allocating and Releasing Relocatable Blocks of Memory

You can use the `NewHandle` function to allocate a relocatable block of memory. If you want to allocate new blocks of memory with their bits precleared to 0, you can use the `NewHandleClear` function.

▲ **WARNING**
You should not call any of these memory-allocation routines at interrupt time. ▲

You can use the `DisposeHandle` procedure to free relocatable blocks of memory you have allocated.

NewHandle

You can use the `NewHandle` function to allocate a relocatable memory block of a specified size.

```
FUNCTION NewHandle (logicalSize: Size): Handle;
```

`logicalSize`
The requested size (in bytes) of the relocatable block.

DESCRIPTION

The `NewHandle` function attempts to allocate a new relocatable block in the current heap zone with a logical size of `logicalSize` bytes and then return a handle to the block. The new block is unlocked and unpurgeable. If `NewHandle` cannot allocate a block of the requested size, it returns `NIL`.

▲ **WARNING**
Do not try to manufacture your own handles without this function by simply assigning the address of a variable of type `Ptr` to a variable of type `Handle`. The resulting "fake handle" would not reference a relocatable block and could cause a system crash. ▲

The `NewHandle` function pursues all available avenues to create a block of the requested size, including compacting the heap zone, increasing its size, and purging blocks from it. If all of these techniques fail and the heap zone has a grow-zone function installed, `NewHandle` calls the function. Then `NewHandle` tries again to free the necessary amount of memory, once more compacting and purging the heap zone if necessary. If memory still cannot be allocated, `NewHandle` calls the grow-zone function again, unless that function had returned 0, in which case `NewHandle` gives up and returns `NIL`.

SPECIAL CONSIDERATIONS

Because `NewHandle` allocates memory, you should not call it at interrupt time.

ASSEMBLY-LANGUAGE INFORMATION

The registers on entry and exit for `NewHandle` are

Registers on entry

A0 Number of logical bytes requested

Registers on exit

A0 Address of the new block's master pointer or `NIL`

D0 Result code

If you want to clear the bytes of a block of memory to 0 when you allocate it with the `NewHandle` function, set bit 9 of the routine trap word. You can usually do this by supplying the word `CLEAR` as the second argument to the routine macro, as follows:

```
_NewHandle ,CLEAR
```

RESULT CODES

`noErr`	0	No error
`memFullErr`	–108	Not enough memory in heap zone

SEE ALSO

If you allocate a relocatable block that you plan to lock for long periods of time, you can prevent heap fragmentation by allocating the block as low as possible in the heap zone. To do this, see the description of the `ReserveMem` procedure on page 1-70.

If you plan to lock a relocatable block for short periods of time, you might want to move it to the top of the heap zone to prevent heap fragmentation. For more information, see the description of the `MoveHHi` procedure on page 1-71.

NewHandleClear

You can use the `NewHandleClear` function to allocate prezeroed memory in a relocatable block of a specified size.

```
FUNCTION NewHandleClear (logicalSize: Size): Handle;
```

`logicalSize`
: The requested size (in bytes) of the relocatable block. The `NewHandleClear` function sets each of these bytes to 0.

DESCRIPTION

The `NewHandleClear` function works much as the `NewHandle` function does but sets all bytes in the new block to 0 instead of leaving the contents of the block undefined.

Currently, `NewHandleClear` clears the block one byte at a time. For a large block, it might be faster to clear the block manually a long word at a time.

RESULT CODES

`noErr`	0	No error
`memFullErr`	–108	Not enough memory in heap zone

DisposeHandle

When you are completely done with a relocatable block, call the `DisposeHandle` procedure to free it and its master pointer for other uses.

```
PROCEDURE DisposeHandle (h: Handle);
```

`h`	A handle to a relocatable block.

DESCRIPTION

The `DisposeHandle` procedure releases the memory occupied by the relocatable block whose handle is `h`. It also frees the handle's master pointer for other uses.

▲ **WARNING**
After a call to `DisposeHandle`, all handles to the released block become invalid and should not be used again. Any subsequent calls to `DisposeHandle` using an invalid handle might damage the master pointer list. ▲

Do not use `DisposeHandle` to dispose of a handle obtained from the Resource Manager (for example, by a previous call to `GetResource`); use `ReleaseResource` instead. If, however, you have called `DetachResource` on a resource handle, you should dispose of the storage by calling `DisposeHandle`.

SPECIAL CONSIDERATIONS

Because `DisposeHandle` purges memory, you should not call it at interrupt time.

ASSEMBLY-LANGUAGE INFORMATION

The registers on entry and exit for `DisposeHandle` are

Registers on entry

A0	Handle to the relocatable block to be disposed of

Registers on exit

D0	Result code

RESULT CODES

`noErr`	0	No error
`memWZErr`	–111	Attempt to operate on a free block

Allocating and Releasing Nonrelocatable Blocks of Memory

You can use the `NewPtr` function to allocate a nonrelocatable block of memory. If you want to allocate new blocks of memory with their bits precleared to 0, you can use the `NewPtrClear` function.

▲ **WARNING**
You should not call any of these memory-allocation routines at interrupt time. ▲

You can use the `DisposePtr` procedure to free nonrelocatable blocks of memory you have allocated.

NewPtr

You can use the `NewPtr` function to allocate a nonrelocatable block of memory of a specified size.

```
FUNCTION NewPtr (logicalSize: Size): Ptr;
```

`logicalSize`
The requested size (in bytes) of the nonrelocatable block.

DESCRIPTION

The `NewPtr` function attempts to allocate, in the current heap zone, a nonrelocatable block with a logical size of `logicalSize` bytes and then return a pointer to the block. If the requested number of bytes cannot be allocated, `NewPtr` returns `NIL`.

The `NewPtr` function attempts to reserve space as low in the heap zone as possible for the new block. If it is able to reserve the requested amount of space, `NewPtr` allocates the nonrelocatable block in the gap `ReserveMem` creates. Otherwise, `NewPtr` returns `NIL` and generates a `memFullErr` error.

SPECIAL CONSIDERATIONS

Because `NewPtr` allocates memory, you should not call it at interrupt time.

ASSEMBLY-LANGUAGE INFORMATION

The registers on entry and exit for `NewPtr` are

Registers on entry

A0	Number of logical bytes requested

Registers on exit

A0	Address of the new block or `NIL`
D0	Result code

If you want to clear the bytes of a block of memory to 0 when you allocate it with the `NewPtr` function, set bit 9 of the routine trap word. You can usually do this by supplying the word `CLEAR` as the second argument to the routine macro, as follows:

```
_NewPtr ,CLEAR
```

RESULT CODES

`noErr`	0	No error
`memFullErr`	–108	Not enough memory

NewPtrClear

You can use the `NewPtrClear` function to allocate prezeroed memory in a nonrelocatable block of a specified size.

```
FUNCTION NewPtrClear (logicalSize: Size): Ptr;
```

`logicalSize`
The requested size (in bytes) of the nonrelocatable block.

DESCRIPTION

The `NewPtrClear` function works much as the `NewPtr` function does, but sets all bytes in the new block to 0 instead of leaving the contents of the block undefined.

Currently, `NewPtrClear` clears the block one byte at a time. For a large block, it might be faster to clear the block manually a long word at a time.

RESULT CODES

`noErr`	0	No error
`memFullErr`	–108	Not enough memory

DisposePtr

When you are completely done with a nonrelocatable block, call the `DisposePtr` procedure to free it for other uses.

```
PROCEDURE DisposePtr (p: Ptr);
```

`p` A pointer to the nonrelocatable block you want to dispose of.

DESCRIPTION

The `DisposePtr` procedure releases the memory occupied by the nonrelocatable block specified by `p`.

▲ **WARNING**
After a call to `DisposePtr`, all pointers to the released block become invalid and should not be used again. Any subsequent use of a pointer to the released block might cause a system error. ▲

SPECIAL CONSIDERATIONS

Because `DisposePtr` purges memory, you should not call it at interrupt time.

ASSEMBLY-LANGUAGE INFORMATION

The registers on entry and exit for `DisposePtr` are

Registers on entry

A0 Pointer to the nonrelocatable block to be disposed of

Registers on exit

D0 Result code

RESULT CODES

`noErr`	0	No error
`memWZErr`	–111	Attempt to operate on a free block

Setting the Properties of Relocatable Blocks

A relocatable block can be either locked or unlocked and either purgeable or unpurgeable. In addition, it can have its resource bit either set or cleared. To determine the state of any of these properties, use the `HGetState` function. To change these properties, use the `HLock`, `HUnlock`, `HPurge`, `HNoPurge`, `HSetRBit`, and `HClrRBit` procedures. To restore these properties, use the `HSetState` procedure.

▲ **WARNING**
Be sure to use these procedures to get and set the properties of relocatable blocks. In particular, do not rely on the structure of master pointers, because their structure in 24-bit mode is different from their structure in 32-bit mode. ▲

HGetState

You can use the `HGetState` function to get the current properties of a relocatable block (perhaps so that you can change and then later restore those properties).

```
FUNCTION HGetState (h: Handle): SignedByte;
```

`h` A handle to a relocatable block.

DESCRIPTION

The `HGetState` function returns a signed byte containing the flags of the master pointer for the given handle. You can save this byte, change the state of any of the flags, and then restore their original states by passing the byte to the `HSetState` procedure, described next.

You can use bit-manipulation functions on the returned signed byte to determine the value of a given attribute. Currently the following bits are used:

Bit	Meaning
0–4	Reserved
5	Set if relocatable block is a resource
6	Set if relocatable block is purgeable
7	Set if relocatable block is locked

If an error occurs during an attempt to get the state flags of the specified relocatable block, `HGetState` returns the low-order byte of the result code as its function result. For example, if the handle `h` points to a master pointer whose value is `NIL`, then the signed byte returned by `HGetState` will contain the value –109.

ASSEMBLY-LANGUAGE INFORMATION

The registers on entry and exit for `HGetState` are

Registers on entry

A0 Handle whose properties you want to get

Registers on exit

D0 Byte containing flags

RESULT CODES

`noErr`	0	No error
`nilHandleErr`	–109	`NIL` master pointer
`memWZErr`	–111	Attempt to operate on a free block

HSetState

You can use the `HSetState` procedure to restore properties of a block after a call to `HGetState`.

```
PROCEDURE HSetState (h: Handle; flags: SignedByte);
```

`h` A handle to a relocatable block.

`flags` A signed byte specifying the properties to which you want to set the relocatable block.

DESCRIPTION

The `HSetState` procedure restores to the handle `h` the properties specified in the `flags` signed byte. See the description of the `HGetState` function for a list of the currently used bits in that byte. Because additional bits of the `flags` byte could become significant in future versions of system software, use `HSetState` only with a byte returned by `HGetState`. If you need to set two or three properties of a relocatable block at once, it is better to use the procedures that set individual properties than to manipulate the bits returned by `HGetState` and then call `HSetState`.

ASSEMBLY-LANGUAGE INFORMATION

The registers on entry and exit for `HSetState` are

Registers on entry

A0	Handle whose properties you want to set
D0	Byte containing flags indicating the handle's new properties

Registers on exit

D0	Result code

RESULT CODES

`noErr`	0	No error
`nilHandleErr`	–109	`NIL` master pointer
`memWZErr`	–111	Attempt to operate on a free block

HLock

You can use the `HLock` procedure to lock a relocatable block so that it does not move in the heap. If you plan to dereference a handle and then allocate, move, or purge memory (or call a routine that does so), then you should lock the handle before using the dereferenced handle.

```
PROCEDURE HLock (h: Handle);
```

`h` A handle to a relocatable block.

DESCRIPTION

The `HLock` procedure locks the relocatable block to which `h` is a handle, preventing it from being moved within its heap zone. If the block is already locked, `HLock` does nothing.

ASSEMBLY-LANGUAGE INFORMATION

The registers on entry and exit for `HLock` are

Registers on entry

A0 Handle to lock

Registers on exit

D0 Result code

RESULT CODES

`noErr`	0	No error
`nilHandleErr`	–109	`NIL` master pointer
`memWZErr`	–111	Attempt to operate on a free block

SEE ALSO

If you plan to lock a relocatable block for long periods of time, you can prevent fragmentation by ensuring that the block is as low as possible in the heap zone. To do this, see the description of the `ReserveMem` procedure on page 1-70.

If you plan to lock a relocatable block for short periods of time, you can prevent heap fragmentation by moving the block to the top of the heap zone before locking. For more information, see the description of the `MoveHHi` procedure on page 1-71.

HUnlock

You can use the `HUnlock` procedure to unlock a relocatable block so that it is free to move in its heap zone.

```
PROCEDURE HUnlock (h: Handle);
```

`h` A handle to a relocatable block.

DESCRIPTION

The `HUnlock` procedure unlocks the relocatable block to which `h` is a handle, allowing it to be moved within its heap zone. If the block is already unlocked, `HUnlock` does nothing.

ASSEMBLY-LANGUAGE INFORMATION

The registers on entry and exit for HUnlock are

Registers on entry

A0 Handle to unlock

Registers on exit

D0 Result code

RESULT CODES

noErr	0	No error
nilHandleErr	–109	NIL master pointer
memWZErr	–111	Attempt to operate on a free block

HPurge

You can use the HPurge procedure to mark a relocatable block so that it can be purged if a memory request cannot be fulfilled after compaction.

```
PROCEDURE HPurge (h: Handle);
```

h A handle to a relocatable block.

DESCRIPTION

The HPurge procedure makes the relocatable block to which h is a handle purgeable. If the block is already purgeable, HPurge does nothing.

The Memory Manager might purge the block when it needs to purge the heap zone containing the block to satisfy a memory request. A direct call to the PurgeMem procedure or the MaxMem function would also purge blocks marked as purgeable.

Once you mark a relocatable block as purgeable, you should make sure that handles to the block are not empty before you access the block. If they are empty, you must reallocate space for the block and recopy the block's data from another source, such as a resource file, before using the information in the block.

If the block to which h is a handle is locked, HPurge does not unlock the block but does mark it as purgeable. If you later call HUnlock on h, the block is subject to purging.

ASSEMBLY-LANGUAGE INFORMATION

The registers on entry and exit for `HPurge` are

Registers on entry

A0	Handle to make purgeable

Registers on exit

D0	Result code

RESULT CODES

`noErr`	0	No error
`nilHandleErr`	–109	`NIL` master pointer
`memWZErr`	–111	Attempt to operate on a free block

SEE ALSO

If the Memory Manager has purged a block, you can reallocate space for it by using the `ReallocateHandle` procedure, described on page 1-68.

You can immediately free the space taken by a handle without disposing of it by calling `EmptyHandle`. This procedure, described on page 1-67, does not require that the block be purgeable.

HNoPurge

You can use the `HNoPurge` procedure to mark a relocatable block so that it cannot be purged.

```
PROCEDURE HNoPurge (h: Handle);
```

`h`	A handle to a relocatable block.

DESCRIPTION

The `HNoPurge` procedure makes the relocatable block to which `h` is a handle unpurgeable. If the block is already unpurgeable, `HNoPurge` does nothing.

The `HNoPurge` procedure does not reallocate memory for a handle if it has already been purged.

ASSEMBLY-LANGUAGE INFORMATION

The registers on entry and exit for `HNoPurge` are

Registers on entry

A0 Handle to make unpurgeable

Registers on exit

D0 Result code

RESULT CODES

`noErr`	0	No error
`nilHandleErr`	–109	`NIL` master pointer
`memWZErr`	–111	Attempt to operate on a free block

SEE ALSO

If you want to reallocate memory for a relocatable block that has already been purged, you can use the `ReallocateHandle` procedure, described in the next section, "Managing Relocatable Blocks."

Managing Relocatable Blocks

The Memory Manager provides routines that allow you to purge and later reallocate space for relocatable blocks and control where in their heap zone relocatable blocks are located.

To free the memory taken up by a relocatable block without releasing the master pointer to the block for other uses, use the `EmptyHandle` procedure. To reallocate space for a handle that you have emptied or the Memory Manager has purged, use the `ReallocateHandle` procedure.

To ensure that a relocatable block that you plan to lock for short or long periods of time does not cause heap fragmentation, use the `MoveHHi` and the `ReserveMem` procedures, respectively.

EmptyHandle

The `EmptyHandle` procedure allows you to free memory taken by a relocatable block without freeing the relocatable block's master pointer for other uses.

```
PROCEDURE EmptyHandle (h: Handle);
```

`h` A handle to a relocatable block.

DESCRIPTION

The `EmptyHandle` procedure purges the relocatable block whose handle is `h` and sets the handle's master pointer to `NIL`. The block whose handle is `h` must be unlocked but need not be purgeable.

Note
If there are multiple handles to the relocatable block, then calling the `EmptyHandle` procedure empties them all, because all of the handles share a common master pointer. When you later use `ReallocateHandle` to reallocate space for the block, the master pointer is updated, and all of the handles reference the new block correctly. ◆

SPECIAL CONSIDERATIONS

Because `EmptyHandle` purges memory, you should not call it at interrupt time.

ASSEMBLY-LANGUAGE INFORMATION

The registers on entry and exit for `EmptyHandle` are

Registers on entry

A0	Handle to relocatable block

Registers on exit

A0	Handle to relocatable block
D0	Result code

RESULT CODES

`noErr`	0	No error
`memWZErr`	–111	Attempt to operate on a free block
`memPurErr`	–112	Attempt to purge a locked block

SEE ALSO

To free the memory taken up by a relocatable block and release the block's master pointer for other uses, use the `DisposeHandle` procedure, described on page 1-57.

ReallocateHandle

To recover space for a relocatable block that you have emptied or the Memory Manager has purged, use the `ReallocateHandle` procedure.

```
PROCEDURE ReallocateHandle (h: Handle; logicalSize: Size);
```

`h` A handle to a relocatable block.

`logicalSize`
The desired new logical size (in bytes) of the relocatable block.

DESCRIPTION

The `ReallocateHandle` procedure allocates a new relocatable block with a logical size of `logicalSize` bytes. It updates the handle `h` by setting its master pointer to point to the new block. The new block is unlocked and unpurgeable.

Usually you use `ReallocateHandle` to reallocate space for a block that you have emptied or the Memory Manager has purged. If the handle references an existing block, `ReallocateHandle` releases that block before creating a new one.

Note
To reallocate space for a resource that has been purged, you should call `LoadResource`, not `ReallocateHandle`. ◆

If many handles reference a single purged, relocatable block, you need to call `ReallocateHandle` on just one of them.

In case of an error, `ReallocateHandle` neither allocates a new block nor changes the master pointer to which handle `h` points.

SPECIAL CONSIDERATIONS

Because `ReallocateHandle` might purge and allocate memory, you should not call it at interrupt time.

ASSEMBLY-LANGUAGE INFORMATION

The registers on entry and exit for `ReallocateHandle` are

Registers on entry

A0	Handle for new relocatable block
D0	Desired logical size, in bytes, of new block

Registers on exit

D0	Result code

RESULT CODES

`noErr`	0	No error
`memROZErr`	–99	Heap zone is read-only
`memFullErr`	–108	Not enough memory
`memWZErr`	–111	Attempt to operate on a free block
`memPurErr`	–112	Attempt to purge a locked block

ReserveMem

Use the `ReserveMem` procedure when you allocate a relocatable block that you intend to lock for long periods of time. This helps prevent heap fragmentation because it reserves space for the block as close to the bottom of the heap as possible. Consistent use of `ReserveMem` for this purpose ensures that all locked, relocatable blocks and nonrelocatable blocks are together at the bottom of the heap zone and thus do not prevent unlocked relocatable blocks from moving about the zone.

```
PROCEDURE ReserveMem (cbNeeded: Size);
```

`cbNeeded` The number of bytes to reserve near the bottom of the heap.

DESCRIPTION

The `ReserveMem` procedure attempts to create free space for a block of `cbNeeded` contiguous logical bytes at the lowest possible position in the current heap zone. It pursues every available means of placing the block as close as possible to the bottom of the zone, including moving other relocatable blocks upward, expanding the zone (if possible), and purging blocks from it.

Because `ReserveMem` does not actually allocate the block, you must combine calls to `ReserveMem` with calls to the `NewHandle` function.

Do not use the `ReserveMem` procedure for a relocatable block you intend to lock for only a short period of time. If you do so and then allocate a nonrelocatable block above it, the relocatable block becomes trapped under the nonrelocatable block when you unlock that relocatable block.

Note

It isn't necessary to call `ReserveMem` to reserve space for a nonrelocatable block, because the `NewPtr` function calls it automatically. Also, you do not need to call `ReserveMem` to reserve memory before you load a locked resource into memory, because the Resource Manager calls `ReserveMem` automatically. ◆

SPECIAL CONSIDERATIONS

Because the `ReserveMem` procedure could move and purge memory, you should not call it at interrupt time.

ASSEMBLY-LANGUAGE INFORMATION

The registers on entry and exit for `ReserveMem` are

Registers on entry

D0	Number of bytes to reserve

Registers on exit

D0	Result code

RESULT CODES

`noErr`	0	No error
`memFullErr`	–108	Not enough memory

MoveHHi

If you plan to lock a relocatable block for a short period of time, use the `MoveHHi` procedure, which moves the block to the top of the heap and thus helps prevent heap fragmentation.

```
PROCEDURE MoveHHi (h: Handle);
```

`h` A handle to a relocatable block.

DESCRIPTION

The `MoveHHi` procedure attempts to move the relocatable block referenced by the handle `h` upward until it reaches a nonrelocatable block, a locked relocatable block, or the top of the heap.

▲ **WARNING**
If you call `MoveHHi` to move a handle to a resource that has its `resChanged` bit set, the Resource Manager updates the resource by using the `WriteResource` procedure to write the contents of the block to disk. If you want to avoid this behavior, call the Resource Manager procedure `SetResPurge(FALSE)` before you call `MoveHHi`, and then call `SetResPurge(TRUE)` to restore the default setting. ▲

By using the `MoveHHi` procedure on relocatable blocks you plan to allocate for short periods of time, you help prevent islands of immovable memory from accumulating in (and thus fragmenting) the heap.

Do not use the `MoveHHi` procedure to move blocks you plan to lock for long periods of time. The `MoveHHi` procedure moves such blocks to the top of the heap, perhaps preventing other blocks already at the top of the heap from moving down once they are unlocked. Instead, use the `ReserveMem` procedure before allocating such blocks, thus keeping them in the bottom partition of the heap, where they do not prevent relocatable blocks from moving.

If you frequently lock a block for short periods of time and find that calling `MoveHHi` each time slows down your application, you might consider leaving the block always locked and calling the `ReserveMem` procedure before allocating it.

Once you move a block to the top of the heap, be sure to lock it if you do not want the Memory Manager to move it back to the middle partition as soon as it can. (The `MoveHHi` procedure cannot move locked blocks; be sure to lock blocks after, not before, calling `MoveHHi`.)

Note
Using the `MoveHHi` procedure without taking other precautionary measures to prevent heap fragmentation is useless, because even one small nonrelocatable or locked relocatable block in the middle of the heap might prevent `MoveHHi` from moving blocks to the top of the heap. ◆

SPECIAL CONSIDERATIONS

Because the `MoveHHi` procedure moves memory, you should not call it at interrupt time.

Don't call `MoveHHi` on blocks in the system heap. Don't call `MoveHHi` from a desk accessory.

ASSEMBLY-LANGUAGE INFORMATION

The registers on entry and exit for `MoveHHi` are

Registers on entry

A0	Handle to move

Registers on exit

D0	Result code

RESULT CODES

`noErr`	0	No error
`nilHandleErr`	–109	`NIL` master pointer
`memLockedErr`	–117	Block is locked

HLockHi

You can use the `HLockHi` procedure to move a relocatable block to the top of the heap and lock it.

```
PROCEDURE HLockHi (h: Handle);
```

`h` A handle to a relocatable block.

DESCRIPTION

The `HLockHi` procedure attempts to move the relocatable block referenced by the handle `h` upward until it reaches a nonrelocatable block, a locked relocatable block, or the top of the heap. Then `HLockHi` locks the block.

The `HLockHi` procedure is simply a convenient replacement for the pair of procedures `MoveHHi` and `HLock`.

SPECIAL CONSIDERATIONS

Because the `HLockHi` procedure moves memory, you should not call it at interrupt time.

Don't call `HLockHi` on blocks in the system heap. Don't call `HLockHi` from a desk accessory.

ASSEMBLY-LANGUAGE INFORMATION

The registers on entry and exit for `HLockHi` are

Registers on entry

A0 Handle to move and lock

Registers on exit

D0 Result code

RESULT CODES

noErr	0	No error
nilHandleErr	–109	NIL master pointer
memWZErr	–111	Attempt to operate on a free block
memLockedErr	–117	Block is locked

Manipulating Blocks of Memory

The Memory Manager provides a routine for copying blocks of memory referenced by pointers. To copy a block of memory to a nonrelocatable block, you can use the `BlockMove` procedure.

BlockMove

To copy a sequence of bytes from one location in memory to another, you can use the `BlockMove` procedure.

```
PROCEDURE BlockMove (sourcePtr, destPtr: Ptr; byteCount: Size);
```

`sourcePtr` The address of the first byte to copy.

`destPtr` The address of the first byte to copy to.

`byteCount` The number of bytes to copy. If the value of `byteCount` is 0, `BlockMove` does nothing.

DESCRIPTION

The `BlockMove` procedure moves a block of `byteCount` consecutive bytes from the address designated by `sourcePtr` to that designated by `destPtr`. It updates no pointers.

The `BlockMove` procedure works correctly even if the source and destination blocks overlap.

SPECIAL CONSIDERATIONS

You can safely call `BlockMove` at interrupt time. Even though it moves memory, `BlockMove` does not move relocatable blocks, but simply copies bytes.

The `BlockMove` procedure currently flushes the processor caches whenever the number of bytes to be moved is greater than 12. This behavior can adversely affect your application's performance. You might want to avoid calling `BlockMove` to move small amounts of data in memory if there is no possibility of moving stale data or instructions. For more information about stale data and instructions, see the discussion of the processor caches in the chapter "Memory Management Utilities" in this book.

ASSEMBLY-LANGUAGE INFORMATION

The registers on entry and exit for `BlockMove` are

Registers on entry

A0 Pointer to source

A1 Pointer to destination

D0 Number of bytes to copy

Registers on exit

D0 Result code

RESULT CODE

`noErr`	0	No error

Assessing Memory Conditions

The Memory Manager provides routines to test how much memory is available. To determine the total amount of free space in the current heap zone or the size of the maximum block that could be obtained after a purge of the heap, call the `PurgeSpace` function.

To find out whether a Memory Manager operation finished successfully, use the `MemError` function.

PurgeSpace

Use the `PurgeSpace` procedure to determine the total amount of free memory and the size of the largest allocatable block after a purge of the heap.

```
PROCEDURE PurgeSpace (VAR total: LongInt; VAR contig: LongInt);
```

`total` On exit, the total amount of free memory in the current heap zone if it were purged.

`contig` On exit, the size of the largest contiguous block of free memory in the current heap zone if it were purged.

DESCRIPTION

The `PurgeSpace` procedure returns, in the `total` parameter, the total amount of space (in bytes) that could be obtained after a general purge of the current heap zone; this amount includes space that is already free. In the `contig` parameter, `PurgeSpace` returns the size of the largest allocatable block in the current heap zone that could be obtained after a purge of the zone.

The `PurgeSpace` procedure does not actually purge the current heap zone.

ASSEMBLY-LANGUAGE INFORMATION

The registers on exit for `PurgeSpace` are

Registers on exit

A0	Maximum number of contiguous bytes after purge
D0	Total free memory after purge

RESULT CODES

`noErr`	0	No error

MemError

To find out whether your application's last direct call to a Memory Manager routine executed successfully, use the MemError function.

```
FUNCTION MemError: OSErr;
```

DESCRIPTION

The MemError function returns the result code produced by the last Memory Manager routine your application called directly.

This function is useful during application debugging. You might also use the function as one part of a memory-management scheme to identify instances in which the Memory Manager rejects overly large memory requests by returning the error code memFullErr.

▲ **WARNING**
Do not rely on the MemError function as the only component of a memory-management scheme. For example, suppose you call NewHandle or NewPtr and receive the result code noErr, indicating that the Memory Manager was able to allocate sufficient memory. In this case, you have no guarantee that the allocation did not deplete your application's memory reserves to levels so low that simple operations might cause your application to crash. Instead of relying on MemError, check before making a memory request that there is enough memory both to fulfill the request and to support essential operations. ▲

ASSEMBLY-LANGUAGE INFORMATION

Because most Memory Manager routines return a result code in register D0, you do not ordinarily need to call the MemError function if you program in assembly language. See the description of an individual routine to find out whether it returns a result code in register D0. If not, you can examine the global variable MemErr. When MemError returns, register D0 contains the result code.

Registers on exit

D0	Result code

RESULT CODES

noErr	0	No error
paramErr	–50	Error in parameter list
memROZErr	–99	Operation on a read-only zone
memFullErr	–108	Not enough memory
nilHandleErr	–109	NIL master pointer
memWZErr	–111	Attempt to operate on a free block
memPurErr	–112	Attempt to purge a locked block
memBCErr	–115	Block check failed
memLockedErr	–117	Block is locked

Grow-Zone Operations

You can implement a grow-zone function that the Memory Manager calls when it cannot fulfill a memory request. You should use the grow-zone function only as a last resort to free memory when all else fails.

The `SetGrowZone` procedure specifies which function the Memory Manager should use for the current zone. The grow-zone function should call the `GZSaveHnd` function to receive a handle to a relocatable block that the grow-zone function must not move or purge.

SetGrowZone

To specify a grow-zone function for the current heap zone, pass a pointer to that function to the `SetGrowZone` procedure. Ordinarily, you call this procedure early in the execution of your application.

If you initialize your own heap zones besides the application and system zones, you can alternatively specify a grow-zone function as a parameter to the `InitZone` procedure.

```
PROCEDURE SetGrowZone (growZone: ProcPtr);
```

`growZone` A pointer to the grow-zone function.

DESCRIPTION

The `SetGrowZone` procedure sets the current heap zone's grow-zone function as designated by the `growZone` parameter. A `NIL` parameter value removes any grow-zone function the zone might previously have had.

The Memory Manager calls the grow-zone function only after exhausting all other avenues of satisfying a memory request, including compacting the zone, increasing its size (if it is the original application zone and is not yet at its maximum size), and purging blocks from it.

See "Grow-Zone Functions" on page 1-80 for a complete description of a grow-zone function.

ASSEMBLY-LANGUAGE INFORMATION

The registers on entry and exit for `SetGrowZone` are

Registers on entry

A0 Pointer to new grow-zone function

Registers on exit

D0 Result code

RESULT CODES

noErr	0	No error

SEE ALSO

See "Defining a Grow-Zone Function" on page 1-48 for a description of a grow-zone function.

GZSaveHnd

Your grow-zone function must call the GZSaveHnd function to obtain a handle to a protected relocatable block that the grow-zone function must not move, purge, or delete.

```
FUNCTION GZSaveHnd: Handle;
```

DESCRIPTION

The GZSaveHnd function returns a handle to a relocatable block that the grow-zone function must not move, purge, or delete. It returns NIL if there is no such block. The returned handle is a handle to the block of memory being manipulated by the Memory Manager at the time that the grow-zone function is called.

ASSEMBLY-LANGUAGE INFORMATION

You can find the same handle in the global variable GZRootHnd.

Setting and Restoring the A5 Register

Any code that runs asynchronously or as a callback routine and that accesses the calling application's A5 world must ensure that the A5 register correctly points to the boundary between the application parameters and the application global variables. To accomplish this, you can call the SetCurrentA5 function at the beginning of any asynchronous or callback code that isn't executed at interrupt time. If the code is executed at interrupt time, you must use the SetA5 function to set the value of the A5 register. (You determine this value at noninterrupt time by calling SetCurrentA5.) Then you must restore the A5 register to its previous value before the interrupt code returns.

SetCurrentA5

You can use the `SetCurrentA5` function to get the current value of the system global variable `CurrentA5`.

```
FUNCTION SetCurrentA5: LongInt;
```

DESCRIPTION

The `SetCurrentA5` function does two things: First, it gets the current value in the A5 register and returns it to your application. Second, `SetCurrentA5` sets register A5 to the value of the low-memory global variable `CurrentA5`. This variable points to the boundary between the parameters and global variables of the current application.

SPECIAL CONSIDERATIONS

You cannot reliably call `SetCurrentA5` in code that is executed at interrupt time unless you first guarantee that your application is the current process (for example, by calling the Process Manager function `GetCurrentProcess`). In general, you should call `SetCurrentA5` at noninterrupt time and then pass the returned value to the interrupt code.

ASSEMBLY-LANGUAGE INFORMATION

You can access the value of the current application's A5 register with the low-memory global variable `CurrentA5`.

SetA5

In interrupt code that accesses application global variables, use the `SetA5` function first to restore a value previously saved using `SetCurrentA5`, and then, at the end of the code, to restore the A5 register to the value it had before the first call to `SetA5`.

```
FUNCTION SetA5 (newA5: LongInt): LongInt;
```

`newA5` The value to which the A5 register is to be changed.

DESCRIPTION

The `SetA5` function performs two tasks: it returns the address in the A5 register when the function is called, and it sets the A5 register to the address specified in `newA5`.

Application-Defined Routines

The techniques illustrated in this chapter use only one application-defined routine, a grow-zone function.

Grow-Zone Functions

The Memory Manager calls your application's grow-zone function whenever it cannot find enough contiguous memory to satisfy a memory allocation request and has exhausted other means of obtaining the space.

MyGrowZone

A grow-zone function should have the following form:

```
FUNCTION MyGrowZone (cbNeeded: Size): LongInt;
```

`cbNeeded` The physical size, in bytes, of the needed block, including the block header. The grow-zone function should attempt to create a free block of at least this size.

DESCRIPTION

Whenever the Memory Manager has exhausted all available means of creating space within your application heap—including purging, compacting, and (if possible) expanding the heap—it calls your application-defined grow-zone function. The grow-zone function can do whatever is necessary to create free space in the heap. Typically, a grow-zone function marks some unneeded blocks as purgeable or releases an emergency memory reserve maintained by your application.

The grow-zone function should return a nonzero value equal to the number of bytes of memory it has freed, or zero if it is unable to free any. When the function returns a nonzero value, the Memory Manager once again purges and compacts the heap zone and tries to reallocate memory. If there is still insufficient memory, the Memory Manager calls the grow-zone function again (but only if the function returned a nonzero value the previous time it was called). This mechanism allows your grow-zone function to release just a little bit of memory at a time. If the amount it releases at any time is not enough, the Memory Manager calls it again and gives it the opportunity to take more drastic measures.

The Memory Manager might designate a particular relocatable block in the heap as protected; your grow-zone function should not move or purge that block. You can determine which block, if any, the Memory Manager has protected by calling the `GZSaveHnd` function in your grow-zone function.

Remember that a grow-zone function is called while the Memory Manager is attempting to allocate memory. As a result, your grow-zone function should not allocate memory itself or perform any other actions that might indirectly cause memory to be allocated (such as calling routines in unloaded code segments or displaying dialog boxes).

You install a grow-zone function by passing its address to the `InitZone` procedure when you create a new heap zone or by calling the `SetGrowZone` procedure at any other time.

SPECIAL CONSIDERATIONS

Your grow-zone function might be called at a time when the system is attempting to allocate memory and the value in the A5 register is not correct. If your function accesses your application's A5 world or makes any trap calls, you need to set up and later restore the A5 register by calling `SetCurrentA5` and `SetA5`.

Because of the optimizations performed by some compilers, the actual work of the grow-zone function and the setting and restoring of the A5 register might have to be placed in separate procedures.

SEE ALSO

See "Defining a Grow-Zone Function" on page 1-48 for a definition of a sample grow-zone function.

Summary of Memory Management

Pascal Summary

Data Types

```
TYPE
   SignedByte          = -128..127;        {arbitrary byte of memory}
   Byte                = 0..255;           {unsigned, arbitrary byte}
   Ptr                 = ^SignedByte;      {pointer to nonrelocatable block}
   Handle              = ^Ptr;             {handle to relocatable block}

   ProcPtr             = Ptr;              {procedure pointer}

   Size                = LongInt;          {size, in bytes, of block}
```

Memory Management Routines

Setting Up the Application Heap

```
PROCEDURE MaxApplZone;
PROCEDURE MoreMasters;
FUNCTION GetApplLimit        : Ptr;
PROCEDURE SetApplLimit       (zoneLimit: Ptr);
```

Allocating and Releasing Relocatable Blocks of Memory

```
FUNCTION NewHandle           (logicalSize: Size): Handle;
FUNCTION NewHandleClear      (logicalSize: Size): Handle;
PROCEDURE DisposeHandle      (h: Handle);
```

Allocating and Releasing Nonrelocatable Blocks of Memory

```
FUNCTION NewPtr              (logicalSize: Size): Ptr;
FUNCTION NewPtrClear         (logicalSize: Size): Ptr;
PROCEDURE DisposePtr         (p: Ptr);
```

Setting the Properties of Relocatable Blocks

```
FUNCTION HGetState           (h: Handle): SignedByte;
PROCEDURE HSetState          (h: Handle; flags: SignedByte);
PROCEDURE HLock              (h: Handle);
PROCEDURE HUnlock            (h: Handle);
PROCEDURE HPurge             (h: Handle);
PROCEDURE HNoPurge           (h: Handle);
```

Managing Relocatable Blocks

```
PROCEDURE EmptyHandle        (h: Handle);
PROCEDURE ReallocateHandle   (h: Handle; logicalSize: Size);
PROCEDURE ReserveMem         (cbNeeded: Size);
PROCEDURE MoveHHi            (h: Handle);
PROCEDURE HLockHi            (h: Handle);
```

Manipulating Blocks of Memory

```
PROCEDURE BlockMove          (sourcePtr, destPtr: Ptr; byteCount: Size);
```

Assessing Memory Conditions

```
PROCEDURE PurgeSpace         (VAR total: LongInt; VAR contig: LongInt);
FUNCTION MemError            : OSErr;
```

Grow-Zone Operations

```
PROCEDURE SetGrowZone        (growZone: ProcPtr);
FUNCTION GZSaveHnd           : Handle;
```

Setting and Restoring the A5 Register

```
FUNCTION SetCurrentA5        : LongInt;
FUNCTION SetA5               (newA5: LongInt) : LongInt;
```

Application-Defined Routines

Grow-Zone Functions

```
FUNCTION MyGrowZone          (cbNeeded: Size): LongInt;
```

C Summary

Data Types

```
typedef char SignedByte;                /*arbitrary byte of memory*/
typedef unsigned char Byte;             /*unsigned, arbitrary byte*/
typedef char *Ptr;                      /*pointer to nonrelocatable block*/
typedef Ptr *Handle;                    /*handle to relocatable block*/

typedef long (*ProcPtr)();              /*procedure pointer*/
typedef long Size;                      /*size in bytes of block*/
```

Memory Management Routines

Setting Up the Application Heap

```
pascal void MaxApplZone      (void);
pascal void MoreMasters      (void);
#define GetApplLimit()       (* (Ptr*) 0x0130)
pascal void SetApplLimit     (void *zoneLimit);
```

Allocating and Releasing Relocatable Blocks of Memory

```
pascal Handle NewHandle      (Size byteCount);
pascal Handle NewHandleClear (Size byteCount);
pascal void DisposeHandle    (Handle h);
```

Allocating and Releasing Nonrelocatable Blocks of Memory

```
pascal Ptr NewPtr            (Size byteCount);
pascal Ptr NewPtrClear       (Size byteCount);
pascal void DisposePtr       (Ptr p);
```

Setting the Properties of Relocatable Blocks

```
pascal char HGetState        (Handle h);
pascal void HSetState        (Handle h, char flags);
pascal void HLock            (Handle h);
pascal void HUnlock          (Handle h);
pascal void HPurge           (Handle h);
pascal void HNoPurge         (Handle h);
```

Managing Relocatable Blocks

```
pascal void EmptyHandle      (Handle h);
pascal void ReallocateHandle (Handle h, Size byteCount);
pascal void ReserveMem       (Size cbNeeded);
pascal void MoveHHi          (Handle h);
pascal void HLockHi          (Handle h);
```

Manipulating Blocks of Memory

```
pascal void BlockMove        (const void *srcPtr, void *destPtr,
                              Size byteCount);
```

Assessing Memory Conditions

```
pascal void PurgeSpace       (long *total, long *contig);
#define MemError()           (* (OSErr*) 0x0220)
```

Grow-Zone Operations

```
pascal void SetGrowZone      (GrowZoneProcPtr growZone);
#define GZSaveHnd()          (* (Handle*) 0x0328)
```

Setting and Restoring the A5 Register

```
long SetCurrentA5            (void);
long SetA5                   (long newA5);
```

Application-Defined Routines

Grow-Zone Functions

```
pascal long MyGrowZone       (Size cbNeeded);
```

Assembly-Language Summary

Global Variables

ApplLimit	long	The application heap limit, beyond which the heap cannot expand.
ApplZone	long	A pointer to the original application heap zone.
BufPtr	long	Address of highest byte of allocatable memory.
CurrentA5	long	Address of the boundary between the application global variables and the application parameters of the current application.
GZRootHnd	long	A handle to a block that the grow-zone function must not move.

Result Codes

noErr	0	No error
paramErr	–50	Error in parameter list
memROZErr	–99	Heap zone is read-only
memFullErr	–108	Not enough memory
nilHandleErr	–109	NIL master pointer
memWZErr	–111	Attempt to operate on a free block
memPurErr	–112	Attempt to purge a locked block
memBCErr	–115	Block check failed
memLockedErr	–117	Block is locked

Memory Manager

Contents

This chapter describes how your application can use the Memory Manager to manage memory both in its own partition and outside its partition. Ordinarily, you allocate memory in your application heap only. You might, however, occasionally need to access memory outside of your application partition, or you might want to create additional heap zones within your application partition.

You need to read this chapter if you want to use Memory Manager routines other than those described in the chapter "Introduction to Memory Management" in this book. That chapter shows how to use the Memory Manager and other system software components to perform the most common memory-manipulation operations while avoiding heap fragmentation and low memory situations. This chapter addresses a number of other important memory-related issues.

This chapter begins with a description of areas of memory that are outside your application's partition and their typical uses. Then it describes how you can

- allocate temporary memory
- allocate memory in and install code into the system heap
- read and change the values of system global variables
- allocate high memory during the startup process
- create additional heap zones within your application's partition
- install a purge-warning procedure for a heap zone

This chapter also addresses some advanced topics that are generally of use only to developers of very specialized applications or memory utilities. These advanced topics include

- how the Memory Manager organizes heap zones
- how the Memory Manager organizes memory blocks

To use this chapter, you should be familiar with ordinary use of the Memory Manager and other system software components that allow you to manage memory, as described in the chapter "Introduction to Memory Management" earlier in this book.

The "Memory Manager Reference" and "Summary of the Memory Manager" sections in this chapter provide a complete reference and summary of the constants, data types, and routines provided by the Memory Manager.

About the Memory Manager

The Memory Manager is the part of the Macintosh Operating System that controls the dynamic **allocation** of memory space. Ordinarily, you need to access information only within your own application's heap, stack, and A5 world. Occasionally, however, you might need to use the Memory Manager to allocate temporary memory outside of your application's partition or to initialize new heap zones within your application partition. You might also need to read a system global variable to obtain information about the environment in which your application is executing.

The Memory Manager provides a large number of routines that you can use to perform various operations on blocks within your application partition. You can use the Memory Manager to

- set up your application partition
- allocate and release both relocatable and nonrelocatable blocks in your application heap
- copy data from nonrelocatable blocks to relocatable blocks, and vice versa
- determine how much space is free in your heap
- determine the location of the top of your stack
- determine the size of a memory block and, if necessary, change that size
- change the properties of relocatable blocks
- install or remove a grow-zone function for your heap
- obtain the result code of the most recent Memory Manager routine executed

The Memory Manager also provides routines that you can use to access areas of memory outside your application partition. You can use the Memory Manager to

- allocate memory outside your partition that is currently unused by any open application or by the Operating System
- allocate memory in the system heap

This section describes the areas of memory that lie outside your application partition. It also describes multiple heap zones.

Temporary Memory

In the Macintosh multitasking environment, your application is limited to a particular memory partition (whose size is determined by information in the `'SIZE'` resource of your application). The size of your application's partition places certain limits on the size of your application heap and hence on the sizes of the buffers and other data structures that your application can use.

If for some reason you need more memory than is currently available in your application heap, you can ask the Operating System to let you use any available memory that is not yet allocated to any other application. This memory, called **temporary memory,** is allocated from the available unused RAM; in general, that memory is not contiguous with the memory in your application's zone

Your application should use temporary memory only for occasional short-term purposes that could be accomplished in less space, though perhaps less efficiently. For example, if you want to copy a large file, you might try to allocate a fairly large buffer of temporary memory. If you receive the temporary memory, you can use the large buffer to copy data from the source file into the destination file. If, however, the request for temporary memory fails, you can instead use a smaller buffer within your application heap. Although the use of a smaller buffer might prolong the copy operation, the file is nonetheless copied.

One good reason for using temporary memory only occasionally is that you cannot assume that you will always receive the temporary memory you request. For example, if two or more applications use all available memory outside the system partition, then a request by any of them for some temporary memory would fail.

Another strategy for using temporary memory is to use it, when possible, for all nonessential memory requests. For example, you could allocate window records and any associated window data using temporary memory. This scheme allows you to keep your application partition relatively small (because you don't need space for nonessential tasks) but assumes that users will not fill up the available memory with other applications.

Multiple Heap Zones

A **heap zone** is a heap (that is, an area in which you can dynamically allocate and release memory on demand) together with a zone header and a zone trailer. The **zone header** is an area of memory that contains essential information about the heap, such as the number of free bytes in the heap and the addresses of the heap's grow-zone function and purge-warning procedure. The **zone trailer** is just a minimum-sized block placed as a marker at the end of the heap zone. (See "Heap Zones" on page 2-19 for a complete description of zone headers and trailers.)

When your application is executing, there exist at least two heap zones: your application's heap zone (created when your application was launched) and the system heap zone (created when the system was started up). The **system heap zone** is the heap zone that contains the system heap. Your **application heap zone** (also known as the **original application heap zone**) is the heap zone initially provided by the Memory Manager for use by your application and any system software routines your application calls.

Ordinarily, you allocate and release blocks of memory in the **current heap zone,** which by default is your application heap zone. Unless you change the current heap zone (for example, by calling the `InitZone` or `SetZone` procedures), you do not need to worry about which is the current zone; all blocks that you access are taken from the current heap zone, that is, your application heap zone.

Occasionally, however, you might need to allocate memory in the system heap zone. System software uses the system heap to store information it needs. Although, in general, you should not allocate memory in the system heap, there are several valid reasons for doing so. First, if you are implementing a system extension, the extension can use the system heap to store information. Second, if you want the Time Manager or Vertical Retrace Manager to execute some interrupt code when your application is not the current application, you might in certain cases need to store the task record and the task code in the system heap. Third, if you write interrupt code that itself uses heap memory, you should either place that memory in the system heap or hold it in real RAM to prevent page faults at interrupt time, as discussed in the chapter "Virtual Memory Manager" in this book.

You can create additional heap zones for your application's own use by calling the `InitZone` procedure. If you do maintain more than one heap zone, you can find out which heap zone is the current one at any time by calling the `GetZone` function, and you can switch zones by calling the `SetZone` procedure. Almost all Memory Manager operations implicitly apply to the current heap zone. To refer to the system heap zone or to the (original) application heap zone, you can call the functions `SystemZone` or `ApplicationZone`. To find out which zone a particular block resides in, you can call the `HandleZone` function (if the block is relocatable) or the `PtrZone` function (if it's nonrelocatable).

▲ **WARNING**
Be sure, when calling routines that access blocks, that the zone in which the block is located is the current zone. If, for example, you attempt to release an empty resource in the system zone when the current zone is not the system zone, the Operating System might incorrectly update the list of free master pointers in your partition. ▲

Once you have created a heap zone, it remains fixed in size and location. For this reason, it usually makes more sense to use the undivided application heap zone for all of your memory-allocation needs. You might, however, choose to initialize an additional heap zone in circumstances like these:

- If you are implementing a software development environment and want to launch applications within the development environment's partition, you can initialize a heap zone for the launched application to use as its heap zone.
- If you want to avoid heap fragmentation but cannot prevent allocation of small nonrelocatable blocks in the middle of your program's execution, you could, soon after your application starts up, allocate a small heap zone to hold the nonrelocatable blocks you allocate during execution.
- If you need to resize a particular handle quite often, you can minimize the resizing time by creating a heap zone whose size is set to the maximum size the handle will ever be assigned. Because there is only one relocatable block in the new heap zone, the resizing is likely to happen more quickly than if that block were in the original heap zone (where other relocatable blocks in the zone might need to be moved).

Before deciding to create additional heap zones, however, make sure that you really need to. Maintaining multiple heap zones requires a considerable amount of extra work. You must always make sure to allocate or release memory in the correct zone, and you must monitor memory conditions in each zone so that your application doesn't run out of memory.

The System Global Variables

Just as the Toolbox stores information about your drawing environment in a set of QuickDraw global variables within your application partition, the Operating System and Toolbox store information about the entire multiple-application environment in a set of **system global variables,** also called low-memory global variables. The system global variables are stored in the lowest part of the physical RAM, in the system partition.

Most system global variables are intended for use by system software only, and you should never need to read or write them directly. Current versions of system software contain functions that return values equivalent to most of the important system global variables. Use those routines whenever they are available. However, you might occasionally need to access the value of a system global variable to maintain compatibility with previous versions of system software, or you might need to access a system global variable whose value no equivalent function returns.

The MPW interface file `SysEqu.p` defines the memory locations at which system global variables are stored in the latest version of system software. For example, `SysEqu.p` contains lines like these:

```
CONST
   RndSeed          = $156;   {random number seed (long)}
   Ticks            = $16A;   {ticks since last boot (unsigned long)}
   DeskHook         = $A6C;   {hook for painting desktop (pointer)}
   MBarHeight       = $BAA;   {height of menu bar (integer)}
```

You can use these memory locations to examine the value of one of these variables. See "Reading and Writing System Global Variables" on page 2-8 for instructions on reading and writing the values of system global variables from a high-level language.

You should avoid relying on the value of a system global variable whenever possible. The meanings of many global variables have changed in the past and will change again in the future. Using the system global variables documented in *Inside Macintosh* is fairly safe, but you risk incompatibility with future versions of system software if you attempt to access global variables defined in the interface files but not explicitly documented.

Even when *Inside Macintosh* does document a particular system global variable, you should use any available routines to access that variable's value instead of examining it directly. For example, you should use the `TickCount` function to find the number of ticks since startup instead of examining the `Ticks` global variable directly.

IMPORTANT

You should read or write the value of a system global variable only when that variable is documented in *Inside Macintosh* and when there is no alternate method of reading or writing the information you need. ▲

Using the Memory Manager

This section discusses the techniques you can use both to deal with memory outside of your application's partition and to manipulate your own application's partition.

You can use the techniques in this section to

- read and write the values of system global variables when there is no Toolbox routine that would accomplish the work for you

- check for the availability of temporary memory and use it to speed operations that depend on memory buffers
- allocate memory in the system heap
- install code into the system heap
- allocate memory at the high end of the available RAM from within a system extension during the startup process
- initialize new heap zones within your application heap zone, on your application's stack, or in the application global variables area
- install a purge-warning procedure for your application heap zone

Reading and Writing System Global Variables

In general, you should avoid relying on the values of system global variables whenever possible. However, you might occasionally need to access the value of one of these variables. Because the actual values associated with global variables in MPW's `SysEqu.p` interface file are memory locations, you can access the value of a low-memory variable simply by dereferencing a memory location.

Many system global variables are process-independent, but some are process-specific. The Operating System swaps the values of the process-specific variables as it switches processes. If you write interrupt code that reads low memory, that code could execute at a time when another process's system global variables are installed. Therefore, before reading low memory from interrupt code, you should call the Process Manager to ensure that your process is the current process. If it is not, you should not rely on the value of system global variables that could conceivably be process-specific.

Note
No available documentation distinguishes process-specific from process-independent system global variables. ◆

The routine defined in Listing 2-1 illustrates how you can read a system global variable, in this case the system global variable `BufPtr`, which gives the address of the highest byte of allocatable memory.

Listing 2-1 Reading the value of a system global variable

```
FUNCTION FindHighestByte: LongInt;
TYPE
   LongPtr = ^LongInt;
BEGIN
   FindHighestByte := LongPtr(BufPtr)^;
END;
```

In Pascal, the main technique for reading system global variables is to define a new data type that points to the variable type you want to read. In this example, the address is stored as a long integer. Thus, the memory location BufPtr is really a pointer to a long integer. Because of Pascal's strict typing rules, you must cast the low-memory address into a pointer to a long integer. Then, you can dereference the pointer and return the long integer itself as the function result.

You can use a similar technique to change the value of a system global variable. For example, suppose you are writing an extension that displays a window at startup time. To maintain compatibility with pre-Macintosh II systems, you need to clear the system global variable named DeskHook. This global variable holds a ProcPtr that references a procedure called by system software to paint the desktop. If the value of the pointer is NIL, the system software uses the standard desktop pattern. If you do not set DeskHook to NIL, the system software might attempt to use whatever random data it contains to call an updating procedure when you move or close your window. The procedure defined in Listing 2-2 sets DeskHook to NIL.

Listing 2-2 Changing the value of a system global variable

```
PROCEDURE ClearDeskHook;
TYPE
   ProcPtrPtr = ^ProcPtr;                   {pointer to ProcPtr}
VAR
   deskHookProc: ProcPtrPtr;
BEGIN
   deskHookProc := ProcPtrPtr(DeskHook);    {initialize variable}
   deskHookProc^ := NIL;                    {clear DeskHook proc}
END;
```

You can use a similar technique to change the value of any other documented system global variable.

Extending an Application's Memory

Rather than using your application's 'SIZE' resource to specify a preferred partition size that is large enough to contain the largest possible application heap, you should specify a smaller but adequate partition size. When you need more memory for temporary use, you can use a set of Memory Manager routines for the allocation of temporary memory.

By using the routines for allocating temporary memory, your application can request some additional memory for occasional short-term needs. For example, the Finder uses these temporary-memory routines to secure buffer space for use during file copy operations. Any available memory (that is, memory currently unallocated to any application's partition) is dedicated to this purpose. The Finder releases this memory as soon as the copy is completed, thus making the memory available to other applications or to the Operating System for launching new applications.

Because the requested amount of memory might not be available, you cannot be sure that every request for temporary memory will be honored. Thus, you should make sure that your application will work even if your request for temporary memory is denied. For example, if the Finder cannot allocate a large temporary copy buffer, it uses a reserved small copy buffer from within its own heap zone, prolonging the copying but performing it nonetheless.

Temporary memory is taken from RAM that is reserved for (but not yet used by) other applications. Thus, if you use too much temporary memory or hold temporary memory for long periods of time, you might prevent the user from being able to launch other applications. In certain circumstances, however, you can hold temporary memory indefinitely. For example, if the temporary memory is used for open files and the user can free that memory simply by closing those files, it is safe to hold onto that memory as long as necessary.

Temporary memory is tracked (or monitored) for each application, and so you must use it only for code that is running on an application's behalf. Moreover, the Operating System frees all temporary memory allocated to an application when the application quits or crashes. As a result, you should not use temporary memory for VBL tasks, Time Manager tasks, or other procedures that should continue to be executed after your application quits. Similarly, it is wise not to use temporary memory for an interprocess buffer (that is, a buffer whose address is passed to another application in a high-level event) because the originating application could crash, quit, or be terminated, thereby causing the temporary memory to be released before (or even while) the receiving application uses that memory.

Although you can usually perform ordinary Memory Manager operations on temporary memory, there are two restrictions. First, you must never lock temporary memory across calls to `GetNextEvent` or `WaitNextEvent`. Second, although you can determine the zone from which temporary memory is generated (using the `HandleZone` function), you should not use this information to make new blocks or perform heap operations on your own.

Allocating Temporary Memory

You can request a block of memory for temporary use by calling the Memory Manager's `TempNewHandle` function. This function attempts to allocate a new relocatable block of the specified size for temporary use. For example, to request a block that is one-quarter megabyte in size, you might issue this command:

```
myHandle := TempNewHandle($40000, myErr); {request temp memory}
```

If the routine succeeds, it returns a handle to the block of memory. The block of memory returned by a successful call to `TempNewHandle` is initially unlocked. If an error occurs and `TempNewHandle` fails, it returns a `NIL` handle. You should always check for `NIL` handles before using any temporary memory. If you detect a `NIL` handle, the second parameter (in this example, `myErr`) contains the result code from the function.

Instead of asking for a specific amount of memory and then checking the returned handle to find out whether it was allocated, you might prefer to determine beforehand how much temporary memory is available. There are two functions that return information on the amount of free memory available for temporary allocation. The first is the `TempFreeMem` function, which you can use as follows:

```
memFree := TempFreeMem;     {find amount of free temporary memory}
```

The result is a long integer containing the amount, in bytes, of free memory available for temporary allocation. It usually isn't possible to allocate a block of this size because of fragmentation. Consequently, you'll probably want to use the second function, `TempMaxMem`, to determine the size of the largest contiguous block of space available. To allocate that block, you can write

```
mySize := TempMaxMem(grow);
myHandle := TempNewHandle(mySize, myErr);
```

The `TempMaxMem` function returns the size, in bytes, of the largest contiguous free block available for temporary allocation. (The `TempMaxMem` function is analogous to the `MaxMem` function.) The `grow` parameter is a variable parameter of type `Size`; after the function returns, it always contains 0, because the temporary memory does not come from the application's heap. Even when you use `TempMaxMem` to determine the size of the available memory, you should check that the handle returned by `TempNewHandle` is not `NIL`.

Determining the Features of Temporary Memory

Only computers running system software version 7.0 and later can use temporary memory as described in this chapter. For this reason, you should always check that the routines are available and that they have the features you require before calling them.

Note

The temporary-memory routines are available in some earlier system software versions when MultiFinder is running. However, the handles to blocks of temporary memory are neither tracked nor real. ◆

The `Gestalt` function includes a selector to determine whether the temporary-memory routines are present in the operating environment and, if they are, whether the temporary-memory handles are tracked and whether they are real. If temporary-memory handles are not tracked, you must release temporary memory before your next call to `GetNextEvent` or `WaitNextEvent`. If temporary-memory handles are not real, then you cannot use normal Memory Manager routines such as `HLock` to manipulate them.

To determine whether the temporary-memory routines are implemented, you can check the value returned by the `TempMemCallsAvailable` function, defined in Listing 2-3.

Listing 2-3 Determining whether temporary-memory routines are available

```
FUNCTION TempMemCallsAvailable: Boolean;
VAR
   myErr:    OSErr;                   {Gestalt result code}
   myRsp:    LongInt;                 {response returned by Gestalt}
BEGIN
   TempMemCallsAvailable := FALSE;
   myErr := Gestalt(gestaltOSAttr, myRsp);
   IF myErr <> noErr THEN
      DoError(myErr)              {Gestalt failed}
   ELSE                           {check bit for temp mem support}
      TempMemCallsAvailable :=
            BAND(myRsp, gestaltTempMemSupport) <> 0;
END;
```

You can use similar code to determine whether temporary-memory handles are real and whether the temporary memory is tracked.

Using the System Heap

The system heap is used to store most of the information needed by the Operating System and other system software components. As a result, it is ideal for storing information needed by a system extension (which by definition extends the capabilities of system software). You might also need to use the system heap to store a task record and the code for an interrupt task that should continue to be executed when your application is not the current application.

Allocating blocks in the system heap is straightforward. Most ordinary Memory Manager routines have counterparts that allocate memory in the system heap zone instead of the current heap zone. For example, the counterpart of the `NewPtr` function is the `NewPtrSys` function. The following line of code allocates a new nonrelocatable block of memory in the system heap to store a Time Manager task record:

```
myTaskPtr := QElemPtr(NewPtrSys(SizeOf(TMTask)));
```

Alternatively, you can change the current zone and use ordinary Memory Manager operations, as follows:

```
SetZone(SystemZone);
myTaskPtr := QElemPtr(NewPtr(SizeOf(TMTask)));
...
SetZone(ApplicationZone);
```

You might also need to store the interrupt code itself in the system heap. For example, when an application that installed a vertical retrace task with the `VInstall` function is in the background, the Vertical Retrace Manager executes the task only if the `vblAddr` field of the task record points to a routine in the system heap.

Unfortunately, manually copying a routine into the system heap is difficult in Pascal. The easiest way to install code into the system heap is to place the code into a separate stand-alone code resource in your application's resource fork. You should set the system heap bit and the locked bit of the code resource's attributes. Then, when you need to use the code, you must load the resource from the resource file and cast the resource handle's master pointer into a procedure pointer (a variable of type `ProcPtr`), as follows:

```
myProcHandle := GetResource(kProcType, kProcID);
IF myProcHandle <> NIL THEN
   myTaskPtr^.vblAddr := ProcPtr(myProcHandle^);
```

Because the resource is locked in memory, you don't have to worry about creating a dangling pointer when you dereference a handle to the resource. If you want the code to remain in the system heap after the user quits your application, you can call the Resource Manager procedure `DetachResource` so that closing your application's resource fork does not destroy the resource data. Note, however, that if you do so and your application crashes, the code still remains in the system heap.

Once you have loaded a code resource into memory and created a `ProcPtr` that references the entry point of the code resource, you can use that `ProcPtr` just as you can use any such variable. For example, you could assign the value of the variable to the `vblAddr` field of a vertical retrace task record (as shown just above). If you are programming in assembly language, you can then call the code directly. To call the routine from a high-level language such as Pascal, you'll need to use some inline assembly-language code. Listing 2-4 defines a routine that you can use to execute a procedure by address.

Listing 2-4 Calling a procedure by address

```
PROCEDURE CallByAddress (aRoutine: ProcPtr);
   INLINE   $205F,            {MOVE.L (SP)+,A0}
            $4ED0;            {JMP (A0)}
```

Allocating Memory at Startup Time

If you are implementing a system extension, you might need to allocate memory at startup time. As explained in the previous section, an ideal place to allocate such memory is in the system heap. To allocate memory in the system heap under system software version 7.0 and later, you merely need to call the appropriate Memory Manager routines, and the system heap expands dynamically to meet your request. In earlier versions of system software, you must use a `'sysz'` resource to indicate how much the Operating System should increase the size of the system zone.

Alternatively, however, you can allocate blocks in high memory. The global variable `BufPtr` always references the highest byte in memory that might become part of an application partition. You can lower the value of `BufPtr` and then use the memory between the old and new values of `BufPtr`.

Note
In general, if you are implementing a system extension, you should allocate memory in the system heap instead of high memory. In this way, you avoid the problems associated with lowering the value of `BufPtr` too far (described in the following paragraphs) and ensure that the extension is not paged out if virtual memory is operating. ◆

Lowering the value of `BufPtr` too far can be dangerous for several reasons. In 128K ROM Macintosh computers running system software version 4.1, you must avoid lowering the value of `BufPtr` so that it points in the system startup blocks. The highest byte of these blocks can always be found relative to the global variable `MemTop`, at `MemTop DIV 2 + 1024`.

In later versions of the Macintosh system software, the system startup blocks were no longer barriers to `BufPtr`, but new barriers arose, including Macintosh IIci video storage, for example. To maintain compatibility with extensions that rely on the ability to lower `BufPtr` relative to `MemTop`, the system software simply adjusts `MemTop` so that the formula still holds. Thus, at startup, the `MemTop` global variable currently does not reference any memory location in particular. Instead, it holds a value that guarantees that the formula allowing you to lower `BufPtr` as low as `MemTop DIV 2 + 1024` but no further still holds.

Beginning in system software version 7.0, the Operating System can detect excessive lowering of `BufPtr`, but only after the fact. When the Operating System does detect that the value of `BufPtr` has fallen too low, it generates an out-of-memory system error.

▲ **WARNING**
Although the above formula has been true since system software version 4.1, a bug in the Macintosh IIci and later ROMs made it invalid in certain versions of system software 6.x. ▲

Because there is no calling interface for lowering `BufPtr`, you must do it manually, by changing the value of the system variable, as explained in "Reading and Writing System Global Variables" on page 2-8. To obtain the value of the `MemTop` global variable, you can use the `TopMem` function.

Creating Heap Zones

You can create heap zones as subzones of your application heap zone or (in rare instances) either in space reserved for the application global variables or on the stack. You can also create heap zones in a block of temporary memory or within the system heap zone. This section describes how to create new heap zones by calling the `InitZone` procedure.

Note
Most applications do not need to create heap zones. ◆

To create a new heap zone in the application heap, you must allocate nonrelocatable blocks in your application heap to hold new subzones of the application heap. In addition to being able to create subzones of the application zone, you can create subzones of any other zone to which you have access, including a zone that is itself a subzone of another zone.

You create a heap zone by calling the `InitZone` procedure, which takes four parameters. The first parameter specifies a grow-zone function for the new zone, or `NIL` if you do not want the zone to have a grow-zone function. The second parameter specifies the number of new master pointers that you want each block of master pointers in the zone to contain. The `InitZone` procedure allocates one such block to start with, and you can allocate more by calling the `MoreMasters` procedure. The third and fourth parameters specify, respectively, the first byte beyond the end of the new zone and the first byte of the zone.

When initializing a zone with the `InitZone` procedure, make sure that you are subdividing the current zone. When `InitZone` returns, the new zone becomes current. Thus, if you subdivide the application zone into several subzones, you must call `SetZone(ApplicationZone)` before you create the second and each of the subsequent subzones. Listing 2-5 shows a technique for creating a single subzone of the original application zone, assuming that the application zone is the current zone. The technique for subdividing subzones is similar.

Listing 2-5 Creating a subzone of the original application heap zone

```
FUNCTION CreateSubZone: THz;
CONST
   kZoneSize = 10240;              {10K zone}
   kNumMasterPointers = 16;        {num of master ptrs for new zone}
VAR
   start:   Ptr;                   {first byte in zone}
   limit:   Ptr;                   {first byte beyond zone}
BEGIN
   start := NewPtr(kZoneSize);     {allocate storage for zone}
   IF MemError <> noErr THEN
   BEGIN                           {allocation successful}
      limit := Ptr(ORD4(start) + kZoneSize);
                                   {compute byte beyond end of zone}
      InitZone(NIL, kNumMasterPointers, limit, start);
                                   {initialize zone header, trailer}
   END;
   CreateSubZone := THz(start);    {cast storage to a zone pointer}
END;
```

To create a subzone in the system heap zone, you can call `SetZone(SystemZone)` at the beginning of the procedure in Listing 2-5. You might find this technique useful if you are implementing a system extension but want to manage your extension's memory much as you manage memory in an application. Instead of simply allocating blocks in the system heap, you can make your zone current whenever your extension is executed. Then, you can call regular Memory Manager routines to allocate memory in your subzone of the system heap, and you can compact and purge your subzone without compacting and purging the entire system heap zone.

When you allocate memory for a subzone, you must allocate that memory in a nonrelocatable block (as in Listing 2-5) or in a locked relocatable block. If you create a subzone within an unlocked relocatable block, the Memory Manager might move your entire subzone during memory operations in the zone containing your subzone. If so, any references to nonrelocatable blocks that you allocated in the subzone would become invalid. Even handles to relocatable blocks in the subzone would no longer be valid, because the Memory Manager does not update the handles' master pointers correctly. This happens because the Memory Manager views a subzone of another zone as a single block. If that subzone is a relocatable block, the Memory Manager updates only that block's master pointer when moving it, and does not update the block's contents (that is, the blocks allocated within the subzone).

If you use a block of temporary memory as a heap zone, you must lock the temporary memory immediately after allocating it. Then, you can pass to `InitZone` a dereferenced copy of a handle to the temporary memory. If you find (after a call to the `Gestalt` function) that temporary memory handles are not real, then you must dispose of the new zone before any calls to `GetNextEvent` or `WaitNextEvent`. You must dispose of the new zone because you cannot lock a handle to temporary memory across event calls if the handle is not real.

Once you have created a subzone as a nonrelocatable block or a locked relocatable block, you can allocate both relocatable and nonrelocatable blocks within it. Although the Memory Manager can move such relocatable blocks only within the subzone, it correctly updates those blocks' master pointers, which are also in the subzone.

Installing a Purge-Warning Procedure

You can define a **purge-warning procedure** that the Memory Manager calls whenever it is about to purge a block from your application heap. You can use this procedure to save the data in the block, if necessary, or to perform other processing in response to this notification.

Note

Most applications don't need to install a purge-warning procedure. This capability is provided primarily for applications that require greater control over their heap. Examples are applications that maintain purgeable handles containing important data and applications that for any other reason need notification when a block is about to be purged. ◆

When your purge-warning procedure is called, the Memory Manager passes it a handle to the block about to be purged. In your procedure, you can test the handle to determine whether it contains data that needs to be saved; if so, you can save the data (possibly by writing it to some open file). Listing 2-6 defines a very simple purge-warning procedure.

Listing 2-6 A purge-warning procedure

```
PROCEDURE MyPurgeProc (h: Handle);
VAR
   theA5:   LongInt;               {value of A5 when procedure is called}
BEGIN
   theA5 := SetCurrentA5;          {remember current value of A5; install ours}
   IF BAND(HGetState(h), $20) = 0 THEN
      BEGIN                        {if the handle isn't a resource handle}
         IF InSaveList(h) THEN
            WriteData(h);          {save the data in the block}
      END;
   theA5 := SetA5(theA5);          {restore previous value of A5}
END;
```

The `MyPurgeProc` procedure defined in Listing 2-6 inspects the handle's properties (using `HGetState`) to see whether its resource bit is clear. If so, the procedure next determines whether the handle is contained in an application-maintained list of handles whose data should be saved before purging. If the handle is in that list, the purge-warning procedure writes its data to disk. (The file into which the data is written should already be open at the time the procedure is called, because opening a file might cause memory to move.)

Note that `MyPurgeProc` sets up the A5 register with the application's A5 value upon entry and restores it to its previous value before exiting. This is necessary because you cannot rely on the A5 register within a purge-warning procedure.

▲ **WARNING**
Because of the optimizations performed by some compilers, the actual work of the purge-warning procedure and the setting and restoring of the A5 register might have to be placed in separate procedures. See the chapter "Vertical Retrace Manager" in *Inside Macintosh: Processes* for an illustration of how you can do this. ▲

To install a purge-warning procedure, you need to install the address of the procedure into the `purgeProc` field of your application's heap zone header. Listing 2-7 illustrates one way to do this.

Listing 2-7 Installing a purge-warning procedure

```
PROCEDURE InstallPurgeProc;
VAR
   myZone:  THz;
BEGIN
   myZone := GetZone;                      {find the current zone header}
   gPrevProc := myZone^.purgeProc;         {remember previous procedure}
   myZone^.purgeProc := @MyPurgeProc;      {install new procedure}
END;
```

The `InstallPurgeProc` procedure defined in Listing 2-7 first obtains the address of the current heap zone by calling the `GetZone` function. Then it saves the address of any existing purge-warning procedure in the global variable `gPrevProc`. Finally, `InstallPurgeProc` installs the new procedure by putting its address directly into the `purgeProc` field of the zone header. (For more information on zone headers, see "Heap Zones" on page 2-19.)

Keep in mind that the Memory Manager calls your purge-warning procedure each time it decides to purge any purgeable block, and it might call your procedure far more often than you would expect. Your purge-warning procedure might be passed handles not only to blocks that you explicitly mark as purgeable (by calling `HPurge`), but also to resources whose purgeable attribute is set. (In general, applications don't need to take any action on handles that belong to the Resource Manager.) Because of the potentially large number of times your purge-warning procedure might be called, it should be able to determine quickly whether a handle that is about to be purged needs additional processing.

Remember that a purge-warning procedure is called during the execution of some Memory Manager routine. As a result, your procedure cannot cause memory to be moved or purged. In addition, it should not dispose of the handle it is passed or change the purge status of the handle. See "Purge-Warning Procedures" on page 2-90 for a complete description of the limitations on purge-warning procedures.

▲ **WARNING**
If your application calls the Resource Manager procedure `SetResPurge` with the parameter `TRUE` (to have the Resource Manager automatically save any modified resources that are about to be purged), you should avoid using a purge-warning procedure. This is because the Resource Manager installs its own purge-warning procedure when you call `SetResPurge` in this way. If you must install your own purge-warning procedure, you should remove your procedure, call `SetResPurge`, then reinstall your procedure as shown in Listing 2-7. You then need to make sure that your procedure calls the Resource Manager's purge-warning procedure (which is saved in the global variable `gPrevProc`) before exiting. Most applications do not need to call `SetResPurge` at all. ▲

If your application does call `SetResPurge(TRUE)`, you should use the version of `MyPurgeProc` defined in Listing 2-8. It is just like the version defined in Listing 2-6 except that it calls the Resource Manager's purge-warning procedure before exiting.

Listing 2-8 A purge-warning procedure that calls the Resource Manager's procedure

```
PROCEDURE MyPurgeProc (h: Handle);
VAR
   theA5:   LongInt;                {value of A5 when procedure is called}
BEGIN
   theA5 := SetCurrentA5;           {remember current value of A5; install ours}
   IF BAND(HGetState(h), $20) = 0 THEN
      BEGIN                         {if the handle isn't a resource handle}
         IF InSaveList(h) THEN
            WriteData(h);           {save the data in the block}
      END
   ELSE IF gPrevProc <> NIL THEN
      CallByAddress(gPrevProc);
   theA5 := SetA5(theA5);           {restore previous value of A5}
END;
```

See Listing 2-4 on page 2-13 for a definition of the procedure `CallByAddress`.

Organization of Memory

This section describes the organization of heap zones and block headers. In general, you do not need to know how the Memory Manager organizes heap zones or block headers if your application simply allocates and releases blocks of memory. The information described in this section is used by the Memory Manager for its own purposes. Developers of some specialized applications and utilities might, however, need to know exactly how zones and block headers are organized. This information is also sometimes useful for debugging.

▲ **WARNING**
This section is provided primarily for informational purposes. The organization and size of heap zones and block headers is subject to change in future system software versions. ▲

Heap Zones

Except for temporary memory blocks, all relocatable and nonrelocatable blocks exist within heap zones. A heap zone consists of a zone header, a zone trailer block, and usable bytes in between. The header contains all of the information the

Memory Manager needs about that heap zone; the trailer is just a minimum-sized free block placed as a marker at the end of the zone.

In Pascal, a heap zone is defined as a **zone record** of type `Zone`. The zone record contains all of the fields of the zone header. A heap zone is always referred to with a **zone pointer** of data type `THz`.

▲ **WARNING**
The fields of the zone header are for the Memory Manager's own internal use. You can examine the contents of the zone's fields, but in general it doesn't make sense for your application to try to change them. The only fields of the zone record that you can safely modify directly are the `moreMast` and `purgeProc` fields. ▲

```
TYPE Zone =
RECORD
   bkLim:         Ptr;          {first usable byte after zone}
   purgePtr:      Ptr;          {used internally}
   hFstFree:      Ptr;          {first free master pointer}
   zcbFree:       LongInt;      {number of free bytes in zone}
   gzProc:        ProcPtr;      {grow-zone function}
   moreMast:      Integer;      {num. of master ptrs to allocate}
   flags:         Integer;      {used internally}
   cntRel:        Integer;      {reserved}
   maxRel:        Integer;      {reserved}
   cntNRel:       Integer;      {reserved}
   maxNRel:       Integer;      {reserved}
   cntEmpty:      Integer;      {reserved}
   cntHandles:    Integer;      {reserved}
   minCBFree:     LongInt;      {reserved}
   purgeProc:     ProcPtr;      {purge-warning procedure}
   sparePtr:      Ptr;          {used internally}
   allocPtr:      Ptr;          {used internally}
   heapData:      Integer;      {first usable byte in zone}
END;
THz = ^Zone;                    {zone pointer}
```

Field descriptions

`bkLim` — A pointer to the byte *following* the last byte of usable space in the zone.

`purgePtr` — Used internally.

`hFstFree` — A pointer to the first free master pointer in the zone. All master pointers that are allocated but not currently in use are linked together into a list. The `hFstFree` field references the head node of this list. The Memory Manager updates this list every time it allocates a new relocatable block or releases one, so that the list contains all unused master pointers. If the Memory Manager needs a new master pointer but this field is set to `NIL`, it allocates a new nonrelocatable block of master pointers. You can check the value of this field to see whether allocating a relocatable block would cause a new block of master pointers to be allocated.

`zcbFree` The number of free bytes remaining in the zone. As blocks are allocated and released, the Memory Manager adjusts this field accordingly. You can use the `FreeMem` function to determine the value of this field for the current heap zone.

`gzProc` A pointer to a grow-zone function that system software uses to maintain control over the heap. The system's grow-zone function subsequently calls the grow-zone function you specify for your heap, if any. You can change a heap zone's grow-zone function at any time but should do so only by calling the `InitZone` or `SetGrowZone` procedures. Note that in current versions of system software, this field does not contain a pointer to the grow-zone function that your application defines.

`moreMast` The number of master pointers the Memory Manager should allocate at a time. The Memory Manager allocates this many automatically when a heap zone is initialized. By default, master pointers are allocated 32 at a time for the system heap zone and 64 at a time for the application heap zone, but this might change in future versions of system software.

`flags` Used internally.

`cntRel` Reserved.

`maxRel` Reserved.

`cntNRel` Reserved.

`maxNRel` Reserved.

`cntEmpty` Reserved.

`cntHandles` Reserved.

`minCBFree` Reserved.

`purgeProc` A pointer to the zone's purge-warning procedure, or `NIL` if there is none. The Memory Manager calls this procedure before it purges a block from the zone. Note that whenever you call the Resource Manager procedure `SetResPurge` with the parameter set to `TRUE`, the Resource Manager installs its own purge-warning procedure, overriding any purge-warning procedure you have specified here.

`sparePtr` Used internally.

`allocPtr` Used internally.

`heapData` A dummy field marking the beginning of the zone's usable memory space. The integer in this field has no significance in itself; it is just the first 2 bytes in the block header of the first block in the zone. For example, if `myZone` is a zone pointer, then `@(myZone^.heapData)` is the address of the first usable byte in the zone, and `myZone^.bkLim` is a pointer to the byte following the last usable byte in the zone.

The structure of a heap zone is the same in both 24-bit and 32-bit addressing modes. The use of several of the fields that are reserved or used internally, however, may differ in 24-bit and 32-bit heap zones.

Block Headers

Every block in a heap zone, whether allocated or free, has a **block header** that the Memory Manager uses to find its way around in the zone. Block headers are completely transparent to your application. All pointers and handles to allocated blocks reference the beginning of the block's logical contents, following the end of the header. Similarly, whenever you use a variable of type `Size`, that variable refers to the number of bytes in the block's logical contents, not including the block header. That size is known as the block's **logical size,** as opposed to its **physical size,** the number of bytes it actually occupies in memory, including the header and any unused bytes at the end of the block.

There are two reasons that a block might contain such unused bytes:

- The Memory Manager allocates space only in even numbers of bytes. (This practice guarantees that both the contents and the address of a master pointer are even.) If a block's logical size is odd, an extra, unused byte is added at the end to make the physical size an even number. On computers containing the MC68020, MC68030, or MC68040 microprocessor, blocks are padded to 4-byte boundaries.
- The minimum number of bytes in a block is 12. This minimum applies to all blocks, free as well as allocated. If allocating the required number of bytes from a free block would leave a fragment of fewer than 12 free bytes, the leftover bytes are included unused at the end of the newly allocated block instead of being returned to free storage.

There is no Pascal record type defining the structure of block headers because you shouldn't normally need to access them directly. In addition, the structure of a block header depends on whether the block is located in a 24-bit or 32-bit zone.

In a 24-bit zone, a block header consists of 8 bytes, which together make up two long words, as shown in Figure 2-1.

Figure 2-1 A block header in a 24-bit zone

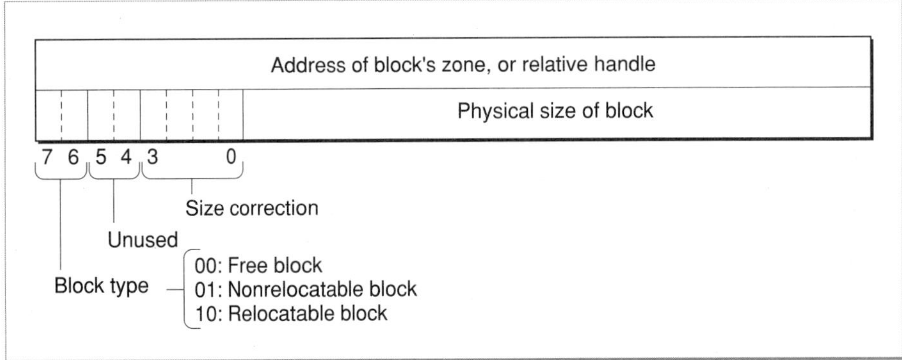

In the first long word, the low-order 3 bytes contain the block's physical size in bytes. Adding this number to the block's address gives the address of the next block in the zone. The first byte of the block header is a **tag byte** that provides other information on the block. The bits in the tag byte have these meanings:

Bit	Meaning
0–3	The block's size correction
4–5	Reserved
6–7	The block type

In the tag byte, the high-order 2 bits determine whether a block is free (binary 00), relocatable (binary 10), or nonrelocatable (binary 01). The low-order 4 bits contain a block's **size correction,** the number of unused bytes at the end of the block, beyond the end of the block's contents. This correction is equal to the difference between the block's logical and physical sizes, excluding the 8 bytes of overhead for the block header, as in the following formula:

```
physicalSize = logicalSize + sizeCorrection + 8
```

The contents of the second long word (4 bytes) in the 24-bit block header depend on the type of block. For relocatable blocks, the second long word contains the block's **relative handle:** a pointer to the block's master pointer, expressed as an offset relative to the start of the heap zone rather than as an absolute memory address. Adding the relative handle to the zone pointer produces a true handle for this block. For nonrelocatable blocks, the second long word of the header is just a pointer to the block's zone. For free blocks, the contents of these 4 bytes are undefined.

In a 32-bit zone, a block header consists of 12 bytes, which together make up three long words, as shown in Figure 2-2.

Figure 2-2 A block header in a 32-bit zone

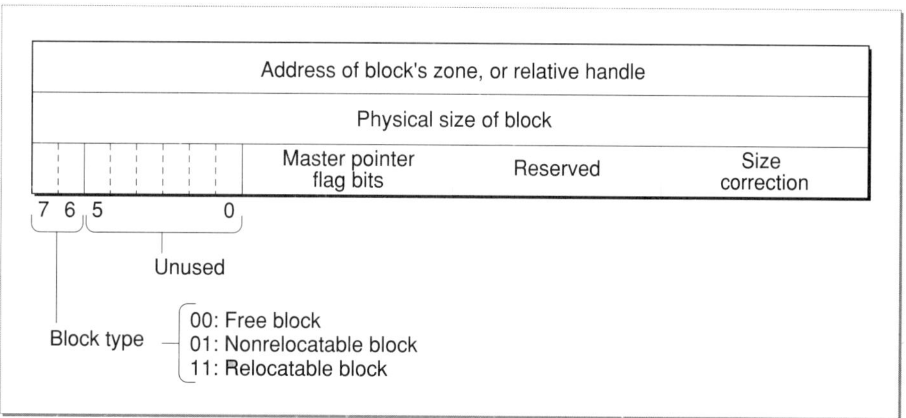

The first byte of the block header is a tag byte that indicates the type of the block. The bits in the tag byte have these meanings:

Bit	Meaning
0–5	Reserved
6–7	The block type

In the tag byte, the high-order 2 bits determine whether a block is free (binary 00), relocatable (binary 10), or nonrelocatable (binary 01).

The second byte in the block header contains the master pointer flag bits, if the block is a relocatable block. Otherwise, this byte is undefined. The bits in this byte have these meanings:

Bit	Meaning
0–4	Reserved
5	If set, block contains resource data
6	If set, block is purgeable
7	If set, block is locked

The low-order byte of the high-order long word contains the block's size correction. This correction is equal to the difference between the block's logical and physical sizes, excluding the 12 bytes of overhead for the block header, as follows:

```
physicalSize = logicalSize + sizeCorrection + 12
```

The second long word in the 32-bit block header contains the block's physical size, and the third long word contains the block's relative handle. These fields have the same meaning as the corresponding fields in the 24-bit block header.

Memory Manager Reference

This section describes the data types and routines provided by the Memory Manager. It describes the general-purpose data types the Memory Manager defines and all routines that relate to manipulating blocks of memory or managing memory in the application heap zone. This section also describes the data structures and routines that allow your application to allocate temporary memory and to use multiple heap zones.

Data Types

This section discusses the general-purpose data types defined by the Memory Manager. Most of these types are used throughout the system software.

The Memory Manager uses pointers and handles to reference nonrelocatable and relocatable blocks, respectively. The data types `Ptr` and `Handle` define pointers and handles as follows:

```
TYPE
   SignedByte      = -128..127;
   Byte            = 0..255;
   Ptr             = ^SignedByte;
   Handle          = ^Ptr;
```

The `SignedByte` type stands for an arbitrary byte in memory, just to give `Ptr` and `Handle` something to point to. The `Byte` type is an alternative definition that treats byte-length data as an unsigned rather than a signed quantity.

Many other data types also use the concept of pointers and handles. For example, the Macintosh system software stores strings in arrays of up to 255 characters, with the first byte of the array storing the length of the string. Some Toolbox routines allow you to pass such a string directly; others require that you pass a pointer or handle to a string. The following type definitions define character strings:

```
TYPE
   Str255          = STRING[255];
   StringPtr       = ^Str255;
   StringHandle    = ^StringPtr;
```

Some Toolbox routines allow you to execute code after a certain amount of time elapses or after a certain condition is met. Any such routine requires you to pass the address of the routine containing the code to be executed so that it knows what routine to call when the time has elapsed or the condition has been met. You use the data type `ProcPtr` to define a pointer to a procedure or function.

```
TYPE ProcPtr = Ptr;
```

For example, after the declarations

```
VAR
   aProcPtr: ProcPtr;

PROCEDURE MyProc;
BEGIN
            ...
END;
```

you can make `aProcPtr` reference the `MyProc` procedure by using the `@` operator, as follows:

```
aProcPtr := @MyProc;
```

With the @ operator, you can assign procedures and functions to variables of type ProcPtr, embed them in data structures, and pass them as arguments to other routines. Notice, however, that the data type ProcPtr technically points to an arbitrary byte, not an actual routine. As a result, there's no direct way in Pascal to access the underlying routine via this pointer in order to call it. (See Listing 2-4 on page 2-13 for some assembly-language code you can use to do so.) The routines in the Operating System and Toolbox, which are written in assembly language, can however, call routines designated by pointers of type ProcPtr.

Note

You can't use the @ operator to reference procedures or functions whose declarations are nested within other routines. ◆

The Memory Manager uses the Size data type to refer to the size, in bytes, of memory blocks. For example, when specifying how large a relocatable block you want to allocate, you pass a parameter of type Size. The Size data type is also defined as a long integer.

```
TYPE Size       = LongInt;
```

Memory Manager Routines

This section describes the routines provided by the Memory Manager. You can use these routines to set up your application's partition, allocate and dispose of relocatable and nonrelocatable blocks, manipulate those blocks, assess the availability of memory in your application's heap, free memory from the heap, and install a grow-zone function for your heap. The Memory Manager also provides routines that allow you to allocate temporary memory and manipulate heap zones.

Note

The result codes listed for Memory Manager routines are usually not directly returned to your application. You need to call the MemError function (or, from assembly language, inspect the MemErr global variable) to get a routine's result code. ◆

You cannot call most Memory Manager routines at interrupt time for several reasons. You cannot allocate memory at interrupt time because the Memory Manager might already be handling a memory-allocation request and the heap might be in an inconsistent state. More generally, you cannot call at interrupt time any Memory Manager routine that returns its result code via the MemError function, even if that routine doesn't allocate or move memory. Resetting the MemErr global variable at interrupt time can lead to unexpected results if the interrupted code depends on the value of MemErr. Note that Memory Manager routines like HLock return their results via MemError and therefore should not be called in interrupt code.

Setting Up the Application Heap

The Operating System automatically initializes your application's heap when your application is launched. To help prevent heap fragmentation, you should call the procedures in this section before you allocate any blocks of memory in your heap.

Use the `MaxApplZone` procedure to extend the application heap zone to the application heap limit so that the Memory Manager does not do so gradually as memory requests require. Use the `MoreMasters` procedure to preallocate enough blocks of master pointers so that the Memory Manager never needs to allocate new master pointer blocks for you.

MaxApplZone

To help ensure that you can use as much of the application heap zone as possible, call the `MaxApplZone` procedure. Call this once near the beginning of your program, after you have expanded your stack.

```
PROCEDURE MaxApplZone;
```

DESCRIPTION

The `MaxApplZone` procedure expands the application heap zone to the application heap limit. If you do not call `MaxApplZone`, the application heap zone grows as necessary to fulfill memory requests. The `MaxApplZone` procedure does not purge any blocks currently in the zone. If the zone already extends to the limit, `MaxApplZone` does nothing.

It is a good idea to call `MaxApplZone` once at the beginning of your program if you intend to maintain an effectively partitioned heap. If you do not call `MaxApplZone` and then call `MoveHHi` to move relocatable blocks to the top of the heap zone before locking them, the heap zone could later grow beyond these locked blocks to fulfill a memory request. If the Memory Manager were to allocate a nonrelocatable block in this new space, your heap would be fragmented.

ASSEMBLY-LANGUAGE INFORMATION

The registers on exit for `MaxApplZone` are

Registers on exit

D0	Result code

RESULT CODES

`noErr`	0	No error

MoreMasters

Call the `MoreMasters` procedure several times at the beginning of your program to prevent the Memory Manager from running out of master pointers in the middle of application execution. If it does run out, it allocates more, possibly causing heap fragmentation.

```
PROCEDURE MoreMasters;
```

DESCRIPTION

The `MoreMasters` procedure allocates another block of master pointers in the current heap zone. In the application heap, a block of master pointers consists of 64 master pointers, and in the system heap, a block consists of 32 master pointers. (These values, however, might change in future versions of system software.) When you initialize additional heap zones, you can specify the number of master pointers you want to have in a block of master pointers.

The Memory Manager automatically calls `MoreMasters` once for every new heap zone, including the application heap zone.

You should call `MoreMasters` at the beginning of your program enough times to ensure that the Memory Manager never needs to call it for you. For example, if your application never allocates more than 300 relocatable blocks in its heap zone, then five calls to the `MoreMasters` should be enough. It's better to call `MoreMasters` too many times than too few. For instance, if your application usually allocates about 100 relocatable blocks but might allocate 1000 in a particularly busy session, call `MoreMasters` enough times at the beginning of the program to accommodate times of greater memory use.

If you are forced to call `MoreMasters` so many times that it causes a significant slowdown, you could change the `moreMast` field of the zone header to the total number of master pointers you need and then call `MoreMasters` just once. Afterward, be sure to restore the `moreMast` field to its original value.

SPECIAL CONSIDERATIONS

Because `MoreMasters` allocates memory, you should not call it at interrupt time.

The calls to `MoreMasters` at the beginning of your application should be in the main code segment of your application or in a segment that the main segment never unloads.

ASSEMBLY-LANGUAGE INFORMATION

The registers on exit for `MoreMasters` are

Registers on exit

D0	Result code

RESULT CODES

`noErr`	0	No error
`memFullErr`	–108	Not enough memory

SEE ALSO

If you initialize a new zone, you can specify the number of master pointers that a master pointer block should contain. See the description of the `InitZone` procedure on page 2-86 for details.

Allocating and Releasing Relocatable Blocks of Memory

You can use the `NewHandle` function to allocate a relocatable block of memory, or the `NewEmptyHandle` function to allocate handles for which you do not yet need blocks of memory. If you want to allocate new blocks of memory in the system heap or with their bits precleared to 0, you can use the functions `NewHandleSys`, `NewHandleClear`, and `NewHandleSysClear`.

▲ **WARNING**
You should not call any of these memory-allocation routines at interrupt time. ▲

You can use the `DisposeHandle` procedure to free relocatable blocks of memory you have allocated.

NewHandle

You can use the `NewHandle` function to allocate a relocatable memory block of a specified size.

```
FUNCTION NewHandle (logicalSize: Size): Handle;
```

`logicalSize`
The requested size (in bytes) of the relocatable block.

DESCRIPTION

The `NewHandle` function attempts to allocate a new relocatable block in the current heap zone with a logical size of `logicalSize` bytes and then return a handle to the block.

The new block is unlocked and unpurgeable. If NewHandle cannot allocate a block of the requested size, it returns NIL.

▲ **WARNING**
Do not try to manufacture your own handles without this function by simply assigning the address of a variable of type Ptr to a variable of type Handle. The resulting "fake handle" would not reference a relocatable block and could cause a system crash. ▲

The NewHandle function pursues all available avenues to create a block of the requested size, including compacting the heap zone, increasing its size, and purging blocks from it. If all of these techniques fail and the heap zone has a grow-zone function installed, NewHandle calls the function. Then NewHandle tries again to free the necessary amount of memory, once more compacting and purging the heap zone if necessary. If memory still cannot be allocated, NewHandle calls the grow-zone function again, unless that function had returned 0, in which case NewHandle gives up and returns NIL.

SPECIAL CONSIDERATIONS

Because NewHandle allocates memory, you should not call it at interrupt time.

ASSEMBLY-LANGUAGE INFORMATION

The registers on entry and exit for NewHandle are

Registers on entry

A0 Number of logical bytes requested

Registers on exit

A0 Address of the new block's master pointer or NIL

D0 Result code

You can specify that the NewHandle function apply to the system heap zone instead of the current zone by setting bit 10 of the routine trap word. In most development systems, you can do this by supplying the word SYS as the second argument to the routine macro, as follows:

```
_NewHandle ,SYS
```

If you want to clear the bytes of a block of memory to 0 when you allocate it with the NewHandle function, set bit 9 of the routine trap word. You can usually do this by supplying the word CLEAR as the second argument to the routine macro, as follows:

```
_NewHandle ,CLEAR
```

You can combine SYS and CLEAR in the same macro call, but SYS must come first.

```
_NewHandle ,SYS,CLEAR
```

RESULT CODES

`noErr`	0	No error
`memFullErr`	–108	Not enough memory in heap zone

SEE ALSO

If you allocate a relocatable block that you plan to lock for long periods of time, you can prevent heap fragmentation by allocating the block as low as possible in the heap zone. To do this, see the description of the `ReserveMem` procedure on page 2-55.

If you plan to lock a relocatable block for short periods of time, you might want to move it to the top of the heap zone to prevent heap fragmentation. For more information, see the description of the `MoveHHi` procedure on page 2-56.

NewHandleSys

You can use the `NewHandleSys` function to allocate a relocatable block of memory of a specified size in the system heap.

```
FUNCTION NewHandleSys (logicalSize: Size): Handle;
```

`logicalSize`
The requested size (in bytes) of the relocatable block.

DESCRIPTION

The `NewHandleSys` function works much as the `NewHandle` function does, but attempts to allocate the requested block in the system heap zone instead of in the current heap zone. If it cannot, it returns `NIL`.

RESULT CODES

`noErr`	0	No error
`memFullErr`	–108	Not enough memory in heap zone

NewHandleClear

You can use the `NewHandleClear` function to allocate prezeroed memory in a relocatable block of a specified size.

```
FUNCTION NewHandleClear (logicalSize: Size): Handle;
```

`logicalSize`
: The requested size (in bytes) of the relocatable block. The `NewHandleClear` function sets each of these bytes to 0.

DESCRIPTION

The `NewHandleClear` function works much as the `NewHandle` function does but sets all bytes in the new block to 0 instead of leaving the contents of the block undefined.

Currently, `NewHandleClear` clears the block one byte at a time. For a large block, it might be faster to clear the block manually a long word at a time.

RESULT CODES

`noErr`	0	No error
`memFullErr`	–108	Not enough memory in heap zone

NewHandleSysClear

You can use the `NewHandleSysClear` function to allocate, in the system heap, prezeroed memory in a relocatable block of a specified size.

```
FUNCTION NewHandleSysClear (logicalSize: Size): Handle;
```

`logicalSize`
: The requested size (in bytes) of the relocatable block. The `NewHandleSysClear` function sets each of these bytes to 0.

DESCRIPTION

The `NewHandleSysClear` function works much as the `NewHandleClear` function does, but attempts to allocate the requested block in the system heap zone instead of in the current heap zone. `NewHandleSysClear` sets all bytes in the new block to 0 instead of leaving the contents of the block undefined.

RESULT CODES

`noErr`	0	No error
`memFullErr`	–108	Not enough memory in heap zone

NewEmptyHandle

If you want to initialize a handle but not allocate any space for it, use the NewEmptyHandle function. The Resource Manager uses this function extensively, but you probably won't need to use it.

```
FUNCTION NewEmptyHandle: Handle;
```

DESCRIPTION

The NewEmptyHandle function initializes a new handle by allocating a master pointer for it, but it does not allocate any memory for the handle to control. NewEmptyHandle sets the handle's master pointer to NIL.

SPECIAL CONSIDERATIONS

Because NewEmptyHandle might need to call the MoreMasters procedure to allocate new master pointers, it might allocate memory. Thus, you should not call NewEmptyHandle at interrupt time.

ASSEMBLY-LANGUAGE INFORMATION

The registers on exit for NewEmptyHandle are

Registers on exit

A0	Address of the new block's master pointer
D0	Result code

You can specify that the NewEmptyHandle function apply to the system heap zone instead of the current zone. To do so, set bit 10 of the routine trap word. In most development systems, you can do this by supplying the word SYS as the second argument to the routine macro, as follows:

```
_NewEmptyHandle ,SYS
```

RESULT CODES

noErr	0	No error
memFullErr	–108	Not enough memory

SEE ALSO

When you want to allocate memory for the empty handle, use the ReallocateHandle procedure, described on page 2-52.

NewEmptyHandleSys

If you want to initialize a handle in the system heap but not allocate any space for it, use the `NewEmptyHandleSys` function. The Resource Manager uses this function extensively, but you probably won't need to use it.

```
FUNCTION NewEmptyHandleSys: Handle;
```

DESCRIPTION

The `NewEmptyHandleSys` function initializes a new handle in the system heap by allocating a master pointer for it, but it does not allocate any memory for the handle to control. `NewEmptyHandleSys` sets the handle's master pointer to `NIL`.

SPECIAL CONSIDERATIONS

Because `NewEmptyHandleSys` might need to call the `MoreMasters` procedure to allocate new master pointers, it might allocate memory. Thus, you should not call `NewEmptyHandleSys` at interrupt time.

ASSEMBLY-LANGUAGE INFORMATION

The registers on exit for `NewEmptyHandleSys` are

Registers on exit

A0	Address of the new block's master pointer
D0	Result code

RESULT CODES

`noErr`	0	No error
`memFullErr`	–108	Not enough memory

SEE ALSO

When you want to allocate memory for the empty handle, use the `ReallocateHandle` procedure, described on page 2-52.

DisposeHandle

When you are completely done with a relocatable block, call the `DisposeHandle` procedure to free it and its master pointer for other uses.

```
PROCEDURE DisposeHandle (h: Handle);
```

h — A handle to a relocatable block.

DESCRIPTION

The `DisposeHandle` procedure releases the memory occupied by the relocatable block whose handle is `h`. It also frees the handle's master pointer for other uses.

▲ **WARNING**
After a call to `DisposeHandle`, all handles to the released block become invalid and should not be used again. Any subsequent calls to `DisposeHandle` using an invalid handle might damage the master pointer list. ▲

Do not use `DisposeHandle` to dispose of a handle obtained from the Resource Manager (for example, by a previous call to `GetResource`); use `ReleaseResource` instead. If, however, you have called `DetachResource` on a resource handle, you should dispose of the storage by calling `DisposeHandle`.

SPECIAL CONSIDERATIONS

Because `DisposeHandle` purges memory, you should not call it at interrupt time.

ASSEMBLY-LANGUAGE INFORMATION

The registers on entry and exit for `DisposeHandle` are

Registers on entry

A0 Handle to the relocatable block to be disposed of

Registers on exit

D0 Result code

RESULT CODES

noErr	0	No error
memWZErr	–111	Attempt to operate on a free block

Allocating and Releasing Nonrelocatable Blocks of Memory

You can use the `NewPtr` function to allocate a nonrelocatable block of memory. If you want to allocate new blocks of memory in the system heap or with their bits precleared to 0, you can use the `NewPtrSys`, `NewPtrClear`, and `NewPtrSysClear` functions.

▲ **WARNING**
You should not call any of these memory-allocation routines at interrupt time. ▲

You can use the `DisposePtr` procedure to free nonrelocatable blocks of memory you have allocated.

NewPtr

You can use the NewPtr function to allocate a nonrelocatable block of memory of a specified size.

```
FUNCTION NewPtr (logicalSize: Size): Ptr;
```

logicalSize
The requested size (in bytes) of the nonrelocatable block.

DESCRIPTION

The NewPtr function attempts to allocate, in the current heap zone, a nonrelocatable block with a logical size of logicalSize bytes and then return a pointer to the block. If the requested number of bytes cannot be allocated, NewPtr returns NIL.

The NewPtr function attempts to reserve space as low in the heap zone as possible for the new block. If it is able to reserve the requested amount of space, NewPtr allocates the nonrelocatable block in the gap ReserveMem creates. Otherwise, NewPtr returns NIL and generates a memFullErr error.

SPECIAL CONSIDERATIONS

Because NewPtr allocates memory, you should not call it at interrupt time.

ASSEMBLY-LANGUAGE INFORMATION

The registers on entry and exit for NewPtr are

Registers on entry

A0 Number of logical bytes requested

Registers on exit

A0 Address of the new block or NIL

D0 Result code

You can specify that the NewPtr function apply to the system heap zone instead of the current zone. To do so, set bit 10 of the routine trap word. In most development systems, you can do this by supplying the word SYS as the second argument to the routine macro, as follows:

```
_NewPtr ,SYS
```

If you want to clear the bytes of a block of memory to 0 when you allocate it with the NewPtr function, set bit 9 of the routine trap word. You can usually do this by supplying the word CLEAR as the second argument to the routine macro, as follows:

```
_NewPtr ,CLEAR
```

You can combine SYS and CLEAR in the same macro call, but SYS must come first.

```
_NewPtr ,SYS,CLEAR
```

RESULT CODES

noErr	0	No error
memFullErr	–108	Not enough memory

NewPtrSys

You can use the NewPtrSys function to allocate a nonrelocatable block of memory of a specified size in the system heap.

```
FUNCTION NewPtrSys (logicalSize: Size): Ptr;
```

logicalSize
The requested size (in bytes) of the nonrelocatable block.

DESCRIPTION

The NewPtrSys function works much as the NewPtr function does, but attempts to allocate the requested block in the system heap zone instead of in the current heap zone.

RESULT CODES

noErr	0	No error
memFullErr	–108	Not enough memory

NewPtrClear

You can use the NewPtrClear function to allocate prezeroed memory in a nonrelocatable block of a specified size.

```
FUNCTION NewPtrClear (logicalSize: Size): Ptr;
```

logicalSize
The requested size (in bytes) of the nonrelocatable block.

DESCRIPTION

The NewPtrClear function works much as the NewPtr function does, but sets all bytes in the new block to 0 instead of leaving the contents of the block undefined.

Currently, `NewPtrClear` clears the block one byte at a time. For a large block, it might be faster to clear the block manually a long word at a time.

RESULT CODES

`noErr`	0	No error
`memFullErr`	–108	Not enough memory

NewPtrSysClear

You can use the `NewPtrSysClear` function to allocate, in the system heap, prezeroed memory in a nonrelocatable block of a specified size.

```
FUNCTION NewPtrSysClear (logicalSize: Size): Ptr;
```

`logicalSize`
The requested size (in bytes) of the nonrelocatable block.

DESCRIPTION

The `NewPtrSysClear` function works much as the `NewPtr` function does, but attempts to allocate the requested block in the system heap zone instead of in the current heap zone. Also, it sets all bytes in the new block to 0 instead of leaving the contents of the block undefined.

RESULT CODES

`noErr`	0	No error
`memFullErr`	–108	Not enough memory

DisposePtr

When you are completely done with a nonrelocatable block, call the `DisposePtr` procedure to free it for other uses.

```
PROCEDURE DisposePtr (p: Ptr);
```

`p` A pointer to the nonrelocatable block you want to dispose of.

DESCRIPTION

The DisposePtr procedure releases the memory occupied by the nonrelocatable block specified by p.

▲ **WARNING**
After a call to DisposePtr, all pointers to the released block become invalid and should not be used again. Any subsequent use of a pointer to the released block might cause a system error. ▲

SPECIAL CONSIDERATIONS

Because DisposePtr purges memory, you should not call it at interrupt time.

ASSEMBLY-LANGUAGE INFORMATION

The registers on entry and exit for DisposePtr are

Registers on entry

A0	Pointer to the nonrelocatable block to be disposed of

Registers on exit

D0	Result code

RESULT CODES

noErr	0	No error
memWZErr	–111	Attempt to operate on a free block

Changing the Sizes of Relocatable and Nonrelocatable Blocks

You can use the GetHandleSize function and the SetHandleSize procedure to find out and change the logical size of a relocatable block, and you can use the GetPtrSize function and the SetPtrSize procedure to find out and change the logical size of a nonrelocatable block.

GetHandleSize

You can use the GetHandleSize function to find out the logical size of the relocatable block corresponding to a handle.

```
FUNCTION GetHandleSize (h: Handle): Size;
```

h	A handle to a relocatable block.

DESCRIPTION

The GetHandleSize function returns the logical size, in bytes, of the relocatable block whose handle is h. In case of an error, GetHandleSize returns 0.

ASSEMBLY-LANGUAGE INFORMATION

The registers on entry and exit for GetHandleSize are

Registers on entry

A0	Handle to the relocatable block

Registers on exit

D0	If >=0, number of bytes in relocatable block
	If <0, result code

The trap dispatcher sets the condition codes before returning from a trap by testing the low-order word of register D0 with a TST.W instruction. Because the block size returned in D0 by _GetHandleSize is a full 32-bit long word, the word-length test sets the condition codes incorrectly in this case. To branch on the contents of D0, use your own TST.L instruction on return from the trap to test the full 32 bits of the register.

SPECIAL CONSIDERATIONS

You shouldn't call GetHandleSize at interrupt time because the heap might be in an inconsistent state.

RESULT CODES

noErr	0	No error
nilHandleErr	–109	NIL master pointer
memWZErr	–111	Attempt to operate on a free block

SetHandleSize

You can use the SetHandleSize procedure to change the logical size of the relocatable block corresponding to a handle.

```
PROCEDURE SetHandleSize (h: Handle; newSize: Size);
```

h	A handle to a relocatable block.
newSize	The desired new logical size, in bytes, of the relocatable block.

DESCRIPTION

The SetHandleSize procedure attempts to change the logical size of the relocatable block whose handle is h. The new logical size is specified by newSize.

SetHandleSize might need to move the relocatable block to obtain enough space for the resized block. Thus, for best results you should unlock a block before resizing it.

An attempt to increase the size of a locked block might fail, because of blocks above and below it that are either nonrelocatable or locked. You should be prepared for this possibility.

SPECIAL CONSIDERATIONS

Because SetHandleSize allocates memory, you should not call it at interrupt time.

ASSEMBLY-LANGUAGE INFORMATION

The registers on entry and exit for SetHandleSize are

Registers on entry

A0	Handle to the relocatable block
D0	Desired new size of relocatable block

Registers on exit

D0	Result code

RESULT CODES

noErr	0	No error
memFullErr	–108	Not enough memory
nilHandleErr	–109	NIL master pointer
memWZErr	–111	Attempt to operate on a free block

SEE ALSO

Instead of using the SetHandleSize procedure to set the size of a handle to 0, you can use the EmptyHandle procedure, described on page 2-51.

GetPtrSize

You can use the GetPtrSize function to find out the logical size of the nonrelocatable block corresponding to a pointer.

```
FUNCTION GetPtrSize (p: Ptr): Size;
```

p A pointer to a nonrelocatable block.

DESCRIPTION

The GetPtrSize function returns the logical size, in bytes, of the nonrelocatable block pointed to by p. In case of an error, GetPtrSize returns 0.

ASSEMBLY-LANGUAGE INFORMATION

The registers on entry and exit for GetPtrSize are

Registers on entry

A0 Pointer to the nonrelocatable block

Registers on exit

D0 If >=0, number of bytes in nonrelocatable block
If <0, result code

The trap dispatcher sets the condition codes before returning from a trap by testing the low-order word of register D0 with a TST.W instruction. Because the block size returned in D0 by _GetPtrSize is a full 32-bit long word, the word-length test sets the condition codes incorrectly in this case. To branch on the contents of D0, use your own TST.L instruction on return from the trap to test the full 32 bits of the register.

RESULT CODES

noErr	0	No error
memWZErr	–111	Attempt to operate on a free block

SetPtrSize

You can use the SetPtrSize procedure to change the logical size of the nonrelocatable block corresponding to a pointer.

```
PROCEDURE SetPtrSize (p: Ptr; newSize: Size);
```

p A pointer to a nonrelocatable block.

newSize The desired new logical size, in bytes, of the nonrelocatable block.

DESCRIPTION

The SetPtrSize procedure attempts to change the logical size of the nonrelocatable block pointed to by p. The new logical size is specified by newSize.

An attempt to increase the size of a nonrelocatable block might fail because of a block above it that is either nonrelocatable or locked. You should be prepared for this possibility.

SPECIAL CONSIDERATIONS

Because `SetPtrSize` allocates memory, you should not call it at interrupt time.

ASSEMBLY-LANGUAGE INFORMATION

The registers on entry and exit for `SetPtrSize` are

Registers on entry

A0	Pointer to the nonrelocatable block
D0	Desired new size of nonrelocatable block

Registers on exit

D0	Result code

RESULT CODES

`noErr`	0	No error
`memFullErr`	–108	Not enough memory
`memWZErr`	–111	Attempt to operate on a free block

Setting the Properties of Relocatable Blocks

A relocatable block can be either locked or unlocked and either purgeable or unpurgeable. In addition, it can have its resource bit either set or cleared. To determine the state of any of these properties, use the `HGetState` function. To change these properties, use the `HLock`, `HUnlock`, `HPurge`, `HNoPurge`, `HSetRBit`, and `HClrRBit` procedures. To restore these properties, use the `HSetState` procedure.

▲ **WARNING**
Be sure to use these procedures to get and set the properties of relocatable blocks. In particular, do not rely on the structure of master pointers, because their structure in 24-bit mode is different from their structure in 32-bit mode. ▲

HGetState

You can use the `HGetState` function to get the current properties of a relocatable block (perhaps so that you can change and then later restore those properties).

```
FUNCTION HGetState (h: Handle): SignedByte;
```

`h` A handle to a relocatable block.

DESCRIPTION

The `HGetState` function returns a signed byte containing the flags of the master pointer for the given handle. You can save this byte, change the state of any of the flags using the routines described on page 2-45 through page 2-50, and then restore their original states by passing the byte to the `HSetState` procedure, described next.

You can use bit-manipulation functions on the returned signed byte to determine the value of a given attribute. Currently the following bits are used:

Bit	Meaning
0–4	Reserved
5	Set if relocatable block is a resource
6	Set if relocatable block is purgeable
7	Set if relocatable block is locked

If an error occurs during an attempt to get the state flags of the specified relocatable block, `HGetState` returns the low-order byte of the result code as its function result. For example, if the handle `h` points to a master pointer whose value is `NIL`, then the signed byte returned by `HGetState` will contain the value –109.

ASSEMBLY-LANGUAGE INFORMATION

The registers on entry and exit for `HGetState` are

Registers on entry

A0 Handle whose properties you want to get

Registers on exit

D0 Byte containing flags

RESULT CODES

`noErr`	0	No error
`nilHandleErr`	–109	`NIL` master pointer
`memWZErr`	–111	Attempt to operate on a free block

HSetState

You can use the `HSetState` procedure to restore properties of a block after a call to `HGetState`.

```
PROCEDURE HSetState (h: Handle; flags: SignedByte);
```

`h` A handle to a relocatable block.

`flags` A signed byte specifying the properties to which you want to set the relocatable block.

DESCRIPTION

The `HSetState` procedure restores to the handle `h` the properties specified in the `flags` signed byte. See the description of the `HGetState` function for a list of the currently used bits in that byte. Because additional bits of the `flags` byte could become significant in future versions of system software, use `HSetState` only with a byte returned by `HGetState`. If you need to set two or three properties of a relocatable block at once, it is better to use the procedures that set individual properties than to manipulate the bits returned by `HGetState` and then call `HSetState`.

ASSEMBLY-LANGUAGE INFORMATION

The registers on entry and exit for `HSetState` are

Registers on entry

A0	Handle whose properties you want to set
D0	Byte containing flags indicating the handle's new properties

Registers on exit

D0	Result code

RESULT CODES

`noErr`	0	No error
`nilHandleErr`	–109	`NIL` master pointer
`memWZErr`	–111	Attempt to operate on a free block

HLock

You can use the `HLock` procedure to lock a relocatable block so that it does not move in the heap. If you plan to dereference a handle and then allocate, move, or purge memory (or call a routine that does so), then you should lock the handle before using the dereferenced handle.

```
PROCEDURE HLock (h: Handle);
```

`h`	A handle to a relocatable block.

DESCRIPTION

The `HLock` procedure locks the relocatable block to which `h` is a handle, preventing it from being moved within its heap zone. If the block is already locked, `HLock` does nothing.

ASSEMBLY-LANGUAGE INFORMATION

The registers on entry and exit for `HLock` are

Registers on entry

A0 Handle to lock

Registers on exit

D0 Result code

RESULT CODES

`noErr`	0	No error
`nilHandleErr`	–109	`NIL` master pointer
`memWZErr`	–111	Attempt to operate on a free block

SEE ALSO

If you plan to lock a relocatable block for long periods of time, you can prevent fragmentation by ensuring that the block is as low as possible in the heap zone. To do this, see the description of the `ReserveMem` procedure on page 2-55.

If you plan to lock a relocatable block for short periods of time, you can prevent heap fragmentation by moving the block to the top of the heap zone before locking. For more information, see the description of the `MoveHHi` procedure on page 2-56.

HUnlock

You can use the `HUnlock` procedure to unlock a relocatable block so that it is free to move in its heap zone.

```
PROCEDURE HUnlock (h: Handle);
```

`h` A handle to a relocatable block.

DESCRIPTION

The `HUnlock` procedure unlocks the relocatable block to which `h` is a handle, allowing it to be moved within its heap zone. If the block is already unlocked, `HUnlock` does nothing.

ASSEMBLY-LANGUAGE INFORMATION

The registers on entry and exit for `HUnlock` are

Registers on entry

A0	Handle to unlock

Registers on exit

D0	Result code

RESULT CODES

`noErr`	0	No error
`nilHandleErr`	–109	`NIL` master pointer
`memWZErr`	–111	Attempt to operate on a free block

HPurge

You can use the `HPurge` procedure to mark a relocatable block so that it can be purged if a memory request cannot be fulfilled after compaction.

```
PROCEDURE HPurge (h: Handle);
```

`h` A handle to a relocatable block.

DESCRIPTION

The `HPurge` procedure makes the relocatable block to which `h` is a handle purgeable. If the block is already purgeable, `HPurge` does nothing.

The Memory Manager might purge the block when it needs to purge the heap zone containing the block to satisfy a memory request. A direct call to the `PurgeMem` procedure or the `MaxMem` function would also purge blocks marked as purgeable.

Once you mark a relocatable block as purgeable, you should make sure that handles to the block are not empty before you access the block. If they are empty, you must reallocate space for the block and recopy the block's data from another source, such as a resource file, before using the information in the block.

If the block to which `h` is a handle is locked, `HPurge` does not unlock the block but does mark it as purgeable. If you later call `HUnlock` on `h`, the block is subject to purging.

ASSEMBLY-LANGUAGE INFORMATION

The registers on entry and exit for `HPurge` are

Registers on entry

A0	Handle to make purgeable

Registers on exit

D0	Result code

RESULT CODES

`noErr`	0	No error
`nilHandleErr`	–109	`NIL` master pointer
`memWZErr`	–111	Attempt to operate on a free block

SEE ALSO

If the Memory Manager has purged a block, you can reallocate space for it by using the `ReallocateHandle` procedure, described on page 2-52.

You can immediately free the space taken by a handle without disposing of it by calling `EmptyHandle`. This procedure, described on page 2-51, does not require that the block be purgeable.

HNoPurge

You can use the `HNoPurge` procedure to mark a relocatable block so that it cannot be purged.

```
PROCEDURE HNoPurge (h: Handle);
```

`h` A handle to a relocatable block.

DESCRIPTION

The `HNoPurge` procedure makes the relocatable block to which `h` is a handle unpurgeable. If the block is already unpurgeable, `HNoPurge` does nothing.

The `HNoPurge` procedure does not reallocate memory for a handle if it has already been purged.

ASSEMBLY-LANGUAGE INFORMATION

The registers on entry and exit for `HNoPurge` are

Registers on entry

A0 Handle to make unpurgeable

Registers on exit

D0 Result code

RESULT CODES

`noErr`	0	No error
`nilHandleErr`	–109	`NIL` master pointer
`memWZErr`	–111	Attempt to operate on a free block

SEE ALSO

If you want to reallocate memory for a relocatable block that has already been purged, you can use the `ReallocateHandle` procedure, described on page 2-52.

HSetRBit

You can use the `HSetRBit` procedure to set the resource flag of a relocatable block. The Resource Manager uses this routine extensively, but you should never need to use it.

```
PROCEDURE HSetRBit (h: Handle);
```

`h` A handle to a relocatable block.

DESCRIPTION

The `HSetRBit` procedure sets the resource flag of the relocatable block to which `h` is a handle. It does nothing if the flag is already set.

▲ **WARNING**
When the resource flag is set, the Resource Manager identifies the associated relocatable block as belonging to a resource. This can cause problems if that block wasn't actually read from a resource. ▲

ASSEMBLY-LANGUAGE INFORMATION

The registers on entry and exit for `HSetRBit` are

Registers on entry

A0 Handle whose resource flag you want to set

Registers on exit

D0 Result code

RESULT CODES

`noErr`	0	No error
`nilHandleErr`	–109	`NIL` master pointer
`memWZErr`	–111	Attempt to operate on a free block

HClrRBit

You can use the `HClrRBit` procedure to clear the resource flag of a relocatable block. The Resource Manager uses this routine extensively, but you probably won't need to use it.

```
PROCEDURE HClrRBit (h: Handle);
```

`h` A handle to a relocatable block.

DESCRIPTION

The `HClrRBit` procedure clears the resource flag of a relocatable block. It does nothing if the flag is already cleared.

ASSEMBLY-LANGUAGE INFORMATION

The registers on entry and exit for `HClrRBit` are

Registers on entry

A0 Handle whose resource flag you want to clear

Registers on exit

D0 Result code

RESULT CODES

`noErr`	0	No error
`nilHandleErr`	–109	`NIL` master pointer
`memWZErr`	–111	Attempt to operate on a free block

SEE ALSO

To disassociate the data in a resource handle from the resource file, you should use the Resource Manager procedure `DetachResource` instead of this procedure.

Managing Relocatable Blocks

The Memory Manager provides routines that allow you to purge and later reallocate space for relocatable blocks, recreate handles to relocatable blocks if you have access to their master pointers, and control where in their heap zone relocatable blocks are located.

To free the memory taken up by a relocatable block without releasing the master pointer to the block for other uses, use the `EmptyHandle` procedure. To reallocate space for a handle that you have emptied or the Memory Manager has purged, use the `ReallocateHandle` procedure.

If, because you have dereferenced a handle, you no longer have access to it but do have access to its master pointer, you can use the `RecoverHandle` function to recreate the handle.

To ensure that a relocatable block that you plan to lock for short or long periods of time does not cause heap fragmentation, use the `MoveHHi` and the `ReserveMem` procedures, respectively.

EmptyHandle

The `EmptyHandle` procedure allows you to free memory taken by a relocatable block without freeing the relocatable block's master pointer for other uses.

```
PROCEDURE EmptyHandle (h: Handle);
```

`h` A handle to a relocatable block.

DESCRIPTION

The `EmptyHandle` procedure purges the relocatable block whose handle is `h` and sets the handle's master pointer to `NIL`. The block whose handle is `h` must be unlocked but need not be purgeable.

Note

If there are multiple handles to the relocatable block, then calling the `EmptyHandle` procedure empties them all, because all of the handles share a common master pointer. When you later use `ReallocateHandle` to reallocate space for the block, the master pointer is updated, and all of the handles reference the new block correctly. ◆

SPECIAL CONSIDERATIONS

Because `EmptyHandle` purges memory, you should not call it at interrupt time.

ASSEMBLY-LANGUAGE INFORMATION

The registers on entry and exit for `EmptyHandle` are

Registers on entry

A0	Handle to relocatable block

Registers on exit

A0	Handle to relocatable block
D0	Result code

RESULT CODES

`noErr`	0	No error
`memWZErr`	–111	Attempt to operate on a free block
`memPurErr`	–112	Attempt to purge a locked block

SEE ALSO

To purge all of the blocks in a heap zone that are marked purgeable, use the `PurgeMem` procedure, described on page 2-73.

To free the memory taken up by a relocatable block and release the block's master pointer for other uses, use the `DisposeHandle` procedure, described on page 2-34.

ReallocateHandle

To recover space for a relocatable block that you have emptied or the Memory Manager has purged, use the `ReallocateHandle` procedure.

```
PROCEDURE ReallocateHandle (h: Handle; logicalSize: Size);
```

`h` A handle to a relocatable block.

`logicalSize`
The desired new logical size (in bytes) of the relocatable block.

DESCRIPTION

The `ReallocateHandle` procedure allocates a new relocatable block with a logical size of `logicalSize` bytes. It updates the handle `h` by setting its master pointer to point to the new block. The new block is unlocked and unpurgeable.

Usually you use `ReallocateHandle` to reallocate space for a block that you have emptied or the Memory Manager has purged. If the handle references an existing block, `ReallocateHandle` releases that block before creating a new one.

Note
To reallocate space for a resource that has been purged, you should call `LoadResource`, not `ReallocateHandle`. ◆

If many handles reference a single purged, relocatable block, you need to call `ReallocateHandle` on just one of them.

In case of an error, `ReallocateHandle` neither allocates a new block nor changes the master pointer to which handle `h` points.

SPECIAL CONSIDERATIONS

Because `ReallocateHandle` might purge and allocate memory, you should not call it at interrupt time.

ASSEMBLY-LANGUAGE INFORMATION

The registers on entry and exit for `ReallocateHandle` are

Registers on entry

A0	Handle for new relocatable block
D0	Desired logical size, in bytes, of new block

Registers on exit

D0	Result code

RESULT CODES

`noErr`	0	No error
`memROZErr`	–99	Heap zone is read-only
`memFullErr`	–108	Not enough memory
`memWZErr`	–111	Attempt to operate on a free block
`memPurErr`	–112	Attempt to purge a locked block

SEE ALSO

Because `ReallocateHandle` releases any existing relocatable block referenced by the handle `h` before allocating a new one, it does not provide an efficient technique for resizing relocatable blocks. To do that, use the `SetHandleSize` procedure, described on page 2-40.

RecoverHandle

The Memory Manager does not allow you to change relocatable blocks into nonrelocatable blocks, or vice-versa. However, if you no longer have access to a handle but still have access to its master pointer, you can use the `RecoverHandle` function to recreate a handle to the relocatable block referenced by the master pointer.

```
FUNCTION RecoverHandle (p: Ptr): Handle;
```

`p` The master pointer to a relocatable block.

DESCRIPTION

The `RecoverHandle` function returns a handle to the relocatable block pointed to by `p`. If `p` doesn't point to a valid block, the results of `RecoverHandle` are undefined.

SPECIAL CONSIDERATIONS

Even though `RecoverHandle` does not move or purge memory, you should not call it at interrupt time.

ASSEMBLY-LANGUAGE INFORMATION

The registers on entry and exit for `RecoverHandle` are

Registers on entry

A0 Master pointer

Registers on exit

A0 Handle to master pointer's relocatable block

D0 Unchanged

Unlike most other Memory Manager routines, `RecoverHandle` does not return a result code in register D0; the previous contents of D0 are preserved unchanged. The result code is, however, returned by `MemError`.

The `RecoverHandle` function looks only in the current heap zone for the relocatable block pointed to by the parameter `p`. If you want to use the `RecoverHandle` function to recover a handle for a relocatable block in the system heap, set bit 10 of the routine trap word. In most development systems, you can do this by supplying the word `SYS` as the second argument to the routine macro, as follows:

```
_RecoverHandle ,SYS
```

RESULT CODES

noErr	0	No error
memBCErr	–115	Block check failed

ReserveMem

Use the ReserveMem procedure when you allocate a relocatable block that you intend to lock for long periods of time. This helps prevent heap fragmentation because it reserves space for the block as close to the bottom of the heap as possible. Consistent use of ReserveMem for this purpose ensures that all locked, relocatable blocks and nonrelocatable blocks are together at the bottom of the heap zone and thus do not prevent unlocked relocatable blocks from moving about the zone.

```
PROCEDURE ReserveMem (cbNeeded: Size);
```

cbNeeded The number of bytes to reserve near the bottom of the heap.

DESCRIPTION

The ReserveMem procedure attempts to create free space for a block of cbNeeded contiguous logical bytes at the lowest possible position in the current heap zone. It pursues every available means of placing the block as close as possible to the bottom of the zone, including moving other relocatable blocks upward, expanding the zone (if possible), and purging blocks from it.

Because ReserveMem does not actually allocate the block, you must combine calls to ReserveMem with calls to the NewHandle function.

Do not use the ReserveMem procedure for a relocatable block you intend to lock for only a short period of time. If you do so and then allocate a nonrelocatable block above it, the relocatable block becomes trapped under the nonrelocatable block when you unlock that relocatable block.

Note

It isn't necessary to call ReserveMem to reserve space for a nonrelocatable block, because the NewPtr function calls it automatically. Also, you do not need to call ReserveMem to reserve memory before you load a locked resource into memory, because the Resource Manager calls ReserveMem automatically. ◆

SPECIAL CONSIDERATIONS

Because the ReserveMem procedure could move and purge memory, you should not call it at interrupt time.

ASSEMBLY-LANGUAGE INFORMATION

The registers on entry and exit for `ReserveMem` are

Registers on entry

D0 Number of bytes to reserve

Registers on exit

D0 Result code

The `ReserveMem` procedure reserves memory in the current heap zone. If you want to reserve memory in the system heap zone rather than in the current heap zone, set bit 10 of the routine trap word. In most development systems, you can do this by supplying the word `SYS` as the second argument to the routine macro, as follows:

```
_ResrvMem ,SYS
```

RESULT CODES

`noErr`	0	No error
`memFullErr`	–108	Not enough memory

ReserveMemSys

If you plan to lock a relocatable block for long periods of time in the system heap zone, use the `ReserveMemSys` procedure to reserve space for the block as low in the system heap as possible.

```
PROCEDURE ReserveMemSys (cbNeeded: Size);
```

`cbNeeded` The number of bytes to reserve near the bottom of the system heap.

DESCRIPTION

The `ReserveMemSys` procedure works much as the `ReserveMem` procedure does, but reserves memory in the system heap zone rather than in the current heap zone.

MoveHHi

If you plan to lock a relocatable block for a short period of time, use the `MoveHHi` procedure, which moves the block to the top of the heap and thus helps prevent heap fragmentation.

```
PROCEDURE MoveHHi (h: Handle);
```

h   A handle to a relocatable block.

DESCRIPTION

The MoveHHi procedure attempts to move the relocatable block referenced by the handle h upward until it reaches a nonrelocatable block, a locked relocatable block, or the top of the heap.

▲ **WARNING**
If you call MoveHHi to move a handle to a resource that has its resChanged bit set, the Resource Manager updates the resource by using the WriteResource procedure to write the contents of the block to disk. If you want to avoid this behavior, call the Resource Manager procedure SetResPurge(FALSE) before you call MoveHHi, and then call SetResPurge(TRUE) to restore the default setting. ▲

By using the MoveHHi procedure on relocatable blocks you plan to allocate for short periods of time, you help prevent islands of immovable memory from accumulating in (and thus fragmenting) the heap.

Do not use the MoveHHi procedure to move blocks you plan to lock for long periods of time. The MoveHHi procedure moves such blocks to the top of the heap, perhaps preventing other blocks already at the top of the heap from moving down once they are unlocked. Instead, use the ReserveMem procedure before allocating such blocks, thus keeping them in the bottom partition of the heap, where they do not prevent relocatable blocks from moving.

If you frequently lock a block for short periods of time and find that calling MoveHHi each time slows down your application, you might consider leaving the block always locked and calling the ReserveMem procedure before allocating it.

Once you move a block to the top of the heap, be sure to lock it if you do not want the Memory Manager to move it back to the middle partition as soon as it can. (The MoveHHi procedure cannot move locked blocks; be sure to lock blocks after, not before, calling MoveHHi.)

Note
Using the MoveHHi procedure without taking other precautionary measures to prevent heap fragmentation is useless, because even one small nonrelocatable or locked relocatable block in the middle of the heap might prevent MoveHHi from moving blocks to the top of the heap. ◆

SPECIAL CONSIDERATIONS

Because the MoveHHi procedure moves memory, you should not call it at interrupt time.

Don't call MoveHHi on blocks in the system heap. Don't call MoveHHi from a desk accessory.

ASSEMBLY-LANGUAGE INFORMATION

The registers on entry and exit for `MoveHHi` are

Registers on entry

A0	Handle to move

Registers on exit

D0	Result code

RESULT CODES

`noErr`	0	No error
`nilHandleErr`	–109	`NIL` master pointer
`memLockedErr`	–117	Block is locked

HLockHi

You can use the `HLockHi` procedure to move a relocatable block to the top of the heap and lock it.

```
PROCEDURE HLockHi (h: Handle);
```

`h`	A handle to a relocatable block.

DESCRIPTION

The `HLockHi` procedure attempts to move the relocatable block referenced by the handle `h` upward until it reaches a nonrelocatable block, a locked relocatable block, or the top of the heap. Then `HLockHi` locks the block.

The `HLockHi` procedure is simply a convenient replacement for the pair of procedures `MoveHHi` and `HLock`.

SPECIAL CONSIDERATIONS

Because the `HLockHi` procedure moves memory, you should not call it at interrupt time.

Don't call `HLockHi` on blocks in the system heap. Don't call `HLockHi` from a desk accessory.

ASSEMBLY-LANGUAGE INFORMATION

The registers on entry and exit for `HLockHi` are

Registers on entry

A0 Handle to move and lock

Registers on exit

D0 Result code

RESULT CODES

noErr	0	No error
nilHandleErr	–109	NIL master pointer
memWZErr	–111	Attempt to operate on a free block
memLockedErr	–117	Block is locked

Manipulating Blocks of Memory

The Memory Manager provides three routines for copying blocks of memory referenced by pointers. To copy a block of memory to a nonrelocatable block, use the `BlockMove` procedure. To copy to a new relocatable block, use the `PtrToHand` function. To copy to an existing relocatable block, use the `PtrToXHand` function. If you want to use any of these routines to copy memory you access with a handle, you must first dereference and lock the handle. A fourth routine, `HandToHand`, allows you to copy information from one handle to another.

To concatenate blocks of memory, you can use the `HandAndHand` and `PtrAndHand` functions.

BlockMove

To copy a sequence of bytes from one location in memory to another, you can use the `BlockMove` procedure.

```
PROCEDURE BlockMove (sourcePtr, destPtr: Ptr; byteCount: Size);
```

`sourcePtr` The address of the first byte to copy.

`destPtr` The address of the first byte to copy to.

`byteCount` The number of bytes to copy. If the value of `byteCount` is 0, `BlockMove` does nothing.

DESCRIPTION

The `BlockMove` procedure moves a block of `byteCount` consecutive bytes from the address designated by `sourcePtr` to that designated by `destPtr`. It updates no pointers.

The `BlockMove` procedure works correctly even if the source and destination blocks overlap.

SPECIAL CONSIDERATIONS

You can safely call `BlockMove` at interrupt time. Even though it moves memory, `BlockMove` does not move relocatable blocks, but simply copies bytes.

The `BlockMove` procedure currently flushes the processor caches whenever the number of bytes to be moved is greater than 12. This behavior can adversely affect your application's performance. You might want to avoid calling `BlockMove` to move small amounts of data in memory if there is no possibility of moving stale data or instructions. For more information about stale data and instructions, see the discussion of the processor caches in the chapter "Memory Management Utilities" in this book.

ASSEMBLY-LANGUAGE INFORMATION

The registers on entry and exit for `BlockMove` are

Registers on entry

A0	Pointer to source
A1	Pointer to destination
D0	Number of bytes to copy

Registers on exit

D0	Result code

RESULT CODE

`noErr`	0	No error

PtrToHand

To copy data referenced by a pointer to a new relocatable block, use the `PtrToHand` function.

```
FUNCTION PtrToHand (srcPtr: Ptr; VAR dstHndl: Handle;
                    size: LongInt): OSErr;
```

`srcPtr`	The address of the first byte to copy.
`dstHndl`	A handle for which you have not yet allocated any memory. The `PtrToHand` function allocates memory for the handle and copies `size` bytes beginning at `srcPtr` into it.
`size`	The number of bytes to copy.

DESCRIPTION

The PtrToHand function returns, in dstHndl, a newly created handle to a copy of the number of bytes specified by the size parameter, beginning at the location specified by srcPtr. The dstHndl parameter must be a handle variable that is not empty and is not a handle to an allocated block of size 0.

SPECIAL CONSIDERATIONS

Because PtrToHand allocates memory, you should not call it at interrupt time.

ASSEMBLY-LANGUAGE INFORMATION

The registers on entry and exit for PtrToHand are

Registers on entry

A0	Pointer to source
D0	Number of bytes to copy

Registers on exit

A0	Destination handle
D0	Result code

RESULT CODES

noErr	0	No error
memFullErr	–108	Not enough memory

SEE ALSO

You can use the PtrToHand function to copy data from one handle to a new handle if you dereference and lock the source handle. However, if you want to copy all of the data from one handle to another, the HandToHand function (described on page 2-62) is more efficient.

PtrToXHand

To copy data referenced by a pointer to an already existing relocatable block, use the PtrToXHand function.

```
FUNCTION PtrToXHand (srcPtr: Ptr; dstHndl: Handle; size: LongInt):
                    OSErr;
```

srcPtr — The address of the first byte to copy.

`dstHndl`	A handle to an already existing relocatable block to which to copy `size` bytes, beginning at `srcPtr`.
`size`	The number of bytes to copy.

DESCRIPTION

The `PtrToXHand` function makes the existing handle, specified by `dstHndl`, a handle to a copy of the number of bytes specified by the `size` parameter, beginning at the location specified by `srcPtr`.

SPECIAL CONSIDERATIONS

Because `PtrToXHand` affects memory, you should not call it at interrupt time.

ASSEMBLY-LANGUAGE INFORMATION

The registers on entry and exit for `PtrToXHand` are

Registers on entry

A0	Pointer to source
A1	Handle to destination
D0	Number of bytes to copy

Registers on exit

A0	Handle to destination
D0	Result code

RESULT CODES

`noErr`	0	No error
`memFullErr`	–108	Not enough memory
`nilHandleErr`	–109	`NIL` master pointer
`memWZErr`	–111	Attempt to operate on a free block

HandToHand

Use the `HandToHand` function to copy all of the data from one relocatable block to a new relocatable block.

```
FUNCTION HandToHand (VAR theHndl: Handle): OSErr;
```

`theHndl`	On entry, a handle to the relocatable block whose data is to be copied. On exit, a handle to a new relocatable block whose data duplicates that of the original.

DESCRIPTION

The HandToHand function attempts to copy the information in the relocatable block to which theHndl is a handle; if successful, HandToHand returns a handle to the new relocatable block in theHndl. The new relocatable block is created in the same heap zone as the original block (which might not be the current heap zone).

Because HandToHand replaces its input parameter with the new handle, you should retain the original value of the input parameter somewhere else, or you won't be able to access it. Here is an example:

```
VAR
   original, copy: Handle;
   myErr: OSErr;
...
   copy := original;           {both handles access same block}
   myErr := HandToHand(copy); {copy now points to copy of block}
```

SPECIAL CONSIDERATIONS

If successful in creating a new relocatable block, the HandToHand function does not duplicate the properties of the original block. The new block is unlocked, unpurgeable, and not a resource. You might need to call HLock, HPurge, or HSetRBit (or the combination of HGetState and HSetState) to adjust the properties of the new block.

Because HandToHand allocates memory, you should not call it at interrupt time.

ASSEMBLY-LANGUAGE INFORMATION

The registers on entry and exit for HandToHand are

Registers on entry

A0	Handle to original data

Registers on exit

A0	Handle to copy of data
D0	Result code

RESULT CODES

noErr	0	No error
memFullErr	–108	Not enough memory
nilHandleErr	–109	NIL master pointer
memWZErr	–111	Attempt to operate on a free block

SEE ALSO

If you want to copy only part of a relocatable block into a new relocatable block, use the `PtrToHand` function, described on page 2-60, after locking and dereferencing a handle to the relocatable block to be copied.

HandAndHand

Use the `HandAndHand` function to concatenate two relocatable blocks.

```
FUNCTION HandAndHand (aHndl, bHndl: Handle): OSErr;
```

`aHndl` A handle to the first relocatable block, whose contents do not change but are concatenated to the end of the second relocatable block.

`bHndl` A handle to the second relocatable block, whose size the Memory Manager expands so that it can concatenate the information from `aHndl` to the end of the contents of this block.

DESCRIPTION

The `HandAndHand` function concatenates the information from the relocatable block to which `aHndl` is a handle onto the end of the relocatable block to which `bHndl` is a handle. The `aHndl` variable remains unchanged.

▲ **WARNING**
The `HandAndHand` function dereferences the handle `aHndl`. You must call the `HLock` procedure to lock the block before calling `HandAndHand`. Afterward, you can call the `HUnlock` procedure to unlock it. Alternatively, you can save the block's original state by calling the `HGetState` function, lock the block by calling `HLock`, and then restore the original settings by calling `HSetState`. ▲

SPECIAL CONSIDERATIONS

Because `HandAndHand` moves memory, you should not call it at interrupt time.

ASSEMBLY-LANGUAGE INFORMATION

The registers on entry and exit for `HandAndHand` are

Registers on entry

A0 Handle to be concatenated

A1 Handle to contain itself, data from A0's handle

Registers on exit

A0 Handle to concatenated data

D0 Result code

RESULT CODES

noErr	0	No error
memFullErr	–108	Not enough memory
nilHandleErr	–109	NIL master pointer
memWZErr	–111	Attempt to operate on a free block

PtrAndHand

Use the PtrAndHand function to concatenate part or all of a memory block to the end of a relocatable block.

```
FUNCTION PtrAndHand (pntr: Ptr; hndl: Handle; size: LongInt):
                    OSErr;
```

pntr — A pointer to the beginning of the data that the Memory Manager is to concatenate onto the end of the relocatable block.

hndl — A handle to the relocatable block, whose size the Memory Manager expands so that it can concatenate the information from pntr onto the end of this block.

size — The number of bytes of the block referenced by pntr to be copied.

DESCRIPTION

The PtrAndHand function takes the number of bytes specified by the size parameter, beginning at the location specified by pntr, and concatenates them onto the end of the relocatable block to which hndl is a handle.

The contents of the source block remain unchanged.

SPECIAL CONSIDERATIONS

Because PtrAndHand allocates memory, you should not call it at interrupt time.

ASSEMBLY-LANGUAGE INFORMATION

The registers on entry and exit for PtrAndHand are

Registers on entry

A0	Pointer to data to copy
A1	Handle to relocatable block at whose end the copied data concatenated
A2	Number of bytes to concatenate

Registers on exit

A0	Handle to now-concatenated relocatable block
D0	Result code

RESULT CODES

noErr	0	No error
memFullErr	–108	Not enough memory
nilHandleErr	–109	NIL master pointer
memWZErr	–111	Attempt to operate on a free block

Assessing Memory Conditions

The Memory Manager provides four routines to test how much memory is available, one routine used after memory operations to determine if an error occurred, and one routine to determine the location in memory of the top of your application's partition.

To determine the total amount of free space in the current heap zone or the size of the maximum block that could be obtained after compacting the heap, use the `FreeMem` and `MaxBlock` functions, respectively. To determine what those values would be after a purge of the heap zone, call the `PurgeSpace` procedure. Finally, to find out how much your stack can grow before it collides with the heap, use the `StackSpace` function.

To find out whether a Memory Manager operation finished successfully, use the `MemError` function.

FreeMem

By calling the `FreeMem` function, you can find out the total amount of free space, in bytes, in the current heap zone.

```
FUNCTION FreeMem: LongInt;
```

DESCRIPTION

The `FreeMem` function returns the total amount of free space (in bytes) in the current heap zone. Note that it usually isn't possible to allocate a block of that size, because of heap fragmentation due to nonrelocatable or locked blocks.

SPECIAL CONSIDERATIONS

Even though `FreeMem` does not move or purge memory, you should not call it at interrupt time because the heap might be in an inconsistent state.

ASSEMBLY-LANGUAGE INFORMATION

The registers on exit for `FreeMem` are

Registers on exit

D0 Number of bytes available in heap zone

The FreeMem function reports the number of free bytes in the current heap zone. If you want to know how many bytes are available in the system heap zone rather than in the current heap zone, set bit 10 of the routine trap word. In most development systems, you can do this by supplying the word SYS as the second argument to the routine macro, as follows:

```
_FreeMem ,SYS
```

RESULT CODES

noErr	0	No error

FreeMemSys

To determine how much free space remains in the system heap zone, use the FreeMemSys function.

```
FUNCTION FreeMemSys: LongInt;
```

DESCRIPTION

The FreeMemSys function works much as the FreeMem function does, but returns the total amount of free memory in the system heap zone instead of in the current heap zone.

RESULT CODES

noErr	0	No error

MaxBlock

Use the MaxBlock function to determine the size of the largest block you could allocate in the current heap zone after a compaction.

```
FUNCTION MaxBlock: LongInt;
```

DESCRIPTION

The MaxBlock function returns the maximum contiguous space, in bytes, that you could obtain after compacting the current heap zone. MaxBlock does not actually do the compaction.

ASSEMBLY-LANGUAGE INFORMATION

The registers on exit for `MaxBlock` are

Registers on exit

D0	Size of largest allocatable block

If you want to know the size of the largest allocatable block in the system heap zone, rather than in the current heap zone, set bit 10 of the routine trap word. In most development systems, you can do this by supplying the word `SYS` as the second argument to the routine macro, as follows:

```
_MaxBlock ,SYS
```

RESULT CODES

`noErr`	0	No error

MaxBlockSys

Use the `MaxBlockSys` function to determine the size of the largest block you could allocate in the system heap after a compaction.

```
FUNCTION MaxBlockSys: LongInt;
```

DESCRIPTION

The `MaxBlockSys` function works much as the `MaxBlock` function does, but returns the maximum contiguous space, in bytes, that you could obtain after compacting the system heap. `MaxBlockSys` does not actually do the compaction.

RESULT CODES

`noErr`	0	No error

PurgeSpace

Use the `PurgeSpace` procedure to determine the total amount of free memory and the size of the largest allocatable block after a purge of the heap.

```
PROCEDURE PurgeSpace (VAR total: LongInt; VAR contig: LongInt);
```

`total` On exit, the total amount of free memory in the current heap zone if it were purged.

`contig` On exit, the size of the largest contiguous block of free memory in the current heap zone if it were purged.

DESCRIPTION

The `PurgeSpace` procedure returns, in the `total` parameter, the total amount of space (in bytes) that could be obtained after a general purge of the current heap zone; this amount includes space that is already free. In the `contig` parameter, `PurgeSpace` returns the size of the largest allocatable block in the current heap zone that could be obtained after a purge of the zone.

The `PurgeSpace` procedure does not actually purge the current heap zone.

ASSEMBLY-LANGUAGE INFORMATION

The registers on exit for `PurgeSpace` are

Registers on exit

A0 Maximum number of contiguous bytes after purge

D0 Total free memory after purge

If you want to test the system heap zone instead of the current zone, set bit 10 of the routine trap word. In most development systems, you can do this by supplying the word `SYS` as the second argument to the routine macro, as follows:

```
_PurgeSpace ,SYS
```

RESULT CODES

noErr	0	No error

StackSpace

Use the `StackSpace` function to find out how much space there is between the bottom of the stack and the top of the application heap.

```
FUNCTION StackSpace: LongInt;
```

DESCRIPTION

The `StackSpace` function returns the current amount of stack space (in bytes) between the current stack pointer and the application heap at the instant of return from the trap.

SPECIAL CONSIDERATIONS

Ordinarily, you determine the maximum amount of stack space you need before you ship your application. In general, therefore, this routine is useful only during debugging to determine how big to make the stack. However, if your application calls a recursive function that conceivably could call itself many times, that function should keep track of the stack space and take appropriate action if it becomes too low.

ASSEMBLY-LANGUAGE INFORMATION

The registers on exit for `StackSpace` are

Registers on exit

D0	Number of bytes between stack and heap

RESULT CODES

`noErr`	0	No error

MemError

To find out whether your application's last direct call to a Memory Manager routine executed successfully, use the `MemError` function.

```
FUNCTION MemError: OSErr;
```

DESCRIPTION

The `MemError` function returns the result code produced by the last Memory Manager routine your application called directly.

This function is useful during application debugging. You might also use the function as one part of a memory-management scheme to identify instances in which the Memory Manager rejects overly large memory requests by returning the error code `memFullErr`.

▲ **WARNING**
Do not rely on the `MemError` function as the only component of a memory-management scheme. For example, suppose you call `NewHandle` or `NewPtr` and receive the result code `noErr`, indicating that the Memory Manager was able to allocate sufficient memory. In this case, you have no guarantee that the allocation did not deplete your application's memory reserves to levels so low that simple operations might cause your application to crash. Instead of relying on `MemError`, check before making a memory request that there is enough memory both to fulfill the request and to support essential operations. ▲

ASSEMBLY-LANGUAGE INFORMATION

Because most Memory Manager routines return a result code in register D0, you do not ordinarily need to call the `MemError` function if you program in assembly language. See the description of an individual routine to find out whether it returns a result code in register D0. If not, you can examine the global variable `MemErr`. When `MemError` returns, register D0 contains the result code.

Registers on exit

D0 Result code

RESULT CODES

`noErr`	0	No error
`paramErr`	–50	Error in parameter list
`memROZErr`	–99	Operation on a read-only zone
`memFullErr`	–108	Not enough memory
`nilHandleErr`	–109	`NIL` master pointer
`memWZErr`	–111	Attempt to operate on a free block
`memPurErr`	–112	Attempt to purge a locked block
`memBCErr`	–115	Block check failed
`memLockedErr`	–117	Block is locked

Freeing Memory

The Memory Manager compacts and purges the heap whenever necessary to satisfy requests for memory. You can also compact or purge the heap manually. To compact the current heap zone manually, use the `CompactMem` function. To purge it manually, use the `PurgeMem` procedure. To do both at once, use the `MaxMem` function. To perform the same operations on the system heap zone, use the `CompactMemSys` function, the `PurgeMemSys` procedure, and the `MaxMemSys` function.

Note

Most applications don't need to call the routines described in this section. Normally you should let the Memory Manager compact or purge your application heap. ◆

CompactMem

The Memory Manager compacts the heap for you when you make a memory request that it can't fill. However, you can use the `CompactMem` function to compact the current heap zone manually.

```
FUNCTION CompactMem (cbNeeded: Size): Size;
```

`cbNeeded` The size, in bytes, of the block for which `CompactMem` should attempt to make room.

DESCRIPTION

The CompactMem function compacts the current heap zone by moving unlocked, relocatable blocks down until they encounter nonrelocatable blocks or locked, relocatable blocks, but not by purging blocks. It continues compacting until it either finds a contiguous block of at least cbNeeded free bytes or has compacted the entire zone.

The CompactMem function returns the size, in bytes, of the largest contiguous free block for which it could make room, but it does not actually allocate that block.

To compact the entire heap zone, call CompactMem(maxSize). The Memory Manager defines the constant maxSize for the largest contiguous block possible in the 24-bit Memory Manager:

```
CONST
   maxSize              = $800000;          {maximum size of a block}
```

SPECIAL CONSIDERATIONS

Because CompactMem moves memory, you should not call it at interrupt time.

ASSEMBLY-LANGUAGE INFORMATION

The registers on entry and exit for CompactMem are

Registers on entry

D0 Size of block to make room for

Registers on exit

D0 Size of largest allocatable block

The CompactMem function compacts the current heap zone. If you want to compact the system heap zone rather than the current heap zone, set bit 10 of the routine trap word. In most development systems, you can do this by supplying the word SYS as the second argument to the routine macro, as follows:

```
_CompactMem ,SYS
```

RESULT CODES

noErr	0	No error

CompactMemSys

You can use the CompactMemSys function to compact the system heap zone manually.

```
FUNCTION CompactMemSys (cbNeeded: Size): Size;
```

`cbNeeded` The size in bytes of the block for which `CompactMemSys` should attempt to make room.

DESCRIPTION

The `CompactMemSys` function works much as the `CompactMem` function does, but compacts the system heap instead of the current heap.

RESULT CODES

`noErr`	0	No error

PurgeMem

The Memory Manager purges the heap for you when you make a memory request that it can't fill. However, you can use the `PurgeMem` procedure to purge the current heap zone manually.

```
PROCEDURE PurgeMem (cbNeeded: Size);
```

`cbNeeded` The size, in bytes, of the block for which `PurgeMem` should attempt to make room.

DESCRIPTION

The `PurgeMem` procedure sequentially purges blocks from the current heap zone until it either allocates a contiguous block of at least `cbNeeded` free bytes or has purged the entire zone. If it purges the entire zone without creating a contiguous block of at least `cbNeeded` free bytes, `PurgeMem` generates a `memFullErr`.

The `PurgeMem` procedure purges only relocatable, unlocked, purgeable blocks.

The `PurgeMem` procedure does not actually attempt to allocate a block of `cbNeeded` bytes.

To purge the entire heap zone, call `PurgeMem(maxSize)`.

SPECIAL CONSIDERATIONS

Because `PurgeMem` purges memory, you should not call it at interrupt time.

ASSEMBLY-LANGUAGE INFORMATION

The registers on entry and exit for `PurgeMem` are

Registers on entry

D0	Size of block to make room for

Registers on exit

D0	Result code

The `PurgeMem` procedure purges the current heap zone. If you want to purge the system heap zone rather than the current heap zone, set bit 10 of the routine trap word. In most development systems, you can do this by supplying the word `SYS` as the second argument to the routine macro, as follows:

```
_PurgeMem ,SYS
```

RESULT CODES

noErr	0	No error
memFullErr	–108	Not enough memory

PurgeMemSys

You can use the `PurgeMemSys` procedure to purge the system heap manually.

```
PROCEDURE PurgeMemSys (cbNeeded: Size);
```

`cbNeeded` The size, in bytes, of the block for which `PurgeMemSys` should attempt to make room.

DESCRIPTION

The `PurgeMemSys` procedure works much as the `PurgeMem` procedure does, but purges the system heap instead of the current heap.

RESULT CODES

noErr	0	No error
memFullErr	–108	Not enough memory

MaxMem

Use the `MaxMem` function to compact and purge the current heap zone.

```
FUNCTION MaxMem (VAR grow: Size): Size;
```

`grow` On exit, the maximum number of bytes by which the current heap zone can grow. After a call to `MaxApplZone`, `MaxMem` always returns 0 in this parameter.

DESCRIPTION

The `MaxMem` function compacts the current heap zone and purges all relocatable, unlocked, and purgeable blocks from the zone. It returns the size, in bytes, of the largest contiguous free block in the zone after the compacting and purging. If the current zone is the original application zone, the `grow` parameter is set to the maximum number of bytes by which the zone can grow. For any other heap zone, `grow` is set to 0. `MaxMem` doesn't actually expand the zone or call the zone's grow-zone function.

SPECIAL CONSIDERATIONS

Because `MaxMem` moves and purges memory, you should not call it at interrupt time.

ASSEMBLY-LANGUAGE INFORMATION

The registers on exit for `MaxMem` are

Registers on exit

A0	Number of bytes zone can grow
D0	Size in bytes of largest allocatable block

The `MaxMem` function compacts the current heap zone. If you want to compact and purge the system heap zone rather than the current heap zone, set bit 10 of the routine trap word. In most development systems, you can do this by supplying the word `SYS` as the second argument to the routine macro, as follows:

```
_MaxMem ,SYS
```

RESULT CODES

noErr	0	No error

MaxMemSys

You can use the `MaxMemSys` function to purge and compact the system heap zone manually.

```
FUNCTION MaxMemSys (VAR grow: Size): Size;
```

`grow` On exit, the `MaxMemSys` function sets this parameter to 0. Ignore this parameter.

DESCRIPTION

The MaxMemSys function works much as the MaxMem function does, but compacts and purges the system heap instead of the current heap. It returns the size, in bytes, of the largest block you can allocate in the system heap.

RESULT CODES

noErr	0	No error

Grow-Zone Operations

You can implement a grow-zone function that the Memory Manager calls when it cannot fulfill a memory request. You should use the grow-zone function only as a last resort to free memory when all else fails. For explanations of how grow-zone functions work and an example of a memory-management scheme that uses a grow-zone function, see the discussion of low-memory conditions in the chapter "Introduction to Memory Management" in this book.

The SetGrowZone procedure specifies which function the Memory Manager should use for the current zone. The grow-zone function should call the GZSaveHnd function to receive a handle to a relocatable block that the grow-zone function must not move or purge.

SetGrowZone

To specify a grow-zone function for the current heap zone, pass a pointer to that function to the SetGrowZone procedure. Ordinarily, you call this procedure early in the execution of your application.

If you initialize your own heap zones besides the application and system zones, you can alternatively specify a grow-zone function as a parameter to the InitZone procedure.

```
PROCEDURE SetGrowZone (growZone: ProcPtr);
```

growZone A pointer to the grow-zone function.

DESCRIPTION

The SetGrowZone procedure sets the current heap zone's grow-zone function as designated by the growZone parameter. A NIL parameter value removes any grow-zone function the zone might previously have had.

The Memory Manager calls the grow-zone function only after exhausting all other avenues of satisfying a memory request, including compacting the zone, increasing its size (if it is the original application zone and is not yet at its maximum size), and purging blocks from it.

See "Grow-Zone Functions" on page 2-89 for a complete description of a grow-zone function.

ASSEMBLY-LANGUAGE INFORMATION

The registers on entry and exit for `SetGrowZone` are

Registers on entry

A0 Pointer to new grow-zone function

Registers on exit

D0 Result code

RESULT CODES

`noErr`	0	No error

GZSaveHnd

Your grow-zone function must call the `GZSaveHnd` function to obtain a handle to a protected relocatable block that the grow-zone function must not move, purge, or delete.

```
FUNCTION GZSaveHnd: Handle;
```

DESCRIPTION

The `GZSaveHnd` function returns a handle to a relocatable block that the grow-zone function must not move, purge, or delete. It returns `NIL` if there is no such block. The returned handle is a handle to the block of memory being manipulated by the Memory Manager at the time that the grow-zone function is called.

ASSEMBLY-LANGUAGE INFORMATION

You can find the same handle in the global variable `GZRootHnd`.

Allocating Temporary Memory

In system software version 7.0 and later, you can manipulate temporary memory with three routines that are counterparts to other Memory Manager routines. The `TempNewHandle` function allocates a new block of relocatable memory, the `TempFreeMem` function returns the total amount of free memory available for temporary allocation, and the TempMaxMem function compacts the heap zone and returns the size of the largest contiguous block available for temporary allocation.

▲ **WARNING**
You should not call any of these memory-allocation routines at interrupt time. ▲

TempNewHandle

To allocate a new relocatable block of temporary memory, call the TempNewHandle function after making sure that there is enough free space to satisfy the request.

```
FUNCTION TempNewHandle (logicalSize: Size;
                        VAR resultCode: OSErr): Handle;
```

logicalSize
: The requested logical size, in bytes, of the new temporary block of memory.

resultCode
: On exit, the result code from the function call.

DESCRIPTION

The TempNewHandle function returns a handle to a block of size logicalSize. If it cannot allocate a block of that size, the function returns NIL. Before you use the returned handle, make sure its value is not NIL.

ASSEMBLY-LANGUAGE INFORMATION

The trap macro and routine selector for TempNewHandle are

Trap macro	Selector
_OSDispatch	$001D

SPECIAL CONSIDERATIONS

Because TempNewHandle might allocate memory, you should not call it at interrupt time.

Note that TempNewHandle returns its result code in a parameter, not through MemError.

RESULT CODES

noErr	0	No error
memFullErr	–108	Not enough memory

TempFreeMem

To find out the total amount of memory available for temporary allocation, use the `TempFreeMem` function.

```
FUNCTION TempFreeMem: LongInt;
```

DESCRIPTION

The `TempFreeMem` function returns the total amount of free temporary memory that you could allocate by calling `TempNewHandle`. The returned value is the total number of free bytes. Because these bytes might be dispersed throughout memory, it is ordinarily not possible to allocate a single relocatable block of that size.

ASSEMBLY-LANGUAGE INFORMATION

The trap macro and routine selector for `TempFreeMem` are

Trap macro	Selector
`_OSDispatch`	$0018

SPECIAL CONSIDERATIONS

Even though `TempFreeMem` does not move or purge memory, you should not call it at interrupt time.

TempMaxMem

To find the size of the largest contiguous block available for temporary allocation, use the `TempMaxMem` function.

```
FUNCTION TempMaxMem (VAR grow: Size): Size;
```

`grow` On exit, this parameter always contains 0 after the function call because temporary memory does not come from the application's heap zone, and only that zone can grow. Ignore this parameter.

DESCRIPTION

The `TempMaxMem` function compacts the current heap zone and returns the size of the largest contiguous block available for temporary allocation.

ASSEMBLY-LANGUAGE INFORMATION

The trap macro and routine selector for `TempMaxMem` are

Trap macro	Selector
`_OSDispatch`	$0015

SPECIAL CONSIDERATIONS

Because `TempMaxMem` could move memory, you should not call it at interrupt time.

Accessing Heap Zones

The majority of applications, which allocate memory in their application heap zone only, do not need to use any of the routines in this section. The few applications that do allocate memory in zones other than the application heap zone can use the `GetZone` function and the `SetZone` procedure to get and set the current zone, the `ApplicationZone` and `SystemZone` functions to obtain pointers to the application and system zones, and the `HandleZone` and `PtrZone` functions to find the zones in which relocatable and nonrelocatable blocks lie.

GetZone

To find which zone is current, use the `GetZone` function.

```
FUNCTION GetZone: THz;
```

DESCRIPTION

The `GetZone` function returns a pointer to the current heap zone.

ASSEMBLY-LANGUAGE INFORMATION

The registers on exit for `GetZone` are

Registers on exit

A0	Pointer to current heap zone
D0	Result code

The global variable `TheZone` contains a pointer to the current heap zone.

RESULT CODES

`noErr`	0	No error

SetZone

To change the current heap zone, you can use the SetZone procedure.

```
PROCEDURE SetZone (hz: THz);
```

hz A pointer to the heap zone to make current.

DESCRIPTION

The SetZone procedure makes the zone to which hz points the current heap zone. Often, you use the SetZone procedure in conjunction with one of the ApplicationZone, SystemZone, HandleZone, and PtrZone functions. For example, the code SetZone(SystemZone) makes the system heap zone current.

ASSEMBLY-LANGUAGE INFORMATION

The registers on entry and exit for SetZone are

Registers on entry

A0 Pointer to new current heap zone

Registers on exit

D0 Result code

RESULT CODES

noErr	0	No error

ApplicationZone

To obtain a pointer to the application heap zone, you can use the ApplicationZone function.

```
FUNCTION ApplicationZone: THz;
```

DESCRIPTION

The ApplicationZone function returns a pointer to the original application heap zone.

ASSEMBLY-LANGUAGE INFORMATION

The global variable ApplZone contains a pointer to the original application heap zone.

SystemZone

To obtain a pointer to the system heap zone, you can use the `SystemZone` function.

```
FUNCTION SystemZone: THz;
```

DESCRIPTION

The `SystemZone` function returns a pointer to the system heap zone.

ASSEMBLY-LANGUAGE INFORMATION

The global variable `SysZone` contains a pointer to the system heap zone.

HandleZone

If you need to know which heap zone contains a particular relocatable block, you can use the `HandleZone` function.

```
FUNCTION HandleZone (h: Handle): THz;
```

`h` A handle to a relocatable block.

DESCRIPTION

The `HandleZone` function returns a pointer to the heap zone containing the relocatable block whose handle is `h`. In case of an error, the result returned by `HandleZone` is undefined and should be ignored.

IMPORTANT
If the handle `h` is empty (that is, if it points to a `NIL` master pointer), `HandleZone` returns a pointer to the heap zone that contains the master pointer. ▲

ASSEMBLY-LANGUAGE INFORMATION

The registers on entry and exit for `HandleZone` are

Registers on entry

A0	Handle whose zone is to be found

Registers on exit

A0	Pointer to handle's heap zone
D0	Result code

RESULT CODES

`noErr`	0	No error
`memWZErr`	–111	Attempt to operate on a free block

PtrZone

If you have allocated a nonrelocatable block and need to know in which zone it lies, you can use the `PtrZone` function.

```
FUNCTION PtrZone (p: Ptr): THz;
```

`p` A pointer to a nonrelocatable block.

DESCRIPTION

The `PtrZone` function returns a pointer to the heap zone containing the nonrelocatable block pointed to by `p`.

In case of an error, the result returned by `PtrZone` is undefined and should be ignored.

ASSEMBLY-LANGUAGE INFORMATION

The registers on entry and exit for `PtrZone` are

Registers on entry

A0 Pointer whose zone is to be found

Registers on exit

A0 Pointer to heap zone of nonrelocatable block

D0 Result code

RESULT CODES

`noErr`	0	No error
`memWZErr`	–111	Attempt to operate on a free block

Manipulating Heap Zones

The Memory Manager provides several routines for initializing and resizing heap zones.

To obtain information about the current application partition, applications can call the `GetApplLimit` function and the `TopMem` function. If your application uses the stack extensively, you might want to ensure that the stack is set to at least some minimum size, at the expense of the heap. To do so, use the `SetApplLimit` procedure to change the application heap limit before you call the `MaxApplZone` procedure.

To initialize a new heap zone, use the `InitZone` procedure. The Operating System automatically initializes the application zone by calling the `SetApplBase` procedure, which subsequently calls the `InitApplZone` procedure.

GetApplLimit

Use the `GetApplLimit` function to get the application heap limit, beyond which the application heap cannot expand.

```
FUNCTION GetApplLimit: Ptr;
```

DESCRIPTION

The `GetApplLimit` function returns the current application heap limit. The Memory Manager expands the application heap only up to the byte preceding this limit.

Nothing prevents the stack from growing below the application limit. If the Operating System detects that the stack has crashed into the heap, it generates a system error. To avoid this, use `GetApplLimit` and the `SetApplLimit` procedure to set the application limit low enough so that a growing stack does not encounter the heap.

Note
The `GetApplLimit` function does not indicate the amount of memory available to your application. ◆

ASSEMBLY-LANGUAGE INFORMATION

The global variable `ApplLimit` contains the current application heap limit.

SetApplLimit

Use the `SetApplLimit` procedure to set the application heap limit, beyond which the application heap cannot expand.

```
PROCEDURE SetApplLimit (zoneLimit: Ptr);
```

`zoneLimit` A pointer to a byte in memory demarcating the upper boundary of the application heap zone. The zone can grow to include the byte preceding `zoneLimit` in memory, but no further.

DESCRIPTION

The `SetApplLimit` procedure sets the current application heap limit to `zoneLimit`. The Memory Manager then can expand the application heap only up to the byte preceding the application limit. If the zone already extends beyond the specified limit, the Memory Manager does not cut it back but does prevent it from growing further.

Note

The `zoneLimit` parameter is not a byte count, but an absolute byte in memory. Thus, you should use the `SetApplLimit` procedure only with a value obtained from the Memory Manager functions `GetApplLimit` or `ApplicationZone`. ◆

You cannot change the limit of zones other than the application heap zone.

ASSEMBLY-LANGUAGE INFORMATION

The registers on entry and exit for `SetApplLimit` are

Registers on entry

A0 Pointer to desired new zone limit

Registers on exit

D0 Result code

RESULT CODES

`noErr`	0	No error
`memFullErr`	–108	Not enough memory

TopMem

To find out the location of the top of an application's partition, you can use the `TopMem` function, which exhibits special behavior during the startup process.

```
FUNCTION TopMem: Ptr;
```

DESCRIPTION

Except during the startup process, the `TopMem` function returns a pointer to the byte at the top of an application's partition, directly above the jump table. The function does this to maintain compatibility with programs that check `TopMem` to find out how much memory is installed in a computer. To obtain this information, you can currently use the `Gestalt` function.

The function exhibits special behavior at startup time, and the value it returns controls the amount by which an extension can lower the value of the global variable `BufPtr` at startup time. If you are writing a system extension, you should not lower the value of `BufPtr` by more than `MemTop DIV 2 + 1024`. If you do lower `BufPtr` too far, the startup process generates an out-of-memory system error.

You should never need to call `TopMem` except during the startup process.

ASSEMBLY-LANGUAGE INFORMATION

The `TopMem` function returns the value of the `MemTop` global variable.

InitZone

If you want to use heap zones other than the original application heap zone, a temporary memory zone, or the system heap zone, you can use the `InitZone` procedure to initialize a new heap zone.

```
PROCEDURE InitZone (pGrowZone: ProcPtr; cMoreMasters: Integer;
                    limitPtr, startPtr: Ptr);
```

`pGrowZone` A pointer to a grow-zone function for the new heap zone. If you do not want the new zone to have a grow-zone function, set this parameter to `NIL`.

`cMoreMasters`
The number of master pointers that should be allocated at a time for the new zone. The Memory Manager allocates this number initially, and, if it needs to allocate more later, allocates them in increments of this same number.

`limitPtr` The first byte beyond the end of the zone.

`startPtr` The first byte of the new zone.

DESCRIPTION

The `InitZone` procedure creates a new heap zone, initializes its header and trailer, and makes it the current zone. Although the new zone occupies memory addresses from `startPtr` through `limitPtr-1`, the new zone includes a zone header and a zone trailer. In addition, the new zone contains a block header for the master pointer block and 4 bytes for each master pointer. If you need to create a zone with some specific number of usable bytes, see "Organization of Memory," beginning on page 2-19, for details on the sizes of the zone header, zone trailer, and block header.

Note
The sizes of zones and block headers may change in future system software versions. You should ensure that your zones are large enough to accommodate a reasonable increase in the sizes of those structures. ◆

SPECIAL CONSIDERATIONS

Because `InitZone` changes the current zone, you should not call it at interrupt time.

ASSEMBLY-LANGUAGE INFORMATION

The registers on entry and exit for `InitZone` are

Registers on entry

A0	Pointer to parameter block

Registers on exit

D0	Result code

The parameter block whose address is passed in register A0 has no Pascal type definition. It has this structure:

Parameter block

→	`startPtr`	`Ptr`	The first byte of the new zone.
→	`limitPtr`	`Ptr`	The first byte beyond the new zone.
→	`cMoreMasters`	`Integer`	The number of master pointers to be allocated at a time.
→	`pGrowZone`	`ProcPtr`	A pointer to the new zone's grow-zone function, or `NIL` if none.

RESULT CODES

`noErr`	0	No error

InitApplZone

The Process Manager calls the `InitApplZone` procedure indirectly when it starts up your application. You should never need to call it. It is documented for completeness only.

```
PROCEDURE InitApplZone;
```

DESCRIPTION

The `InitApplZone` procedure initializes the application heap zone and makes it the current zone. The Memory Manager discards the contents of any previous application zone and discards all previously existing blocks in that zone. The procedure sets the zone's grow-zone function to `NIL`.

▲ **WARNING**

Reinitializing the application zone from within a running program is dangerous, because the application's code itself normally resides in the application zone. To do so safely, you must make sure that the code containing the `InitApplZone` call is not in the application zone. ▲

SPECIAL CONSIDERATIONS

You should not call `InitApplZone` at all, but, if you must, be sure not to call it at interrupt time because it could purge and allocate memory.

ASSEMBLY-LANGUAGE INFORMATION

The registers on exit for `InitApplZone` are

Registers on exit

D0 Result code

RESULT CODES

`noErr`	0	No error

SetApplBase

The Process Manager calls the `SetApplBase` procedure when it starts up your application. You should never need to call it. It is documented for completeness only.

```
PROCEDURE SetApplBase (startPtr: Ptr);
```

`startPtr` The starting address for the application heap zone to be initialized.

DESCRIPTION

The `SetApplBase` procedure sets the starting address of the application heap zone for the application being initialized to the address designated by `startPtr`, and then calls the `InitApplZone` procedure.

▲ **WARNING**
Like `InitApplZone`, `SetApplBase` is a potentially dangerous operation, because the program's code itself normally resides in the application heap zone. To do so safely, you must make sure that the code containing the `SetApplBase` call is not in the application zone. ▲

SPECIAL CONSIDERATIONS

You should not call `SetApplBase` at all, but, if you must, be sure not to call it at interrupt time because it affects memory.

ASSEMBLY-LANGUAGE INFORMATION

The registers on exit for `SetApplBase` are

Registers on exit

D0 Result code

RESULT CODES

`noErr`	0	No error

Application-Defined Routines

The Memory Manager provides a means for you to intervene in its otherwise automatic operations by allowing you to define a grow-zone function and a purge-warning procedure.

Note

Many applications use a grow-zone function as part of a general strategy to prevent low-memory situations. Most applications, however, do not need to use purge-warning procedures. ◆

Grow-Zone Functions

The Memory Manager calls your application's grow-zone function whenever it cannot find enough contiguous memory to satisfy a memory allocation request and has exhausted other means of obtaining the space.

MyGrowZone

A grow-zone function should have the following form:

```
FUNCTION MyGrowZone (cbNeeded: Size): LongInt;
```

`cbNeeded` The physical size, in bytes, of the needed block, including the block header. The grow-zone function should attempt to create a free block of at least this size.

DESCRIPTION

Whenever the Memory Manager has exhausted all available means of creating space within your application heap—including purging, compacting, and (if possible) expanding the heap—it calls your application-defined grow-zone function. The grow-zone function can do whatever is necessary to create free space in the heap. Typically, a grow-zone function marks some unneeded blocks as purgeable or releases an emergency memory reserve maintained by your application.

The grow-zone function should return a nonzero value equal to the number of bytes of memory it has freed, or zero if it is unable to free any. When the function returns a nonzero value, the Memory Manager once again purges and compacts the heap zone and tries to reallocate memory. If there is still insufficient memory, the Memory Manager calls the grow-zone function again (but only if the function returned a nonzero value the previous time it was called). This mechanism allows your grow-zone function to release just a little bit of memory at a time. If the amount it releases at any time is not enough, the Memory Manager calls it again and gives it the opportunity to take more drastic measures.

The Memory Manager might designate a particular relocatable block in the heap as protected; your grow-zone function should not move or purge that block. You can determine which block, if any, the Memory Manager has protected by calling the `GZSaveHnd` function in your grow-zone function.

Remember that a grow-zone function is called while the Memory Manager is attempting to allocate memory. As a result, your grow-zone function should not allocate memory itself or perform any other actions that might indirectly cause memory to be allocated (such as calling routines in unloaded code segments or displaying dialog boxes).

You install a grow-zone function by passing its address to the `InitZone` procedure when you create a new heap zone or by calling the `SetGrowZone` procedure at any other time.

SPECIAL CONSIDERATIONS

Your grow-zone function might be called at a time when the system is attempting to allocate memory and the value in the A5 register is not correct. If your function accesses your application's A5 world or makes any trap calls, you need to set up and later restore the A5 register by calling `SetCurrentA5` and `SetA5`. See the chapter "Memory Management Utilities" in this book for a description of these two functions.

Because of the optimizations performed by some compilers, the actual work of the grow-zone function and the setting and restoring of the A5 register might have to be placed in separate procedures.

SEE ALSO

See the chapter "Introduction to Memory Management" in this book for a definition of a sample grow-zone function.

Purge-Warning Procedures

The Memory Manager calls your application's purge-warning procedure whenever it is about to purge a relocatable block from your application heap.

MyPurgeProc

A purge-warning procedure should have the following form:

```
PROCEDURE MyPurgeProc (h: Handle);
```

`h` A handle to the block that is about to be purged.

DESCRIPTION

Whenever the Memory Manager needs to purge a block from the application heap, it first calls any application-defined purge-warning procedure that you have installed. The purge-warning procedure can, if necessary, save the contents of that block or otherwise respond to the warning.

Your purge-warning procedure is called during a memory-allocation request. As a result, you should not call any routines that might cause memory to be moved or purged. In particular, if you save the data of the block in a file, the file should already be open when your purge-warning procedure is called, and you should write the data synchronously.

You should not dispose of or change the purgeable status of the block whose handle is passed to your procedure.

To install a purge-warning procedure, you need to assign its address to the `purgeProc` field of the associated zone header.

Note
If you call the Resource Manager procedure `SetResPurge` with the parameter `TRUE`, any existing purge-warning procedure is replaced by a purge-warning procedure installed by the Resource Manager. You can execute both warning procedures by calling `SetResPurge`, saving the existing value of the `purgeProc` field of the zone header, and then reinstalling your purge-warning procedure. Your purge-warning procedure should call the Resource Manager's purge-warning procedure internally. ◆

SPECIAL CONSIDERATIONS

Your purge-warning procedure might be called at a time when the system is attempting to allocate memory and the value in the A5 register is not correct. If your function accesses your application's A5 world or makes any trap calls, you need to set up and later restore the A5 register by calling `SetCurrentA5` and `SetA5`.

Because of the optimizations performed by some compilers, the actual work of the purge-warning procedure and the setting and restoring of the A5 register might have to be placed in separate procedures.

Your purge-warning procedure is called for *every* handle that is about to be purged (not necessarily for every purgeable handle in your heap, however). Your procedure should be able to determine quickly whether the handle it is passed is one whose associated data needs to be saved or otherwise processed.

SEE ALSO

See "Installing a Purge-Warning Procedure" on page 2-16 for a definition of a sample purge-warning procedure and for instructions on installing the procedure.

Summary of the Memory Manager

Pascal Summary

Constants

```
CONST
   {Gestalt constants}
   gestaltOSAttr              = 'os  ';     {O/S attributes}
   gestaltTempMemSupport      = 4;          {temp memory support present}
   gestaltRealTempMemory      = 5;          {temp memory handles are real}
   gestaltTempMemTracked      = 6;          {temp memory handles tracked}

   maxSize                    = $800000;    {maximum size of a block}
```

Data Types

```
TYPE
   SignedByte           = -128..127;        {arbitrary byte of memory}
   Byte                 = 0..255;           {unsigned, arbitrary byte}
   Ptr                  = ^SignedByte;      {pointer to nonrelocatable block}
   Handle               = ^Ptr;             {handle to relocatable block}

   Str255               = STRING[255];      {Pascal string}
   StringPtr            = ^Str255;
   StringHandle         = ^StringPtr;

   ProcPtr              = Ptr;              {procedure pointer}

   Size                 = LongInt;          {size in bytes of block}
```

```
Zone =
RECORD
   bkLim:          Ptr;                   {first usable byte after zone}
   purgePtr:       Ptr;                   {used internally}
   hFstFree:       Ptr;                   {first free master pointer}
   zcbFree:        LongInt;               {number of free bytes}
   gzProc:         ProcPtr;               {grow-zone function}
   moreMast:       Integer;               {number of master ptrs to allocate}
   flags:          Integer;               {used internally}
   cntRel:         Integer;               {reserved}
   maxRel:         Integer;               {reserved}
   cntNRel:        Integer;               {reserved}
   maxNRel:        Integer;               {reserved}
   cntEmpty:       Integer;               {reserved}
   cntHandles:     Integer;               {reserved}
   minCBFree:      LongInt;               {reserved}
   purgeProc:      ProcPtr;               {purge-warning procedure}
   sparePtr:       Ptr;                   {used internally}
   allocPtr:       Ptr;                   {used internally}
   heapData:       Integer;               {first usable byte in zone}
END;

THz = ^Zone;                              {zone pointer}
```

Memory Manager Routines

Setting Up the Application Heap

```
PROCEDURE MaxApplZone;
PROCEDURE MoreMasters;
```

Allocating and Releasing Relocatable Blocks of Memory

```
FUNCTION NewHandle           (logicalSize: Size): Handle;
FUNCTION NewHandleSys        (logicalSize: Size): Handle;
FUNCTION NewHandleClear      (logicalSize: Size): Handle;
FUNCTION NewHandleSysClear   (logicalSize: Size): Handle;
FUNCTION NewEmptyHandle      : Handle;
FUNCTION NewEmptyHandleSys   : Handle;
PROCEDURE DisposeHandle      (h: Handle);
```

Allocating and Releasing Nonrelocatable Blocks of Memory

```
FUNCTION NewPtr                (logicalSize: Size): Ptr;
FUNCTION NewPtrSys             (logicalSize: Size): Ptr;
FUNCTION NewPtrClear           (logicalSize: Size): Ptr;
FUNCTION NewPtrSysClear        (logicalSize: Size): Ptr;
PROCEDURE DisposePtr           (p: Ptr);
```

Changing the Sizes of Relocatable and Nonrelocatable Blocks

```
FUNCTION GetHandleSize         (h: Handle): Size;
PROCEDURE SetHandleSize        (h: Handle; newSize: Size);
FUNCTION GetPtrSize            (p: Ptr): Size;
PROCEDURE SetPtrSize           (p: Ptr; newSize: Size);
```

Setting the Properties of Relocatable Blocks

```
FUNCTION HGetState             (h: Handle): SignedByte;
PROCEDURE HSetState            (h: Handle; flags: SignedByte);
PROCEDURE HLock                (h: Handle);
PROCEDURE HUnlock              (h: Handle);
PROCEDURE HPurge               (h: Handle);
PROCEDURE HNoPurge             (h: Handle);
PROCEDURE HSetRBit             (h: Handle);
PROCEDURE HClrRBit             (h: Handle);
```

Managing Relocatable Blocks

```
PROCEDURE EmptyHandle          (h: Handle);
PROCEDURE ReallocateHandle     (h: Handle; logicalSize: Size);
FUNCTION RecoverHandle         (p: Ptr): Handle;
PROCEDURE ReserveMem           (cbNeeded: Size);
PROCEDURE ReserveMemSys        (cbNeeded: Size);
PROCEDURE MoveHHi              (h: Handle);
PROCEDURE HLockHi              (h: Handle);
```

Manipulating Blocks of Memory

```
PROCEDURE BlockMove            (sourcePtr, destPtr: Ptr; byteCount: Size);
FUNCTION PtrToHand             (srcPtr: Ptr; VAR dstHndl: Handle;
                                size: LongInt): OSErr;
FUNCTION PtrToXHand            (srcPtr: Ptr; dstHndl: Handle; size: LongInt):
                                OSErr;
```

```
FUNCTION HandToHand          (VAR theHndl: Handle): OSErr;
FUNCTION HandAndHand         (aHndl, bHndl: Handle): OSErr;
FUNCTION PtrAndHand          (pntr: Ptr; hndl: Handle; size: LongInt): OSErr;
```

Assessing Memory Conditions

```
FUNCTION FreeMem             : LongInt;
FUNCTION FreeMemSys          : LongInt;
FUNCTION MaxBlock            : LongInt;
FUNCTION MaxBlockSys         : LongInt;
PROCEDURE PurgeSpace         (VAR total: LongInt; VAR contig: LongInt);
FUNCTION StackSpace          : LongInt;
FUNCTION MemError            : OSErr;
```

Freeing Memory

```
FUNCTION CompactMem          (cbNeeded: Size): Size;
FUNCTION CompactMemSys       (cbNeeded: Size): Size;
PROCEDURE PurgeMem           (cbNeeded: Size);
PROCEDURE PurgeMemSys        (cbNeeded: Size);
FUNCTION MaxMem              (VAR grow: Size): Size;
FUNCTION MaxMemSys           (VAR grow: Size): Size;
```

Grow-Zone Operations

```
PROCEDURE SetGrowZone        (growZone: ProcPtr);
FUNCTION GZSaveHnd           : Handle;
```

Allocating Temporary Memory

```
FUNCTION TempNewHandle       (logicalSize: Size; VAR resultCode: OSErr):
                              Handle;
FUNCTION TempFreeMem         : LongInt;
FUNCTION TempMaxMem          (VAR grow: Size): Size;
```

Accessing Heap Zones

```
FUNCTION GetZone             : THz;
PROCEDURE SetZone            (hz: THz);
FUNCTION ApplicationZone     : THz;
FUNCTION SystemZone          : THz;
FUNCTION HandleZone          (h: Handle): THz;
FUNCTION PtrZone             (p: Ptr): THz;
```

Manipulating Heap Zones

```
FUNCTION GetApplLimit        : Ptr;
PROCEDURE SetApplLimit       (zoneLimit: Ptr);
FUNCTION TopMem              : Ptr;
PROCEDURE InitZone           (pGrowZone: ProcPtr; cMoreMasters: Integer;
                              limitPtr, startPtr: Ptr);
PROCEDURE InitApplZone;
PROCEDURE SetApplBase        (startPtr: Ptr);
```

Application-Defined Routines

Grow-Zone Functions

```
FUNCTION MyGrowZone          (cbNeeded: Size): LongInt;
```

Purge-Warning Procedures

```
PROCEDURE MyPurgeProc        (h: Handle);
```

C Summary

Constants

```
/*Gestalt constants*/
#define gestaltOSAttr             'os  ';     /*O/S attributes*/
#define gestaltTempMemSupport     4;          /*temp memory support present*/
#define gestaltRealTempMemory     5;          /*temp memory handles are real*/
#define gestaltTempMemTracked     6;          /*temp memory handles tracked*/

#define maxSize                   0x800000;   /*maximum size of a block*/
```

Data Types

```
typedef char SignedByte;               /*arbitrary byte of memory*/
typedef unsigned char Byte;            /*unsigned, arbitrary byte*/
typedef char *Ptr;                     /*pointer to nonrelocatable block*/
typedef Ptr *Handle;                   /*handle to relocatable block*/
```

```
typedef unsigned char Str255[256];      /*Pascal string*/
typedef unsigned char *StringPtr;
typedef unsigned char **StringHandle;

typedef long (*ProcPtr)();              /*procedure pointer*/
typedef long Size;                      /*size in bytes of block*/

struct Zone {
   Ptr               bkLim;             /*first usable byte after zone*/
   Ptr               purgePtr;          /*used internally*/
   Ptr               hFstFree;          /*first free master pointer*/
   long              zcbFree;           /*number of free bytes*/
   GrowZoneProcPtr   gzProc;            /*grow-zone function*/
   short             moreMast;          /*number of master ptrs to allocate*/
   short             flags;             /*used internally*/
   short             cntRel;            /*reserved*/
   short             maxRel;            /*reserved*/
   short             cntNRel;           /*reserved*/
   short             maxNRel;           /*reserved*/
   short             cntEmpty;          /*reserved*/
   short             cntHandles;        /*reserved*/
   long              minCBFree;         /*reserved*/
   ProcPtr           purgeProc;         /*purge-warning procedure*/
   Ptr               sparePtr;          /*used internally*/
   Ptr               allocPtr;          /*used internally*/
   short             heapData;          /*first usable byte in zone*/
};
typedef struct Zone Zone;
typedef Zone *THz;                      /*zone pointer*/
```

Memory Manager Routines

Setting Up the Application Heap

```
pascal void MaxApplZone      (void);
pascal void MoreMasters      (void);
```

Allocating and Releasing Relocatable Blocks of Memory

```
pascal Handle NewHandle      (Size byteCount);
pascal Handle NewHandleSys   (Size byteCount);
pascal Handle NewHandleClear (Size byteCount);
```

```
pascal Handle NewHandleSysClear
                             (Size byteCount);
pascal Handle NewEmptyHandle (void);
pascal Handle NewEmptyHandleSys
                             (void);
pascal void DisposeHandle    (Handle h);
```

Allocating and Releasing Nonrelocatable Blocks of Memory

```
pascal Ptr NewPtr            (Size byteCount);
pascal Ptr NewPtrSys         (Size byteCount);
pascal Ptr NewPtrClear       (Size byteCount);
pascal Ptr NewPtrSysClear    (Size byteCount);
pascal void DisposePtr       (Ptr p);
```

Changing the Sizes of Relocatable and Nonrelocatable Blocks

```
pascal Size GetHandleSize    (Handle h);
pascal void SetHandleSize    (Handle h, Size newSize);
pascal Size GetPtrSize       (Ptr p);
pascal void SetPtrSize       (Ptr p, Size newSize);
```

Setting the Properties of Relocatable Blocks

```
pascal char HGetState        (Handle h);
pascal void HSetState        (Handle h, char flags);
pascal void HLock            (Handle h);
pascal void HUnlock          (Handle h);
pascal void HPurge           (Handle h);
pascal void HNoPurge         (Handle h);
pascal void HSetRBit         (Handle h);
pascal void HClrRBit         (Handle h);
```

Managing Relocatable Blocks

```
pascal void EmptyHandle      (Handle h);
pascal void ReallocateHandle (Handle h, Size byteCount);
pascal Handle RecoverHandle  (Ptr p);
pascal void ReserveMem       (Size cbNeeded);
pascal void ReserveMemSys    (Size cbNeeded);
pascal void MoveHHi          (Handle h);
pascal void HLockHi          (Handle h);
```

Manipulating Blocks of Memory

```
pascal void BlockMove          (const void *srcPtr, void *destPtr,
                                Size byteCount);
pascal OSErr PtrToHand         (Ptr srcPtr, Handle *dstHndl, long size);
pascal OSErr PtrToXHand        (Ptr srcPtr, Handle dstHndl, long size);
pascal OSErr HandToHand        (Handle *theHndl);
pascal OSErr HandAndHand       (Handle hand1, Handle hand2);
pascal OSErr PtrAndHand        (Ptr ptr1, Handle hand2, long size);
```

Assessing Memory Conditions

```
pascal long FreeMem            (void);
pascal long FreeMemSys         (void);
pascal long MaxBlock           (void);
pascal long MaxBlockSys        (void);
pascal void PurgeSpace         (long *total, long *contig);
pascal long StackSpace         (void);
#define MemError()             (* (OSErr*) 0x0220)
```

Freeing Memory

```
pascal Size CompactMem         (Size cbNeeded);
pascal Size CompactMemSys      (Size cbNeeded);
pascal void PurgeMem           (Size cbNeeded);
pascal void PurgeMemSys        (Size cbNeeded);
pascal Size MaxMem             (Size *grow);
pascal Size MaxMemSys          (Size *grow);
```

Grow-Zone Operations

```
pascal void SetGrowZone        (GrowZoneProcPtr growZone);
#define GZSaveHnd()            (* (Handle*) 0x0328)
```

Allocating Temporary Memory

```
pascal Handle TempNewHandle (Size logicalSize, OSErr *resultCode);
pascal long TempFreeMem        (void);
pascal Size TempMaxMem         (Size *grow);
```

Accessing Heap Zones

```
pascal THz GetZone              (void);
pascal void SetZone             (THz hz);
#define ApplicationZone()       (* (THz*) 0x02AA)
#define SystemZone()            (* (THz*) 0x02A6)
pascal THz HandleZone           (Handle h);
pascal THz PtrZone              (Ptr p);
```

Manipulating Heap Zones

```
#define GetApplLimit()          (* (Ptr*) 0x0130)
pascal void SetApplLimit        (void *zoneLimit);
#define TopMem()                (* (Ptr*) 0x0108)
pascal void InitZone            (GrowZoneProcPtr pgrowZone, short cmoreMasters,
                                 void *limitPtr, void *startPtr);
pascal void InitApplZone        (void);
pascal void SetApplBase         (void *startPtr);
```

Application-Defined Routines

Grow-Zone Functions

```
pascal long MyGrowZone          (Size cbNeeded);
```

Purge-Warning Procedures

```
pascal void MyPurgeProc         (Handle h);
```

Assembly-Language Summary

Constants

```
;flags in trap words
CLEAR               EQU     $200        ;set all bytes in block to 0
SYS                 EQU     $400        ;use the system heap

;values for the tag byte of a block header
tyBkFree            EQU     0           ;free block
tyBkNRel            EQU     1           ;nonrelocatable block
tyBkRel             EQU     2           ;relocatable block
```

```
;flags for the high-order byte of a 24-bit master pointer
lock            EQU     7       ;lock bit
purge           EQU     6       ;purge bit
resource        EQU     5       ;resource bit
```

Data Structures

Zone Data Structure

0	bkLim	long	pointer to first usable byte after zone
4	purgePtr	long	used internally
8	hFstFree	long	first free master pointer
12	zcbFree	4 bytes	number of free bytes in zone
16	gzProc	long	grow-zone function
20	mAllocCnt	word	number of master pointers to allocate
22	flags	word	used internally
24	cntRel	word	reserved
26	maxRel	word	reserved
28	cntNRel	word	reserved
30	maxNRel	word	reserved
32	cntEmpty	word	reserved
34	cntHandles	word	reserved
36	minCBFree	long	reserved
40	purgeProc	long	purge-warning procedure
44	sparePtr	long	used internally
48	allocPtr	long	used internally
52	heapData	word	first usable byte in zone

Parameter Block for InitZone Procedure

0	startPtr	long	first byte of new zone
4	limitPtr	long	first byte beyond new zone
8	cMoreMasters	word	number of master pointers to be allocated at a time
10	pGrowZone	long	pointer to grow-zone function for new zone

Trap Macros

Trap Macro Names

Pascal name	Trap macro name
BlockMove	_BlockMove
CompactMem	_CompactMem
CompactMemSys	_CompactMem
DisposeHandle	_DisposeHandle
DisposePtr	_DisposePtr

Pascal name	Trap macro name
EmptyHandle	_EmptyHandle
FreeMem	_FreeMem
FreeMemSys	_FreeMem
GetHandleSize	_GetHandleSize
GetPtrSize	_GetPtrSize
GetZone	_GetZone
HandAndHand	_HandAndHand
HandleZone	_HandleZone
HandToHand	_HandToHand
HClrRBit	_HClrRBit
HGetState	_HGetState
HLock	_HLock
HNoPurge	_HNoPurge
HPurge	_HPurge
HSetRBit	_HSetRBit
HSetState	_HSetState
HUnlock	_HUnlock
InitApplZone	_InitApplZone
InitZone	_InitZone
MaxApplZone	_MaxApplZone
MaxBlock	_MaxBlock
MaxBlockSys	_MaxBlock
MaxMem	_MaxMem
MaxMemSys	_MaxMem
MoreMasters	_MoreMasters
MoveHHi	_MoveHHi
NewEmptyHandle	_NewEmptyHandle
NewEmptyHandleSys	_NewEmptyHandle
NewHandle	_NewHandle
NewHandleClear	_NewHandle
NewHandleSys	_NewHandle
NewHandleSysClear	_NewHandle
NewPtr	_NewPtr
NewPtrClear	_NewPtr
NewPtrSys	_NewPtr
NewPtrSysClear	_NewPtr

Pascal name	Trap macro name
PtrAndHand	_PtrAndHand
PtrToHand	_PtrToHand
PtrToXHand	_PtrToXHand
PtrZone	_PtrZone
PurgeMem	_PurgeMem
PurgeMemSys	_PurgeMem
PurgeSpace	_PurgeSpace
ReallocateHandle	_ReallocHandle
RecoverHandle	_RecoverHandle
ReserveMem	_ResrvMem
ReserveMemSys	_ResrvMem
SetApplBase	_SetApplBase
SetApplLimit	_SetApplLimit
SetGrowZone	_SetGrowZone
SetHandleSize	_SetHandleSize
SetPtrSize	_SetPtrSize
SetZone	_SetZone
StackSpace	_StackSpace

Trap Macro Requiring Routine Selectors

_OSDispatch

Selector	Routine
$0015	TempMaxMem
$0018	TempFreeMem
$001D	TempNewHandle

Global Variables

ApplLimit	long	The application heap limit, beyond which the heap cannot expand.
ApplZone	long	A pointer to the original application heap zone.
BufPtr	long	Address of highest byte of allocatable memory.
CurStackBase	long	Address of base of stack; start of application global variables.
GZRootHnd	long	A handle to a block that the grow-zone function must not move.
HeapEnd	long	Address of end of application heap zone.
MemErr	word	The current value that MemError would return.
MemTop	long	After startup time, the address at the end of an application's partition.
SysZone	long	A pointer to the system heap zone.
TheZone	long	A pointer to the current heap zone.

Result Codes

noErr	0	No error
paramErr	–50	Error in parameter list
memROZErr	–99	Operation on a read-only zone
memFullErr	–108	Not enough memory
nilHandleErr	–109	NIL master pointer
memWZErr	–111	Attempt to operate on a free block
memPurErr	–112	Attempt to purge a locked block
memBCErr	–115	Block check failed
memLockedErr	–117	Block is locked

Virtual Memory Manager

Contents

This chapter describes the Virtual Memory Manager, the part of the Operating System that allows memory to be extended beyond the limits of the physical address space provided by the available RAM. A user can select (in the Memory control panel) whether to enable this larger or "virtual" address space.

Most applications are completely unaffected by the operation of the Virtual Memory Manager and have no need to know whether any virtual memory is available. You might, however, need to intervene in the otherwise automatic workings of the Virtual Memory Manager if your application has critical timing requirements, executes code at interrupt time, or performs debugging operations.

The Virtual Memory Manager also offers services that might be of use to software components even if virtual memory is not enabled on a particular computer. On some Macintosh computers, the physical address space is discontiguous and is therefore not identical with the logical address space. In normal operations, the Operating System uses the MMU coprocessor to map logical addresses to their corresponding physical addresses. In some cases, however, you might need to perform this address mapping yourself. For example, if you are writing software that runs in the Macintosh Operating System but communicates addresses to NuBus™ expansion cards with bus master or direct memory access (DMA) capabilities, you need to pass physical and not logical addresses. You can use the Virtual Memory Manager to determine those physical addresses.

To use this chapter, you should be familiar with the normal operation of the Memory Manager, as described in the chapter "Introduction to Memory Management" in this book. If your application or other software executes code at interrupt time, you should also be familiar with the process of scheduling interrupt code, as described in the chapter "Introduction to Processes and Tasks" in *Inside Macintosh: Processes.*

This chapter begins with a description of how the Virtual Memory Manager provides virtual memory. It explains how the logical and physical address spaces are mapped to one another and when you might need to use the services provided by the Virtual Memory Manager. Then it explains how you can use the Virtual Memory Manager to

- make portions of the logical address space resident in physical RAM
- make portions of the logical address space immovable in physical RAM
- map logical to physical addresses
- defer execution of application-defined interrupt code until a safe time

This chapter also provides information about a number of routines that are useful only for the implementation of debuggers that operate under virtual memory.

About the Virtual Memory Manager

The Virtual Memory Manager is the part of the Operating System that provides **virtual memory,** addressable memory beyond the limits of the available physical RAM. The principal benefit of using virtual memory is that a user can run more applications at once and work with larger amounts of data than would be possible if the logical address space were limited to the available RAM. Instead of equipping a computer with amounts of RAM large enough to handle all possible needs, the user can install only enough RAM to meet average needs. Then, during those occasional times when more memory is needed for large tasks or many applications, the user can take advantage of virtual memory. When virtual memory is present, the perceived amount of RAM can be extended to as much as 14 MB on systems with 24-bit addressing and as much as 1 GB on systems with 32-bit addressing.

The Virtual Memory Manager also provides a number of routines that your software can use to modify or get information about its operations. You can use the Virtual Memory Manager to

- hold portions of the logical address space in physical RAM
- lock portions of the logical address space in their physical RAM locations
- determine whether a particular portion of the logical address space is currently in physical RAM
- determine, from a logical address, the physical address of a block of memory

This section describes how the Virtual Memory Manager provides virtual memory. It also explains why you might need to use certain Virtual Memory Manager routines even when virtual memory is not available.

Virtual Memory

The Virtual Memory Manager extends the logical address space by using part of the available secondary storage (such as a hard disk) to hold portions of applications and data that are not currently in use in physical memory. When an application needs to operate on portions of memory that have been transferred to disk, the Virtual Memory Manager loads those portions back into physical memory by making them trade places with other, unused segments of memory. This process of moving portions (or **pages**) of memory between physical RAM and the hard disk is called **paging.**

For the most part, the Virtual Memory Manager operates invisibly to applications and to the user. Most applications do not need to know whether virtual memory is installed unless they have critical timing requirements, execute code at interrupt time, or perform debugging operations. The only time that users need to know about virtual memory is when they configure it in the Memory control panel. One visible cost of this extra memory is the use of an equivalent amount of storage on a storage device, such as a SCSI hard disk. Another cost of using virtual memory is a possible perception of sluggishness as paged-out segments of memory are pulled back into physical memory. Performance degradation due to the use of virtual memory ranges from unnoticeable to severe, depending on the ratio of virtual memory to physical RAM and the behavior of the actual applications running.

There are two main requirements for running virtual memory. First, the computer must be running system software version 7.0 or later. Second, the computer must be equipped with an **MMU** or **PMMU** coprocessor. Apple's 68040- and 68030-based machines have an MMU built into the CPU and are ready to run virtual memory with no additional hardware. A Macintosh II (68020-based) computer can take advantage of virtual memory if it has the 68851 PMMU coprocessor on its main logic board in place of the standard **Address Management Unit (AMU).** (The PMMU is the same coprocessor needed to run A/UX.) Apple's 68000-based machines cannot take advantage of virtual memory.

Users control and configure virtual memory through the Memory control panel. Controls in this panel allow the user to turn virtual memory on or off, set the size of virtual memory, and set the volume on which the invisible backing-store file resides. (The **backing-store file** is the file in which the Operating System stores the contents of nonresident pages of memory.) Other memory-related user controls appear in this control panel. These include settings for the disk cache and for 24-bit or 32-bit Memory Manager addressing. If users change the virtual memory, addressing, or disk cache settings, they must restart the computer for the changes to take effect.

The virtual memory setting in the control panel reflects the total amount of memory available to the system (and not simply the amount of memory to be added to available RAM). Also, the backing-store file is as large as the amount of virtual memory. This backing-store file can be located on any HFS volume that allows block-level access. (This volume is known as the **paging device** or **backing volume.**) Because the paging device must support block-level access, users cannot select as the paging device a volume mounted through AppleShare. Also, users cannot select removable disks, including floppy disks, as paging devices.

The Logical Address Space

When virtual memory is present, the logical address space is larger than the physical address space provided by the available RAM. The actual size of the logical address space, and hence the amount of virtual memory, depends on a number of factors, including

- the addressing mode currently used by the Memory Manager
- the amount of space available on a secondary storage device for use by the backing-store file
- if 24-bit addressing is in operation, the number of NuBus expansion cards, if any, installed in the computer

24-Bit Addressing

When running with **24-bit addressing,** the Memory Manager can address at most 2^{24} bytes, or 16 MB. Of these 16 MB, at most 8 MB can be used to address physical RAM. The remaining 8 MB are devoted to ROM addresses, I/O device addresses, and NuBus slot addresses. Figure 3-1 illustrates the logical address space mapping used by the 24-bit Memory Manager.

Note
In some Macintosh computers, the ROM is mapped to the address range $01000000 to $010FFFFF (indicated as belonging to slot $A in Figure 3-1). In these computers, the maximum amount of physical RAM is 10 MB instead of 8 MB. The remainder of this section describes the original layout of the 24-bit logical address space only. ◆

Figure 3-1 24-bit Memory Manager logical address space

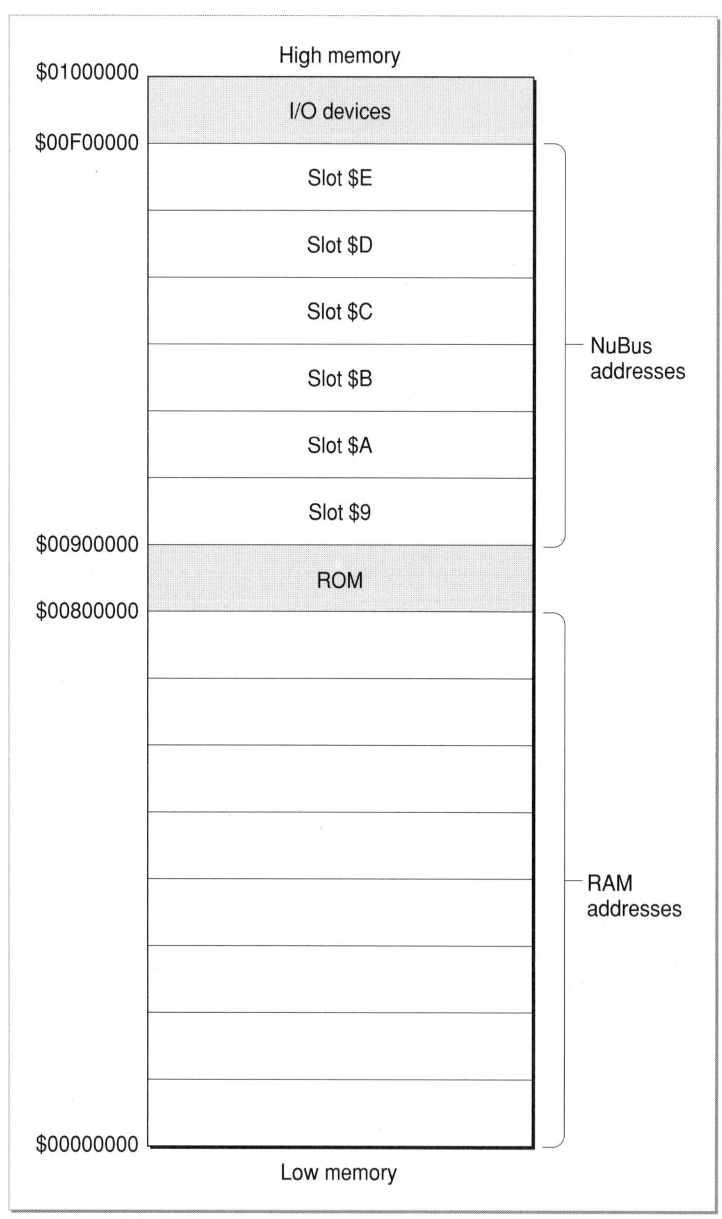

When 24-bit addressing is in operation and virtual memory is available, the Virtual Memory Manager uses, as part of the addressable application memory, any 1 MB segments not assigned to a NuBus card. For example, if a Macintosh computer has three NuBus expansion cards installed, that computer can address at most 11 MB of virtual memory. The maximum amount of virtual memory possible in a 24-bit environment is 14 MB (that is, 8 MB of physical RAM + 6 MB of additional space previously reserved for the NuBus); this maximum is achievable only on a computer with no NuBus expansion cards installed.

Notice in Figure 3-1 that addresses from $00800000 to $008FFFFF are reserved for ROM. In other words, the largest contiguous block of space that an application can allocate when virtual memory is available is somewhat less than 8 MB, even though the total amount of virtual memory available can be as large as 14 MB. The rest of the virtual memory can be in a contiguous block as large as 4 or 5 MB, unless the user has fragmented the NuBus space by making a poor choice of slots in which to install expansion cards. To maximize the amount of contiguous virtual memory, users should place cards in consecutive slots at either end of the expansion bus. A haphazard placement of NuBus cards may result in a number of 1 MB or 2 MB "islands" in the upper portion of the 24-bit address space; in general, this kind of fragmentation reduces the effectiveness of a large virtual address space.

Note

Some Macintosh computers have fewer than six NuBus slots, and the numbering of the slots is not consistent across different models. In a Macintosh IIcx, the three available slots are numbered $9 through $B, so expansion cards should be grouped toward the lowest-numbered slot (contiguous with the ROM space). In a Macintosh IIci, the slots are numbered $C through $E, so expansion cards should be grouped toward the highest-numbered slot (contiguous with the I/O space). However, the RAM-based video on the Macintosh IIci occupies addresses reserved for slot $B; as a result, it is impossible to avoid some degree of fragmentation of the virtual address space when you use the RAM-based video option on that computer. ◆

32-Bit Addressing

When running with **32-bit addressing,** the Memory Manager can address at most 2^{32} bytes, or 4 GB. Of these 4 GB, at most 1 GB can be used to address physical RAM. The remaining 3 GB are devoted to ROM addresses, I/O device addresses, and NuBus slot addresses. Figure 3-2 illustrates the logical address space mapping used by the 32-bit Memory Manager.

Figure 3-2 32-bit Memory Manager logical address space

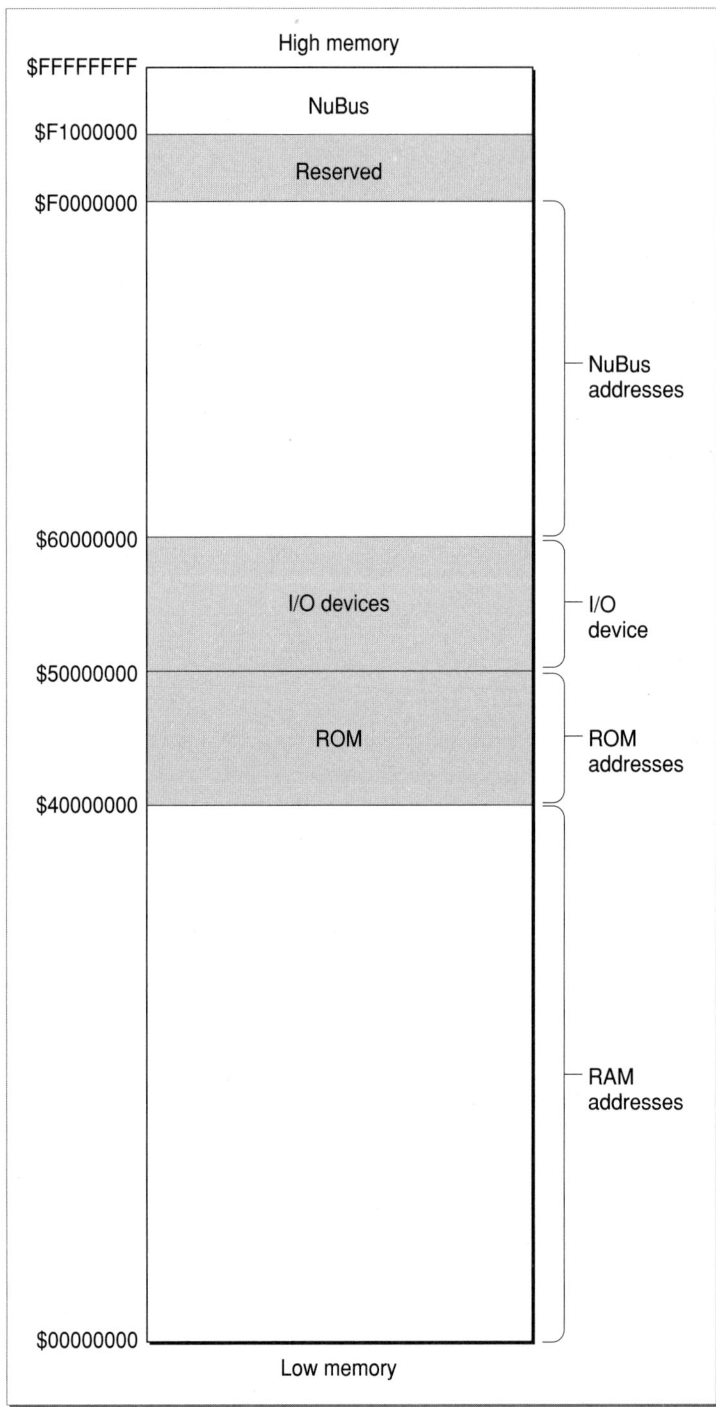

Note
The fragmentation of the virtual address space that sometimes occurs when 24-bit addressing is in operation is never a problem when 32-bit addressing is in operation. In the 32-bit address space, virtual memory and the NuBus slots do not share space. ◆

The Physical Address Space

The original versions of the Macintosh Operating System used physical addresses exclusively. A particular location in RAM could be accessed by its physical address, regardless of whether that address was generated by an application, by the system software, or even by a NuBus expansion card. In short, there was no difference between the logical and the physical address spaces.

However, both hardware and software advances have forced the Operating System to abstract the logical address space from the physical address space. As you have seen, the logical address space is larger than the physical address space when virtual memory is available. The Operating System uses the MMU coprocessor to map logical addresses to their corresponding physical addresses.

In addition, some Macintosh computers have a discontiguous physical address space. For example, on a Macintosh IIci with 8 MB of physical RAM, the physical memory appears to the CPU and to the NuBus expansion bus as two separate 4 MB ranges (see Figure 3-3). As you can see, the physical RAM occupies two separate ranges: the RAM installed in bank A, ranging from $00000000 to $003FFFFF, and the RAM installed in bank B, ranging from $04000000 to $043FFFFF.

Figure 3-3 The physical address space on a Macintosh IIci with 8 MB of RAM

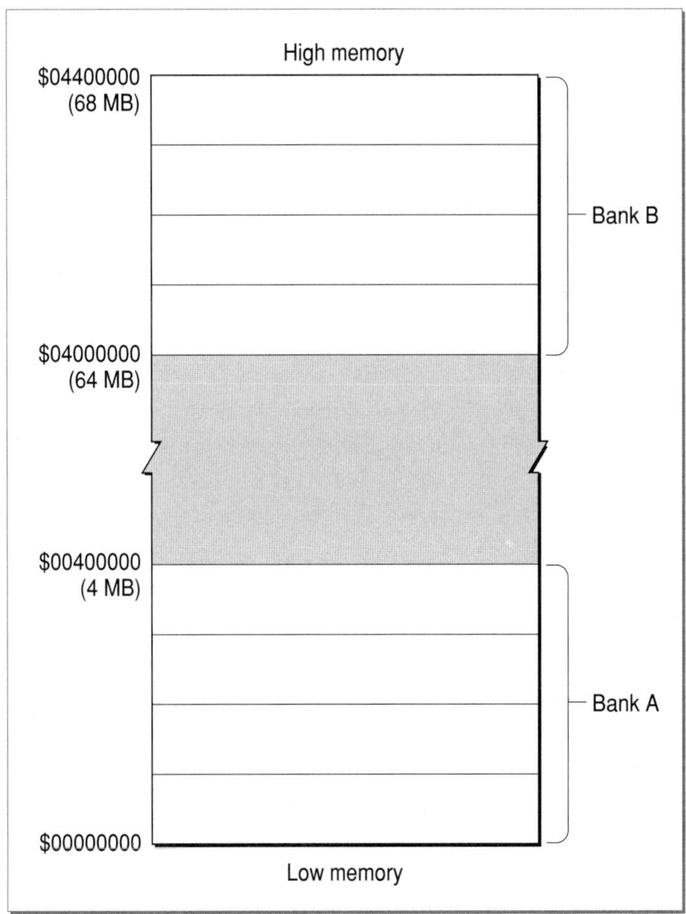

In most cases, a discontiguous physical address space causes no problems, because the Operating System uses the MMU coprocessor to map the available physical memory into a single contiguous logical address space. All memory addresses returned to your application by the Memory Manager (for instance, when you allocate a new block by calling `NewHandle`) are logical addresses. When you read or write a logical memory address, the Operating System uses the MMU coprocessor to determine the physical address corresponding to your logical address. This address translation is completely transparent to your application. For example, if you read the system global variable located at address $10C, it doesn't matter that the CPU actually looks at the physical address $0400010C.

In some cases, however, you can run into problems if you don't account for the possibility that the logical address space and the physical address space might differ. Suppose, for instance, that you are developing a driver that passes addresses to NuBus master hardware. In this case, you need to take care to pass it *physical* addresses only, because NuBus hardware does not use the MMU to translate logical addresses into physical addresses. If your driver passes a logical address, the NuBus hardware cannot translate it into a physical address because it does not have access to the MMU's address-mapping tables. If your hardware then attempts to write data to that address, it is likely to overwrite some other portion of physical memory.

To prevent this problem, you need to make certain that you always convert logical addresses to their corresponding physical addresses before you pass those addresses to any alternate bus master. You can do this by calling the `GetPhysical` function, as described later in "Mapping Logical to Physical Addresses," which begins on page 3-16. The `GetPhysical` function is implemented in ROM on all machines that have a discontiguous physical address space—whether or not virtual memory is available. Accordingly, before you pass addresses to an alternate bus master, you should check for the availability of the `GetPhysical` call; if it's available, you should use it to translate logical to physical addresses.

Note

Passive or slave NuBus cards (such as video cards) that do not read or write physical RAM are not likely to be affected by the presence of virtual memory or by a discontiguous physical address space. ◆

Page Faults

When an application or other software component tries to access data in a page of memory that is not currently resident in RAM, the Operating System issues a special kind of bus error known as a **page fault.** The Virtual Memory Manager intercepts page faults and tries to load the affected page or pages into memory. It does so by executing its own internal page-fault handler, which handles page faults and passes other bus errors to the standard bus-error vector in low memory.

To load the required pages into memory, the Virtual Memory Manager's page-fault handler takes over the SCSI bus and makes calls directly to the driver of the backing-store file. While the Virtual Memory Manager is handling a page fault, it is essential that no other page faults occur. If a page fault did occur during page-fault handling—a condition known as a **double page fault**—the Virtual Memory Manager would have to interrupt the driver of the paging device to make a further request to load the needed page. Unless the driver of the paging device is **concurrent** (that is, able to handle several requests at once), the driver cannot handle this second request. Unfortunately, current versions of most SCSI disk drivers are not concurrent. As a result, a double page fault results in a system crash.

The Virtual Memory Manager takes special steps to avoid double page faults caused by user code (that is, code that is not executed as the result of an exception). It defers all user code while the driver of the paging device is busy. In particular, the Virtual Memory Manager defers until a safe time the following types of code:

- VBL tasks
- Slot-based VBL tasks
- Time Manager tasks
- I/O completion routines

Note
Because these types of tasks may be deferred under virtual memory, any application or device driver that uses them to achieve real-time performance might be adversely affected by the operation of the Virtual Memory Manager. ◆

Other software components must take care not to cause page faults at interrupt time. In particular, device drivers, which commonly run at interrupt time, should make certain that any data structures or buffers that they reference at interrupt time are in physical memory at that time. You can make sure that this happens by holding the required data in physical memory, as described in "Holding and Releasing Memory" on page 3-14.

In an effort to maintain compatibility with existing drivers, the Operating System automatically keeps the entire system heap in physical memory at all times. Therefore, if your device driver and its associated data structures are loaded into the system heap, you do not need to worry about causing page faults at interrupt time.

▲ **WARNING**
Future versions of the system software are not guaranteed to keep the entire system heap in physical memory. To be safe, you should explicitly hold in physical memory any code or data that you know might be accessed at interrupt time. ▲

The Virtual Memory Manager provides this further level of protection against page faults caused by device drivers at interrupt time: it automatically holds in physical memory any buffers used by the Device Manager `_Read` and `_Write` operations. Any driver that uses the `_Read` and `_Write` calls to move data between main memory and the driver's associated hardware device is therefore automatically compatible with virtual memory. If, however, you use `_Status` or `_Control` calls to move data at interrupt time, you must explicitly hold or lock all buffers that are referenced in the `_Status` or `_Control` parameter block. If possible, you should rewrite your driver so that it uses `_Read` and `_Write` calls instead of `_Status` and `_Control` calls to move data.

The Virtual Memory Manager provides one other routine that you can use to help prevent double page faults. If your application or other code installs interrupt routines other than those handled automatically by the Virtual Memory Manager (such as VBL tasks, Time Manager tasks, and Device Manager completion calls), you can explicitly defer the execution of the routine by calling it via the function `DeferUserFn`. See "Deferring User Interrupt Handling" on page 3-20 for details on calling `DeferUserFn`.

Using the Virtual Memory Manager

The routines described in this section allow drivers and applications with critical timing needs to intervene in the otherwise automatic workings of the Virtual Memory Manager's paging mechanism.

Note
The vast majority of applications do not need to use these routines. They are used primarily by drivers, debuggers, and other interrupt-servicing code. ◆

If necessary, your software can request that a range of memory be held in physical memory. **Holding** means that the specified memory range cannot be paged out to disk, although it might be moved within physical RAM. As a result, no page faults can result from reading or writing memory addresses of pages that are held in memory.

Similarly, a page or range of pages can be locked in physical memory. **Locking** means that the specified memory cannot be paged out to disk and that the memory cannot change its real (physical) RAM location. You can also request that a range of pages be locked in a contiguous range of physical memory, although contiguity is not guaranteed. The need to lock pages in a contiguous area of memory arises primarily when external hardware transfers data directly into physical RAM. In this case, locking might be useful for keeping a contiguous range of memory stationary during operations of an external CPU (on a NuBus card, for example) that cannot support a DMA action.

Most applications do not need to hold or lock pages in physical RAM. The Virtual Memory Manager usually works quickly enough that your application is not affected by any delay that might result from paging. Device drivers or sound and animation applications with critical timing requirements usually need only to hold memory, not lock it. Here are some general rules regarding when to hold or lock memory:

- Avoid executing tasks that could cause page faults at interrupt time. The less work done at interrupt time, the better for all applications running.
- You cannot hold or lock memory (or call any Memory Manager routines that move or purge memory) at interrupt time.
- Don't lock or hold everything in RAM. Sometimes you do need to hold or lock pages in RAM, but if you are in doubt, then probably you need to do neither.
- Your application must explicitly release or unlock whatever it held or locked. If for some reason an area of RAM is held and locked, or held twice, then it must be released and unlocked, or released twice.

The last directive is especially important. Your application is responsible for undoing the effects of locking or holding ranges of memory. In particular, the Virtual Memory Manager does not automatically unlock pages that have been locked. If you do not undo these effects in a timely fashion, you are likely to degrade performance. In the worst case, you could cause the system to run out of physical memory.

Obtaining Information About Virtual Memory

You should always determine whether virtual memory is available before attempting to use any Virtual Memory Manager routines. To do this, pass the `Gestalt` function the `gestaltVMAttr` selector. The `Gestalt` function's response indicates the version of virtual memory, if any, installed. If bit 0 of the response is set to 1, then the system software version 7.0 implementation of virtual memory is installed.

Note
Sometimes you don't need to check whether virtual memory is actually available before calling some Virtual Memory Manager routines. For example, you might need to call the `GetPhysical` function even if virtual memory is not enabled. Instead of calling `Gestalt` to see whether virtual memory is available, you should simply test whether the appropriate trap is available. In the case of the `GetPhysical` function, you should check that the `_MemoryDispatchA0Result` trap is available. ◆

You can also use the `Gestalt` function to obtain information about the memory configuration of the system, in particular, information about the amount of physical memory installed in a computer, the amount of logical memory available in a computer, the version of virtual memory installed (if any), and the size of a logical page. By obtaining this information from `Gestalt`, you can help insulate your applications or drivers from possible future changes in the details of the virtual memory implementation.

Holding and Releasing Memory

You can use the `HoldMemory` function to make a portion of the address space resident in physical memory and ineligible for paging. This function is intended primarily for use by drivers that access user data buffers at interrupt level, whether transferring data to or from them. Calling `HoldMemory` on the appropriate memory ranges thus prevents them from causing page faults at interrupt level and effectively prevents them from generating fatal double page faults. The contents of the specified range of virtual addresses can move in physical memory, but they are guaranteed always to be in physical memory when accessed.

Note
If you use the device-level `_Read` and `_Write` functions when doing data transfers, the Virtual Memory Manager automatically ensures that the data buffers and parameter blocks are held before the transfer of data. ◆

The following sample code instructs the Virtual Memory Manager to hold in RAM an 8192-byte range of memory starting at address $32500:

```
myAddress := $32500;
myLength := 8192;
myErr := HoldMemory(myAddress, myLength);
```

Note that whole pages of the virtual address space are held, regardless of the starting address and length parameters you supply. If the starting address parameter supplied to the HoldMemory function is not on a page boundary, then it is rounded down to the nearest page boundary. Similarly, if the specified range does not end on a page boundary, the length parameter is rounded up so that one or more whole pages are held. This rounding might result in the holding of several pages of physical memory, even if the specified range is less than a page in length.

To release memory held as a result of a call to HoldMemory, you must use the UnholdMemory function, which simply reverses the effects of the HoldMemory function. For example, the page or pages held in memory in the previous example can be released as follows:

```
myErr := UnholdMemory(myAddress, myLength);
```

Like holding, releasing applies to whole pages of the virtual address space. Similar rounding of the address and length parameters is performed, as required, to make the range begin and end on page boundaries.

Note
In current versions of system software, the system heap is always held in memory and is never paged out. ◆

Locking and Unlocking Memory

You can use the LockMemory function to make a portion of the address space immovable in physical memory and ineligible for paging. The Operating System may move the contents of the specified range of logical addresses to a more convenient location in physical memory during the locking operation, but on completion, the contents of the specified range of logical addresses are resident and do not move in physical memory.

Locking a range of memory is a more drastic measure than just holding it. Locking not only forces the range to be held resident in RAM but also prevents its logical address from moving with respect to its physical address. The LockMemory function is used by drivers and other code when hardware other than the Macintosh CPU is transferring data to or from user buffers, such as any NuBus master peripheral card or DMA hardware. This function prevents both paging and physical relocation of a specified memory area and allows the physical addresses of a memory area to be exported to the non-CPU hardware. Typically, you would use this service for the duration of a single I/O request. However, you could use this service to lock data structures that are permanently shared between a driver (or other code) and a NuBus master.

Note
Don't confuse locking address ranges in RAM (using LockMemory) with locking a handle (using HLock). A locked handle can still be paged out. ◆

The main reason to disable movement of pages in physical memory is to allow translation of virtual memory addresses to physical addresses. This translation is needed by bus masters, which must write to memory in the physical address space. To avoid stale data, the memory locked in RAM is marked as noncacheable in the MMU page tables.

You can lock a range of memory in a contiguous range of physical memory by calling the `LockMemoryContiguous` function. This function can be used by driver and NuBus master or driver and DMA hardware combinations when a non-CPU device accessing memory cannot handle physically discontiguous data transfers. You can also use this service when the transfer of physically discontiguous data would degrade performance. However, the call to `LockMemoryContiguous` may be expensive, because sometimes entire pages must be copied to make a range contiguous.

Note

It might not be possible to make a range physically contiguous if any of the pages in the range are already locked. Because a call to `LockMemoryContiguous` is not guaranteed to return the desired results, you must include in your code an alternate method for locking the necessary ranges of memory. In general, you should avoid calling `LockMemoryContiguous` if at all possible. If you must call it, do so as early as possible—preferably at system startup time—to increase the likelihood of finding enough contiguous memory. ◆

To unlock a range of previously locked pages, use the `UnlockMemory` function. This function reverses the effects of `LockMemory` or `LockMemoryContiguous`. Unlocked pages are marked as cacheable.

Locking, contiguous locking, and unlocking operations are applied to ranges of the logical address space. If necessary to force the ranges onto page boundaries, the Virtual Memory Manager performs rounding of addresses and sizes, as described in "Holding and Releasing Memory" on page 3-14.

Mapping Logical to Physical Addresses

To obtain information about page mapping between logical and physical addresses, use the `GetPhysical` function, which translates logical addresses into their corresponding physical addresses. It provides drivers and other software with the actual physical memory addresses of a specified logical address range. Non-CPU devices need this information to access memory mapped by the CPU.

The GetPhysical function allows you to obtain the physical addresses that correspond to any logically addressable range of main memory. To specify the logical address range to be translated, you use a **memory-block record,** defined by the MemoryBlock data type.

```
TYPE MemoryBlock =
RECORD
   address:    Ptr;              {start of block}
   count:      LongInt;          {size of block}
END;
```

A memory-block record identifies a single contiguous block of memory by specifying the first byte in the block and the length of the block.

Note
Don't confuse the blocks of memory defined by the MemoryBlock data type with memory blocks as manipulated by the Memory Manager. The portion of the logical address space to be translated by GetPhysical can overlap several Memory Manager memory blocks or be just a part of one. Typically, however, that range coincides with the contents of a single Memory Manager block. ◆

A single logical address range sometimes corresponds to more than one range of physical addresses. As a result, GetPhysical needs to pass back to your application an array of memory-block records. You pass a logical address range to GetPhysical, and it returns an array of physical address ranges. This operation requires the use of a logical-to-physical **translation table,** defined by the LogicalToPhysicalTable data type.

```
TYPE LogicalToPhysicalTable =
RECORD
   logical:    MemoryBlock;           {a logical block}
   physical:   ARRAY[0..defaultPhysicalEntryCount-1] OF
                      MemoryBlock;    {equivalent physical blocks}
END;
```

To call GetPhysical, you need to pass a translation table whose logical field specifies the logical address range you want to translate. You also need to specify how many contiguous physical address ranges you want returned. In this way, you can adjust the number of elements in the array to suit your own needs. By default, a translation table contains enough space for eight physical memory blocks.

```
CONST    defaultPhysicalEntryCount  = 8;
```

If the variable `myTable` is of type `LogicalToPhysicalTable` and `myCount` is of type `LongInt`, you can call `GetPhysical` as follows:

```
myCount := (SizeOf(myTable) DIV SizeOf(MemoryBlock)) - 1;
myErr := GetPhysical(myTable, myCount);
```

The algorithm used here to calculate the number of physical entries returned (`myCount`) allows you to change the size (and hence the type) of the `myTable` variable to include more or fewer memory blocks. The default size of the translation table is sufficient for most purposes. Before you do the translation, you can determine how many physical blocks you need to accommodate the entire logical address space specified in the table's `logical` parameter. To determine this, you pass a variable whose initial value is 0:

```
myCount := 0;         {get number of blocks needed for given range}
myErr := GetPhysical(myTable, myCount);
```

If the value of its second parameter is 0, `GetPhysical` returns in that parameter the total number of physical blocks that would be required to translate the entire logical address range. In this case, both the `logical` and `physical` fields of the translation table are unchanged.

If the value of its second parameter is not 0, `GetPhysical` returns in the `physical` field of the translation table an array specifying the physical blocks that correspond to the logical address specified in the `logical` field. The `GetPhysical` function returns in its second parameter the number of entries in that array (which may be fewer than were asked for). If the translation table was not large enough to contain all the physical blocks corresponding to the logical block, `GetPhysical` updates the fields of the `logical` memory block to reflect the remaining number of bytes in the logical range left to translate (`count` field) and the next address in the logical address range to translate (`start` field).

Note

You must lock (using `LockMemory`) the address range passed to `GetPhysical` to guarantee that the translation data returned are accurate (that is, that the logical pages do not move around in physical memory and that paging activity has not invalidated the translation data). An error is returned if you call `GetPhysical` on an address range that is not locked. ◆

Recall that you sometimes need to call `GetPhysical` even if virtual memory is not available. (See "The Physical Address Space" on page 3-9 for details.) In general, if `GetPhysical` is available in the operating environment, then you should call it any time your software exports addresses to a NuBus expansion card that can read or write physical RAM directly. Listing 3-1 defines a general algorithm for implementing driver calls to a generic NuBus master card. To maximize compatibility with virtual memory, make sure that your hardware and device drivers support this method of issuing driver calls.

Listing 3-1 Translating logical to physical addresses

```
PROGRAM GetPhysicalUsage;
USES Types, Traps, Memory, Utilities;
CONST
   kTestPtrSize = $100000;
VAR
   myPtr:            Ptr;
   myPtrSize:        LongInt;
   hasGetPhysical:   Boolean;       {does this machine have GetPhysical?}
   lockOK:           Boolean;       {was the block successfully locked?}
   myErr:            OSErr;
   myTable:          LogicalToPhysicalTable;
   myCount:          LongInt;
   index:            Integer;

   PROCEDURE SendDMACmd (addr: Ptr; count: LongInt);
      BEGIN
         {This is where you would probably make a driver call }
         { to initiate DMA from a NuBus master or similar hardware.}
      END;
BEGIN
   myPtrSize := kTestPtrSize;
   myPtr := NewPtr(myPtrSize);
   IF myPtr <> NIL THEN
   BEGIN
      hasGetPhysical := TrapAvailable(_MemoryDispatch);
      IF hasGetPhysical THEN
      BEGIN
         myErr := LockMemory(myPtr, myPtrSize);
         lockOK := (myErr = noErr);
         IF lockOK THEN
         BEGIN
            myTable.logical.address := myPtr;
            myTable.logical.count := myPtrSize;
            myErr := noErr;
            WHILE (myErr = noErr) & (myTable.logical.count <> 0) DO
            BEGIN
               myCount := SizeOf(myTable) DIV SizeOf(MemoryBlock) - 1;
               myErr := GetPhysical(myTable, myCount);
               IF myErr = noErr THEN
                  FOR index := 0 TO (myCount - 1) DO
                     WITH myTable DO
                        SendDMACmd(physical[index].address,
```

```
                                                    physical[index].count)
            ELSE
            BEGIN
               {Handle GetPhysical error indicated by myErr.}
               {Loop will terminate unless myErr is reset to noErr.}
            END;
         END; {WHILE}
         {Always unlock a range you locked; ignore any error here.}
         myErr := UnlockMemory(myPtr, myPtrSize);
      END
      ELSE     {not lockOK}
      BEGIN
         {handle LockMemory error indicated by myErr}
      END;
   END
   ELSE                              {GetPhysical not available}
      SendDMACmd(myPtr, myPtrSize);
END; {IF myPtr}
END.
```

If the `GetPhysical` function is not available, the program defined in Listing 3-1 simply calls your routine to send a DMA command to the NuBus hardware. In that case, no address translation is necessary. If, however, `GetPhysical` is available, you need to lock the logical address range whose physical addresses you want to get. If you successfully lock the range, you can call `GetPhysical` as illustrated earlier. Be sure to unlock the range you previously locked before exiting the program.

▲ **WARNING**
Some Macintosh computers contain the `_MemoryDispatch` trap in ROM, even though they do not contain an MMU coprocessor. In this case, the system software patches the `_MemoryDispatch` trap to make it appear unimplemented. However, software that executes before system patches are installed cannot use this as a test of whether to call `GetPhysical` or not. If your code is executed before the installation of system patches, you should use the `Gestalt` function to test directly for the existence of an MMU coprocessor. ▲

Deferring User Interrupt Handling

During the time that the Macintosh is handling a page fault, it is critical that no other page faults occur. Because the system performs no other work while it is handling a page fault, only code that runs as a result of an interrupt can generate a second page fault. For this reason, you must call the `HoldMemory` function on buffers or code that are to be referenced by any interrupt service routine. You must call this function at noninterrupt level because the `MemoryDispatch` calls may cause movement of logical memory or physical memory and possible I/O.

The use of procedure pointers (variables of type `ProcPtr`) in specifying I/O completion routines, socket listeners, and so forth makes it impossible for drivers to know the exact location and size of all code or buffers that might be referenced when these routines are invoked. However, these routines must still be called only at a safe time, when paging is not currently in progress. Because the locations of all needed pages cannot be known, an alternate strategy is used to prevent a fatal double page fault.

The `DeferUserFn` function is provided to allow interrupt service routines to defer, until a safe time, code that might cause page faults. This function determines whether the call can be made immediately and, if it is safe, makes the call. If a page fault is in progress, the address of the service routine and its parameter are saved, and the routine is deferred until page faults are again permitted.

Virtual Memory and Debuggers

Note
You need the information in this section only if you are writing a debugger that is to operate under virtual memory. ◆

Debuggers running under virtual memory can use any of the virtual memory routines discussed in the previous sections. For example, if a debugger is in a situation where page faulting would be fatal, it can use `DeferUserFn` to defer the debugging until paging is safe. However, debuggers running under virtual memory might require a few routines that differ from those available to other applications. In addition, debuggers might depend on some specific features of virtual memory that other applications should not depend on.

For example, because debugger code might be entered at a time when paging would be unsafe, you should lock (and not just hold) the debugger and all of its data and buffer space in memory. Normally, the locking operation is used to allow NuBus masters or other DMA devices to transfer data directly into physical memory. This requires that data caching be disabled on the locked page. You might, however, want your debugger to benefit from the performance of the data cache on pages belonging solely to the debugger. The `DebuggerLockMemory` function does exactly what `LockMemory` does, except that it leaves data caching enabled on the affected pages. You can call the `DebuggerUnlockMemory` function to reverse the effects of `DebuggerLockMemory`.

Other special debugger support functions

- determine whether paging is safe
- allow the debugger to enter supervisor mode
- enter and exit the debugging state
- obtain keyboard input while in the debugging state
- determine the state of a page of logical memory

All of these functions are implemented as extensions of `_DebugUtil`, a trap intended for use by debuggers to allow greater machine independence. This trap is not present in the Macintosh II, Macintosh IIx, Macintosh IIcx, or Macintosh SE/30 models, but it is present in all later models. The Virtual Memory Manager implements this trap for all machines that it supports, so a debugger can use `_DebugUtil` (and functions defined in terms of `_DebugUtil`) if `Gestalt` reports that virtual memory is present.

When the virtual memory extensions to `_DebugUtil` are not present (that is, when the computer supports virtual memory but is *not* a Macintosh II, Macintosh IIx, Macintosh IIcx, or Macintosh SE/30), `_DebugUtil` provides functions that can determine the highest `_DebugUtil` function supported, enter the debugging state, poll the keyboard for input, and exit the debugging state.

Bus-Error Vectors

The Operating System needs to intercept page faults and do the necessary paging. In addition, various applications and pieces of system software need to handle other kinds of bus errors. Virtual memory takes care of the complications of bus-error handling by providing two bus-error vectors. The vector that applications and other system software see is the one in low memory (at address $8). The vector that virtual memory uses (the one actually used by the processor) is in virtual memory's private storage and is pointed to by the Vector Base Register (VBR). Virtual memory's bus-error handler handles page faults and passes other bus errors to the vector in low memory at address $8.

When a debugger wants the contents of a page to be loaded into memory, it can read a byte from that page. The Operating System detects the page fault and loads the appropriate page (perhaps swapping another page to disk).

Note that a debugger will probably temporarily replace one or both of the bus-error vectors while it is executing. A debugger that wants virtual memory to continue paging while the debugger runs can put a handler only in the low-memory bus-error vector. A debugger that displays memory without allowing virtual memory to continue paging can put a handler in the virtual memory's bus-error vector (at VBR + $8).

Because the current version of virtual memory is not reentrant, there are times when trying to load a page into memory would be fatal. To allow for this, you can use the `PageFaultFatal` function to determine whether a page fault would be fatal at that time. If this function returns `TRUE`, the debugger should not allow the virtual memory's bus-error handler to detect any page faults. Thus, you should always replace the virtual memory's bus-error vector if the `PageFaultFatal` function returns `TRUE`.

Special Nonmaskable Interrupt Needs

Because a debugger can be triggered with a nonmaskable interrupt (level 7, triggered by the interrupt switch), it has special needs that other code in the system does not. For example, because a nonmaskable interrupt might occur while virtual memory is moving pages (to make them contiguous, for example), debugger code must be locked (instead of held, like most other code that must run at a time when page faults would be fatal).

Unfortunately, the LockMemory function is intended for use by device drivers and automatically disables data caching for the locked pages. Because this is not desirable for the debugger, the functions DebuggerLockMemory and DebuggerUnlockMemory lock pages without inhibiting the caching of those pages. Note that both stack, code, and other storage used by the debugger might need to be locked in this way.

Supervisor Mode

Because a debugger is typically activated through one of the processor vectors, it usually executes in supervisor mode, allowing it access to all of memory and all processor registers. When the debugger is entered in another way—for example, through the _Debugger or _DebugStr trap or when it is first loaded—it is necessary to enter supervisor mode. You can accomplish this with the following assembly-language instructions:

```
MOVEQ #EnterSupervisorMode,D0
_DebugUtil                    ;OS trap to DebugUtils
                              ;on exit, D0 still holds old SR
```

The code switches the caller into supervisor mode, and the previous status register is returned in register D0. Thus, when the debugger returns to the interrupted code, you can restore the previous interrupt level, condition codes, and so forth. When the debugger is ready to return to user mode, it simply loads the status register with the result returned in D0. Entering supervisor mode also switches the stack pointer from the user stack pointer (USP) to the interrupt stack pointer (ISP); reentering user mode changes the stack pointer back to the user stack pointer.

The Debugging State

When activated by an exception, _Debug or _DebugStr trap, or any other means, the debugger should call the DebuggerEnter procedure to notify _DebugUtil that the debugger is entering the debugging state. Then _DebugUtil can place hardware in a quiescent state and prepare for subsequent _DebugUtil calls.

Before returning to the interrupted application code, the debugger must call the DebuggerExit procedure to allow _DebugUtil to return hardware affected by DebuggerEnter to its previous state.

Keyboard Input

A debugger can obtain the user's keyboard input by calling the DebuggerPoll procedure. This routine can obtain keyboard input even when interrupts are disabled. After you call this service, you must then obtain keyboard events through the normal event-queue mechanism.

Page States

Debuggers need a way to display the contents of memory without paging or to display the contents of pages currently on disk. The GetPageState function returns one of these values to specify the state of a page containing a virtual address:

```
TYPE PageState = Integer;

CONST
   kPageInMemory      = 0;          {page is in RAM}
   kPageOnDisk        = 1;          {page is on disk}
   kNotPaged          = 2;          {address is not paged}
```

A debugger can use this information to determine whether certain memory addresses should be referenced. Note that ROM and I/O space are not pageable and therefore are considered not paged.

Virtual Memory Manager Reference

This section describes the data structures and routines that are provided by the Virtual Memory Manager.

Data Structures

The Virtual Memory Manager defines two data structures for use with the GetPhysical function, the memory-block record and the translation table.

Memory-Block Record

The GetPhysical function uses a memory-block record to hold information about a block of memory, either logical or physical. The memory-block record is a data structure of type MemoryBlock.

```
TYPE MemoryBlock =
RECORD
   address:    Ptr;              {start of block}
   count:      LongInt;          {size of block}
END;
```

Field descriptions

address — A pointer to the beginning of a block of memory.

count — The number of bytes in the block of memory.

Translation Table

The `GetPhysical` function uses a translation table to hold information about a logical address range and its corresponding physical addresses. A translation table is defined by the data type `LogicalToPhysicalTable`.

```
TYPE LogicalToPhysicalTable =
RECORD
   logical:    MemoryBlock;          {a logical block}
   physical:   ARRAY[0..defaultPhysicalEntryCount-1] OF
                      MemoryBlock;   {equivalent physical blocks}
END;
```

Field descriptions

`logical` — A logical block of memory whose corresponding physical blocks are to be determined.

`physical` — A physical translation table that identifies the blocks of physical memory corresponding to the logical block identified in the `logical` field.

Routines

This section describes the routines you can use to control virtual memory. The section "Virtual Memory Management" describes the routines that allow you to control pages in physical memory, and the section "Virtual Memory Debugger Support Routines" describes the routines that only programmers implementing debuggers need to use.

Virtual Memory Management

This section describes the routines you can use to hold logical pages in physical memory and let go of them, lock and unlock pages in physical memory, obtain information about page mapping, and handle interrupts. To hold and release pages, use the `HoldMemory` and `UnholdMemory` functions. To lock and unlock pages, use the `LockMemory`, `LockMemoryContiguous`, and `UnlockMemory` functions. To obtain page-mapping information, use the `GetPhysical` function. To defer user interrupt handling, use the `DeferUserFn` function.

HoldMemory

To make a portion of the address space resident in physical memory and ineligible for paging, use the `HoldMemory` function.

```
FUNCTION HoldMemory (address: UNIV Ptr; count: LongInt): OSErr;
```

`address`	The starting address of the range of memory to be held in RAM.
`count`	The size, in bytes, of the range of memory to be held in RAM.

DESCRIPTION

The `HoldMemory` function makes the portion of the address space beginning at `address` and having a size of `count` bytes resident in physical memory and ineligible for paging.

If the `address` parameter supplied to the `HoldMemory` function is not on a page boundary, then it is rounded down to the nearest page boundary. Similarly, if the specified range does not end on a page boundary, the `count` parameter is rounded up so that the entire range of memory is held.

SPECIAL CONSIDERATIONS

Even though `HoldMemory` does not move or purge memory, you should not call it at interrupt time.

ASSEMBLY-LANGUAGE INFORMATION

The trap macro and routine selector for the `HoldMemory` function are

Trap macro	Selector
`_MemoryDispatch`	$0000

The registers on entry and exit for this routine are

Registers on entry

D0	Selector code
A0	Starting address
A1	Number of bytes to hold

Registers on exit

D0	Result code

RESULT CODES

`noErr`	0	No error
`paramErr`	–50	Error in parameter list
`notEnoughMemoryErr`	–620	Insufficient physical memory
`interruptsMaskedErr`	–624	Called with interrupts masked

UnholdMemory

To make a currently held range of memory eligible for paging again, use the `UnholdMemory` function.

```
FUNCTION UnholdMemory (address: UNIV Ptr; count: LongInt): OSErr;
```

`address`	The starting address of the range of memory to be released.
`count`	The size, in bytes, of the range of memory to be released.

DESCRIPTION

The `UnholdMemory` function makes the portion of the address space beginning at `address` and having a size of `count` bytes eligible for paging.

If the `address` parameter supplied to the `UnholdMemory` function is not on a page boundary, then it is rounded down to the nearest page boundary. Similarly, if the specified range does not end on a page boundary, the `count` parameter is rounded up so that the entire range of memory is released.

ASSEMBLY-LANGUAGE INFORMATION

The trap macro and routine selector for the `UnholdMemory` function are

Trap macro	Selector
`_MemoryDispatch`	$0001

The registers on entry and exit for this routine are

Registers on entry

D0	Selector code
A0	Starting address
A1	Number of bytes to release

Registers on exit

D0	Result code

RESULT CODES

`noErr`	0	No error
`paramErr`	–50	Error in parameter list
`notHeldErr`	–621	Specified range of memory is not held
`interruptsMaskedErr`	–624	Called with interrupts masked

Virtual Memory Manager

LockMemory

To make a portion of the address space immovable in physical memory and ineligible for paging, use the `LockMemory` function.

```
FUNCTION LockMemory (address: UNIV Ptr; count: LongInt): OSErr;
```

`address` The starting address of the range of memory to be locked in RAM.

`count` The size, in bytes, of the range of memory to be locked in RAM.

DESCRIPTION

The `LockMemory` function makes the portion of the address space beginning at `address` and having a size of `count` bytes immovable in physical memory and ineligible for paging.

If the `address` parameter supplied to the `LockMemory` function is not on a page boundary, it is rounded down to the nearest page boundary. Similarly, if the specified range does not end on a page boundary, the `count` parameter is rounded up so that the entire range of memory is locked.

The CPU marks locked pages as noncacheable. On Macintosh computers containing the Macintosh IIci ROM, all physical RAM is marked noncacheable.

ASSEMBLY-LANGUAGE INFORMATION

The trap macro and routine selector for the `LockMemory` function are

Trap macro	Selector
`_MemoryDispatch`	$0002

The registers on entry and exit for this routine are

Registers on entry

D0	Selector code
A0	Starting address
A1	Number of bytes to lock

Registers on exit

D0	Result code

RESULT CODES

`noErr`	0	No error
`paramErr`	–50	Error in parameter list
`notEnoughMemoryErr`	–620	Insufficient physical memory
`interruptsMaskedErr`	–624	Called with interrupts masked

LockMemoryContiguous

The `LockMemoryContiguous` function is exactly like the `LockMemory` function, except that it attempts to obtain a contiguous block of physical memory associated with the specified logical address range.

```
FUNCTION LockMemoryContiguous (address: UNIV Ptr; count: LongInt):
                                OSErr;
```

`address` The starting address of the range of memory to be locked in RAM.

`count` The size, in bytes, of the range of memory to be locked in RAM.

DESCRIPTION

The `LockMemoryContiguous` function makes the portion of the address space beginning at `address` and having a size of `count` bytes immovable in physical memory and ineligible for paging. The function attempts to obtain a contiguous block of physical memory associated with the specified logical address range. It might not be possible to make a range physically contiguous if any of the pages contained in the range are already locked.

If the `address` parameter supplied to the `LockMemoryContiguous` function is not on a page boundary, it is rounded down to the nearest page boundary. Similarly, if the specified range does not end on a page boundary, the `count` parameter is rounded up so that the entire range of memory is locked.

The CPU marks locked pages as noncacheable. On Macintosh computers containing the Macintosh IIci ROM, all physical RAM is marked noncacheable.

SPECIAL CONSIDERATIONS

Because a call to `LockMemoryContiguous` is not guaranteed to succeed, all code that uses `LockMemoryContiguous` must have an alternate method for locking the necessary ranges of memory. In general, you should avoid using `LockMemoryContiguous` if at all possible. If you must call it, do so as early as possible—preferably at system startup time—to increase the likelihood that enough contiguous memory can be found.

ASSEMBLY-LANGUAGE INFORMATION

The trap macro and routine selector for the `LockMemoryContiguous` function are

Trap macro	Selector
`_MemoryDispatch`	$0004

The registers on entry and exit for this routine are

Registers on entry

D0	Selector code
A0	Starting address
A1	Number of bytes to unlock

Registers on exit

D0	Result code

RESULT CODES

`noErr`	0	No error
`paramErr`	–50	Error in parameter list
`notEnoughMemoryErr`	–620	Insufficient physical memory
`cannotMakeContiguousErr`	–622	Cannot make specified range contiguous
`interruptsMaskedErr`	–624	Called with interrupts masked

UnlockMemory

To undo the effects of either `LockMemory` or `LockMemoryContiguous`, use the `UnlockMemory` function.

```
FUNCTION UnlockMemory (address: UNIV Ptr; count: LongInt): OSErr;
```

`address`	The starting address of the range of memory to be unlocked.
`count`	The size, in bytes, of the range of memory to be unlocked.

DESCRIPTION

The `UnlockMemory` function makes the portion of the address space beginning at `address` and having a size of `count` bytes movable in real memory and eligible for paging again.

If the `address` parameter supplied to the `UnlockMemory` function is not on a page boundary, then it is rounded down to the nearest page boundary. Similarly, if the specified range does not end on a page boundary, the `count` parameter is rounded up so that the entire range of memory is unlocked.

ASSEMBLY-LANGUAGE INFORMATION

The trap macro and routine selector for the `UnlockMemory` function are

Trap macro	Selector
`_MemoryDispatch`	$0003

The registers on entry and exit for this routine are

Registers on entry

D0	Selector code
A0	Starting address
A1	Number of bytes to unlock

Registers on exit

D0	Result code

RESULT CODES

noErr	0	No error
paramErr	–50	Error in parameter list
notLockedErr	–623	Specified range of memory is not locked
interruptsMaskedErr	–624	Called with interrupts masked

GetPhysical

To translate logical addresses into their corresponding physical addresses, use the `GetPhysical` function.

```
FUNCTION GetPhysical (VAR addresses: LogicalToPhysicalTable;
                        VAR physicalEntryCount: LongInt): OSErr;
```

`addresses` A translation table. On entry, set the `logical` field of this record to the block of memory to translate. On exit, the `physical` field of this record holds the corresponding physical address blocks.

`physicalEntryCount`
The number of physical entries to translate. On entry, set this field to 0 if you want `GetPhysical` to return the number of table entries needed to translate the entire logical address range.

DESCRIPTION

The `GetPhysical` function translates a logical address range into its corresponding physical address ranges. The `logical` field of the `addresses` translation table specifies the logical address range to be translated. `GetPhysical` translates up to the size of the physical table or until it completes the translation, whichever occurs first.

If you call `GetPhysical` with the `physicalEntryCount` parameter set to 0, it returns in `physicalEntryCount` the number of table entries needed to translate the entire address range. In this case, the translation table specified by the `addresses` parameter is unchanged.

If you call `GetPhysical` with the `physicalEntryCount` parameter set to a number greater than 0, it returns in the `physical` field of the `addresses` translation table an array specifying the physical blocks that correspond to the logical address specified in the `logical` field. In the `physicalEntryCount` parameter, `GetPhysical` returns the number of entries in that array (which may be fewer than were asked for). If the `physical` field of the translation table was not large enough to contain all the physical blocks corresponding to the logical block, `GetPhysical` updates the fields of the `logical` memory block to reflect the remaining number of bytes in the logical range left to translate (`count` field) and the next address in the logical address range to translate (`start` field).

Note

The logical address range must be locked to ensure validity of the translation data. ◆

SPECIAL CONSIDERATIONS

The `GetPhysical` function as currently implemented under virtual memory supports only logical RAM. You cannot use `GetPhysical` to translate addresses in the address spaces of the ROM, I/O devices, or NuBus slots. Some Macintosh computers map a portion of the physical RAM into NuBus space, to simulate the presence of a video expansion card. `GetPhysical` returns the result code `paramErr` if you attempt to read that memory.

ASSEMBLY-LANGUAGE INFORMATION

The trap macro and routine selector for the `GetPhysical` function are

Trap macro	Selector
`_MemoryDispatchA0Result`	$0005

The registers on entry and exit for this routine are

Registers on entry

D0	Selector code
A0	Pointer to a translation table
A1	`physicalEntryCount` in table

Registers on exit

A0	`physicalEntryCount` translated
D0	Result code

RESULT CODES

`noErr`	0	No error
`paramErr`	–50	Error in parameter list
`notLockedErr`	–623	Specified range of memory is not locked
`interruptsMaskedErr`	–624	Called with interrupts masked

SEE ALSO

See "Mapping Logical to Physical Addresses," beginning on page 3-16, for a method of calling GetPhysical to translate addresses to be sent to a NuBus master card.

DeferUserFn

To determine whether code that might cause page faults can safely be called immediately, use the DeferUserFn function.

```
FUNCTION DeferUserFn (userFunction: ProcPtr;
                              argument: UNIV Ptr): OSErr;
```

userFunction
The address of the routine to run.

argument A pointer to the argument to pass to the specified routine.

DESCRIPTION

The DeferUserFn function determines whether or not code that might call page faults can safely be called immediately. If the code can be called safely, DeferUserFn calls the routine designated by userFunction with register A0 containing the value designated by argument. If a page fault is in progress, however, the routine address and its parameter are saved, and the routine is deferred until page faults are again permitted.

Note that the routine might be called immediately (before returning to the caller of DeferUserFn). Deferred functions must follow the register conventions used by interrupt handlers: they can use registers A0–A3 and D0–D3, and they must restore all other registers used.

ASSEMBLY-LANGUAGE INFORMATION

The registers on entry and exit for the DeferUserFn function are

Registers on entry

A0 Address of function

D0 Argument for function

Registers on exit

D0 Result code

RESULT CODES

noErr	0	No error
cannotDeferErr	–625	Unable to defer additional user functions

Virtual Memory Debugger Support Routines

This section describes the virtual-memory routines that pertain primarily to debuggers. You need to read this section only if you are implementing a debugger. To determine which debugger functions are present, use the `DebuggerGetMax` function. When entering and exiting the debugging state, use the `DebuggerEnter` and the `DebuggerExit` procedures. To determine whether paging is safe, use the `PageFaultFatal` function. To lock and unlock memory with caching enabled, use the `DebuggerLockMemory` and the `DebuggerUnlockMemory` functions. To poll for keyboard input, use the `DebuggerPoll` procedure. To determine the state of a page of logical memory, use the `GetPageState` function.

DebuggerGetMax

The Memory Manager includes a special routine that debuggers use, instead of the `Gestalt` function, to determine which debugger functions are present.

```
FUNCTION DebuggerGetMax: LongInt;
```

DESCRIPTION

The `DebuggerGetMax` function returns the highest selector number of the debugger routines that are defined in terms of the `_DebugUtil` trap. The numbers correspond to the following routines:

Selector	Routine
$0000	`DebuggerGetMax`
$0001	`DebuggerEnter`
$0002	`DebuggerExit`
$0003	`DebuggerPoll`
$0004	`GetPageState`
$0005	`PageFaultFatal`
$0006	`DebuggerLockMemory`
$0007	`DebuggerUnlockMemory`
$0008	`EnterSupervisorMode`

Of course, you should use the `Gestalt` function to check whether virtual memory is available at all before you call the `DebuggerGetMax` function.

ASSEMBLY-LANGUAGE INFORMATION

The trap macro and routine selector for the `DebuggerGetMax` function are

Trap macro	Selector
`_DebugUtil`	$0000

The registers on entry and exit for this routine are

Registers on entry

D0 Selector code

Registers on exit

D0 Highest available selector

DebuggerEnter

Before entering the debugging state, call the DebuggerEnter procedure.

```
PROCEDURE DebuggerEnter;
```

DESCRIPTION

Call the DebuggerEnter procedure to enter the debugging state. This allows the _DebugUtil trap to make preparations for subsequent debugging calls.

ASSEMBLY-LANGUAGE INFORMATION

The trap macro and routine selector for the DebuggerEnter procedure are

Trap macro	Selector
_DebugUtil	$0001

The registers on entry for this routine are

Registers on entry

D0 Selector code

DebuggerExit

Before exiting the debugging state, call the DebuggerExit procedure.

```
PROCEDURE DebuggerExit;
```

DESCRIPTION

The DebuggerExit procedure allows the _DebugUtil trap to clean up after all debugging calls are completed.

ASSEMBLY-LANGUAGE INFORMATION

The trap macro and routine selector for the `DebuggerExit` procedure are

Trap macro	Selector
`_DebugUtil`	$0002

The registers on entry for this routine are

Registers on entry

D0	Selector code

PageFaultFatal

A debugger can use the `PageFaultFatal` function to determine whether it should capture all bus errors or whether it is safe to allow them to flow through to virtual memory. When paging is safe, the debugger can allow virtual memory to continue servicing page faults, and the user can view all of memory.

```
FUNCTION PageFaultFatal: Boolean;
```

DESCRIPTION

The `PageFaultFatal` function returns `TRUE` if the debugger should not allow the virtual memory's bus-error handler to detect any page faults.

ASSEMBLY-LANGUAGE INFORMATION

The trap macro and routine selector for the `PageFaultFatal` function are

Trap macro	Selector
`_DebugUtil`	$0005

The registers on entry and exit for this routine are

Registers on entry

D0	Selector code

Registers on exit

D0	Returned value

DebuggerLockMemory

To lock a portion of the address space (as the LockMemory function does) while leaving data caching enabled on the affected pages, use the DebuggerLockMemory function.

```
FUNCTION DebuggerLockMemory (address: UNIV Ptr; count: LongInt):
                              OSErr;
```

address — The start address of the range of memory that is to be locked in RAM.

count — The size in bytes of the range of memory that is to be locked in RAM.

DESCRIPTION

The DebuggerLockMemory function makes the portion of the address space beginning at address and having a size of count bytes immovable in physical memory and ineligible for paging. The function leaves data caching enabled on the affected pages.

If the address parameter supplied to the DebuggerLockMemory function is not on a page boundary, then it is rounded down to the nearest page boundary. Similarly, if the specified range does not end on a page boundary, the count parameter is rounded up so that the entire range of memory is locked.

ASSEMBLY-LANGUAGE INFORMATION

The trap macro and routine selector for the DebuggerLockMemory function are

Trap macro	Selector
_DebuggerLockMemory	$0006

The registers on entry and exit for this routine are

Registers on entry

D0	Selector code
A0	Starting address
A1	Number of bytes to hold

Registers on exit

D0	Result code

RESULT CODES

noErr	0	No error
paramErr	–50	Error in parameter list
notEnoughMemoryErr	–620	Insufficient physical memory

DebuggerUnlockMemory

To reverse the effects of DebuggerLockMemory, use the DebuggerUnlockMemory function.

```
FUNCTION DebuggerUnlockMemory (address: UNIV Ptr; count: LongInt):
                                OSErr;
```

address	The starting address of the range of memory that is to be unlocked.
count	The size, in bytes, of the range of memory that is to be unlocked.

DESCRIPTION

The DebuggerUnlockMemory function makes the portion of the address space beginning at address and having a size of count bytes movable in real memory and eligible for paging again.

If the address parameter supplied to the DebuggerUnlockMemory function is not on a page boundary, then it is rounded down to the nearest page boundary. Similarly, if the specified range does not end on a page boundary, the count parameter is rounded up so that the entire range of memory is unlocked.

ASSEMBLY-LANGUAGE INFORMATION

The trap macro and routine selector for the DebuggerUnlockMemory function are

Trap macro	Selector
_DebugUtil	$0007

The registers on entry and exit for this routine are

Registers on entry

D0	Selector code
A0	Starting address
A1	Number of bytes to hold

Registers on exit

D0	Result code

RESULT CODES

noErr	0	No error
paramErr	–50	Error in parameter list
notLockedErr	–623	Specified range of memory is not locked

DebuggerPoll

To poll for keyboard input, use the `DebuggerPoll` procedure.

```
PROCEDURE DebuggerPoll;
```

DESCRIPTION

Call the `DebuggerPoll` procedure, which you can use even if interrupts are disabled, to poll for keyboard input.

ASSEMBLY-LANGUAGE INFORMATION

The trap macro and routine selector for the `DebuggerPoll` procedure are

Trap macro	Selector
`DebugUtil`	$0003

The registers on entry and exit for this routine are

Registers on entry

D0 Selector code

Registers on exit

D0 Result code

GetPageState

To obtain the state of a page of logical memory, use the `GetPageState` function.

```
FUNCTION GetPageState (address: UNIV Ptr): PageState;
```

`address` An address in the page whose state you want to determine.

DESCRIPTION

The `GetPageState` function returns the page state of the page containing the address passed in the `address` parameter. The returned value is one of these constants:

```
TYPE PageState = Integer;

CONST
   kPageInMemory   = 0;           {page is in RAM}
   kPageOnDisk     = 1;           {page is on disk}
   kNotPaged       = 2;           {address is not paged}
```

ASSEMBLY-LANGUAGE INFORMATION

The trap macro and routine selector for the `GetPageState` function are

Trap macro	Selector
`_DebugUtil`	$0004

The registers on entry and exit for this routine are

Registers on entry

A0	Address in the page whose state is to be determined
D0	Selector code

Registers on exit

D0	Page state

Summary of the Virtual Memory Manager

Pascal Summary

Constants

```
CONST
   {Gestalt constants}
   gestaltVMAttr              = 'vm  ';     {virtual memory attributes}
   gestaltVMPresent           = 0;          {bit set if virtual memory present}

   {default number of physical blocks in a translation table}
   defaultPhysicalEntryCount  = 8;

   {page states}
   kPageInMemory              = 0;          {page is in RAM}
   kPageOnDisk                = 1;          {page is on disk}
   kNotPaged                  = 2;          {address is not paged}
```


Data Types

```
TYPE
   PageState            = Integer;


   LogicalToPhysicalTable =            {translation table}
   RECORD
      logical:       MemoryBlock;      {logical block}
      physical:      ARRAY[0..defaultPhysicalEntryCount-1] OF MemoryBlock;
                                       {equivalent physical blocks}
   END;

   MemoryBlock =                       {memory-block record}
   RECORD
      address:       Ptr;              {start of block}
      count:         LongInt;          {size of block}
   END;
```

Routines

Virtual Memory Management

```
FUNCTION HoldMemory           (address: UNIV Ptr; count: LongInt): OSErr;
FUNCTION UnholdMemory         (address: UNIV Ptr; count: LongInt): OSErr;
FUNCTION LockMemory           (address: UNIV Ptr; count: LongInt): OSErr;
FUNCTION LockMemoryContiguous
                              (address: UNIV Ptr; count: LongInt): OSErr;
FUNCTION UnlockMemory         (address: UNIV Ptr; count: LongInt): OSErr;
FUNCTION GetPhysical          (VAR addresses: LogicalToPhysicalTable;
                               VAR physicalEntryCount: LongInt): OSErr;
FUNCTION DeferUserFn          (userFunction: ProcPtr; argument: UNIV Ptr):
                               OSErr;
```

Virtual Memory Debugger Support Routines

```
FUNCTION DebuggerGetMax       : LongInt;
PROCEDURE DebuggerEnter;
PROCEDURE DebuggerExit;
FUNCTION PageFaultFatal       : Boolean;
FUNCTION DebuggerLockMemory  (address: UNIV Ptr; count: LongInt): OSErr;
FUNCTION DebuggerUnlockMemory
                              (address: UNIV Ptr; count: LongInt): OSErr;
PROCEDURE DebuggerPoll;
FUNCTION GetPageState         (address: UNIV Ptr): PageState;
```

C Summary

Constants

```
/*Gestalt constants*/
#define gestaltVMAttr          'vm  ';  /*virtual memory attributes*/
#define gestaltVMPresent        0;      /*bit set if virtual memory present*/

/*default number of physical blocks in table*/
enum {
   defaultPhysicalEntryCount      = 8
};
```

```
/*page states*/
enum {
   kPageInMemory                  = 0,     /*page is in RAM*/
   kPageOnDisk                    = 1,     /*page is on disk*/
   kNotPaged                      = 2      /*address is not paged*/
};
```

Data Types

```
typedef short PageState;

struct LogicalToPhysicalTable {                /*translation table*/
      MemoryBlock        logical;              /*logical block*/
      MemoryBlock        physical[defaultPhysicalEntryCount];
                                               /*equivalent physical blocks*/
   };
typedef struct LogicalToPhysicalTable LogicalToPhysicalTable;

struct MemoryBlock {                           /*memory-block record*/
      void               *address;             /*start of block*/
      unsigned long      count;                /*size of block*/
};
typedef struct MemoryBlock MemoryBlock;
```

Routines

Virtual Memory Management

```
pascal OSErr HoldMemory      (void *address, unsigned long count);
pascal OSErr UnholdMemory    (void *address, unsigned long count);
pascal OSErr LockMemory      (void *address, unsigned long count);
pascal OSErr LockMemoryContiguous
                             (void *address, unsigned long count);
pascal OSErr UnlockMemory    (void *address, unsigned long count);
pascal OSErr GetPhysical     (LogicalToPhysicalTable *addresses,
                              unsigned long *physicalEntryCount);
pascal OSErr DeferUserFn     (ProcPtr userFunction, void *argument);
```

Virtual Memory Debugger Support Routines

```
pascal long DebuggerGetMax   (void);
pascal void DebuggerEnter    (void);
pascal void DebuggerExit     (void);
pascal Boolean PageFaultFatal
                             (void);
pascal OSErr DebuggerLockMemory
                             (void *address, unsigned long count);
pascal OSErr DebuggerUnlockMemory
                             (void *address, unsigned long count);
pascal void DebuggerPoll     (void);
pascal PageState GetPageState
                             (const void *address);
```

Assembly-Language Summary

Data Types

Memory-Block Data Structure

0	`address`	long	start of block
4	`count`	4 bytes	size of block

Translation Table Data Structure

0	`logical`	8 bytes	logical block
8	`physical`	64 bytes	equivalent physical blocks

Trap Macros

Trap Macros Requiring Routine Selectors

`_MemoryDispatch`

Selector	Routine
$0000	`HoldMemory`
$0001	`UnholdMemory`
$0002	`LockMemory`
$0003	`UnlockMemory`
$0004	`LockMemoryContiguous`

_MemoryDispatchA0Result

Selector	Routine
$0005	GetPhysical

_DebugUtil

Selector	Routine
$0000	DebuggerGetMax
$0001	DebuggerEnter
$0002	DebuggerExit
$0003	DebuggerPoll
$0004	GetPageState
$0005	PageFaultFatal
$0006	DebuggerLockMemory
$0007	DebuggerUnlockMemory
$0008	EnterSupervisorMode

Result Codes

noErr	0	No error
paramErr	–50	Error in parameter list
notEnoughMemoryErr	–620	Insufficient physical memory
notHeldErr	–621	Specified range of memory is not held
cannotMakeContiguousErr	–622	Cannot make specified range contiguous
notLockedErr	–623	Specified range of memory is not locked
interruptsMaskedErr	–624	Called with interrupts masked
cannotDeferErr	–625	Unable to defer additional user functions

Memory Management Utilities

Contents

This chapter describes a number of utility routines you can use to control certain aspects of the memory environment in Macintosh computers. Some features of the memory environment are controlled by the user through the Memory control panel; others are controlled by the Process Manager or other parts of the Macintosh Operating System and Toolbox. The utility routines described in this chapter allow you to modify some of the normal operations of the Operating System or the Toolbox.

You need to read this chapter if your application or driver

- installs completion routines or interrupt tasks that are executed by the Operating System or Toolbox, not directly by your application
- modifies the addressing mode or converts addresses from one form to another
- moves executable code in memory, or performs DMA operations

To use this chapter, you should be familiar with the information in the chapter "Introduction to Memory Management" earlier in this book. Also, you can read the chapter "Introduction to Processes and Tasks" in *Inside Macintosh: Processes* for a related discussion of the A5 register.

This chapter begins with a brief description of the Memory control panel, which allows users to alter several aspects of the Operating System's memory configuration. Then it shows how you can use the Memory Management Utilities to

- set up the A5 register so that your application-defined completion routines and interrupt tasks can access your application's global variables
- get the value of the A5 register so that you can read your application's QuickDraw global variables from within stand-alone code
- get or set a computer's address-translation mode
- strip the flag bits from a master pointer or other memory address
- convert 24-bit addresses to 32-bit addresses
- flush the microprocessor's instruction and data caches

The Memory Control Panel

A user can alter several aspects of the system memory configuration by setting certain controls in the Memory control panel. This panel contains controls governing the operation of the disk cache, virtual memory, and the addressing mode used by the Memory Manager. Figure 4-1 shows the Memory control panel.

Figure 4-1 The Memory control panel

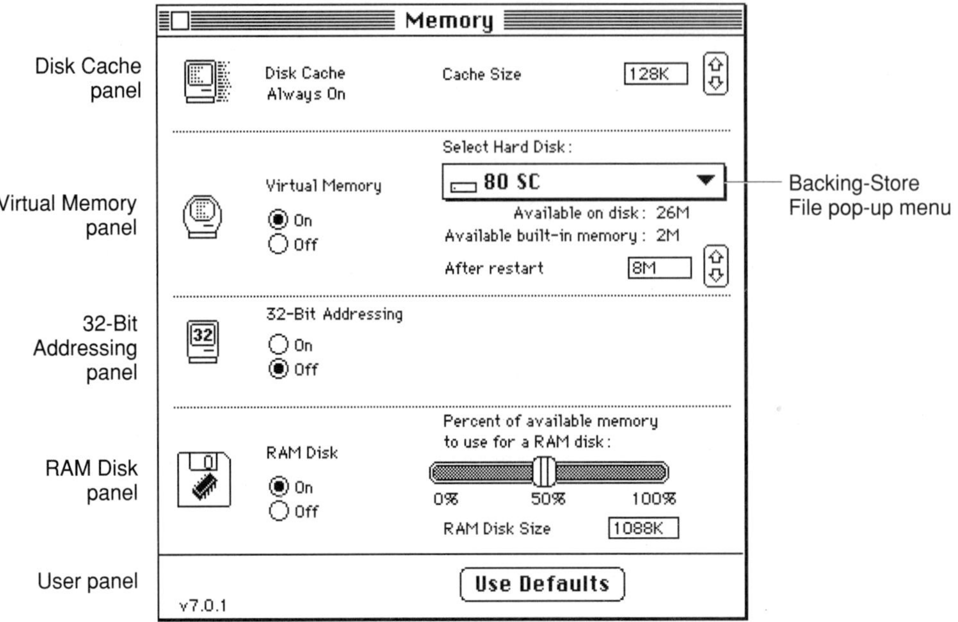

The Disk Cache panel replaces the HFS RAM Cache panel (part of the General control panel) used in earlier versions of system software. A **disk cache** is a part of RAM that acts as an intermediate buffer when data is read from and written to file systems on secondary storage devices. Data is saved there in case it is needed again in the very near future. If it is, the Operating System reads the data from the disk cache rather than the secondary storage device (which would take considerably longer). By increasing the cache size, the user increases the likelihood that data recently read from or written to the file system will be in the cache. The controls in the Disk Cache panel allow the user to configure the size of the disk cache used by the Operating System during file access operations. In system software version 7.0, unlike earlier versions, the user cannot turn off disk caching.

In system software version 7.0, the minimum cache size is 16 KB. The default size is 32 KB per megabyte of installed RAM (thus, the default disk cache size for a computer with 4 MB of RAM is 128 KB). The maximum disk cache size is 320 KB per megabyte of installed RAM (thus, the maximum disk cache size for a computer with 4 MB of RAM is 1280 KB). The operation of the disk cache is completely transparent to your application.

Note

These cache size values are provided for informational purposes only and may differ in later system software versions or on different Macintosh computers. In addition, the use of RAM for a RAM-based video interface or a RAM disk affects the amount of RAM available for the disk cache. ◆

The Virtual Memory panel allows the user to set various features of virtual memory, including whether virtual memory is turned on and, if so, how much is available. The user can also specify the volume of the **backing-store file,** in which the Virtual Memory Manager stores unused portions of code and data. Changes to the virtual memory configuration do not take effect until the user restarts the computer. Note that the Virtual Memory panel appears only on computers that support virtual memory. For information on how your application can interact with virtual memory, see the chapter "Virtual Memory Manager" in this book.

Using the 32-Bit Addressing controls, the user can select the maximum size of the address space used in the computer. The maximum size of the address space is determined by the number of bits used to store memory addresses, as explained in the chapter "Virtual Memory Manager" in this book. The 32-Bit Addressing panel appears only on computers that support 32-bit addressing mode. By clicking the panel's controls, the user can turn 32-bit addressing off and on. Changes made in this panel do not go into effect until the user restarts the computer.

Using the RAM Disk controls, the user can determine the amount of the available RAM that is to be treated as a **RAM disk,** a portion of RAM reserved for use as a temporary storage device. It is most useful to create a RAM disk on battery-powered computers (such as the Macintosh PowerBook computers) because the computer uses less energy to access RAM than to access a hard disk or a floppy disk.

About the Memory Management Utilities

You can use the Memory Management Utilities to ensure that

- your application's callback routines, interrupt tasks, and stand-alone code can access application global variables or QuickDraw global variables
- your application or driver functions properly in both 24- and 32-bit modes
- data or instructions in the microprocessor's internal caches remain consistent with data or instructions in RAM

This section explains when and why you might need to use these utilities; for actual implementation details, see the section "Using the Memory Management Utilities," which begins on page 4-13.

The A5 Register

If you write code that accesses your application's A5 world (usually to read or write the application global variables) at a time that your application is not the current application, you must ensure that the A5 register points to the boundary between your application's parameters and global variables. Because the Operating System accesses your A5 world relative to the address stored in the A5 register, you can obtain unpredictable results if you attempt to read or write data in your A5 world when the contents of A5 are not valid.

There are two general cases in which code might execute when the contents of the A5 register are invalid:

- when you install a completion routine that is executed when some other operation (for instance, writing data to disk or playing a sound) is completed
- when you install a routine (for instance, a VBL task) that is called in response to an interrupt

If you install code that is to be executed at either of these times, you must make sure to set up the A5 register upon entry and to restore it before exit. The sections "Accessing the A5 World in Completion Routines" on page 4-14 and "Accessing the A5 World in Interrupt Tasks" on page 4-16 describe how to do this in each case.

You might also need to determine the location of your application's A5 world if you want to read information in it from within a stand-alone code segment. You might want to do this in application-defined definition procedures called on behalf of your application. These include

- control definition functions
- window definition functions
- menu definition functions

The problem with these kinds of stand-alone code segments is *not* that the value in the A5 register is incorrect at the time they are executed; rather, it is that they have no A5 world at all. During execution, these stand-alone code segments can effectively "borrow" the A5 world of the current application. However, they must be compiled and linked separately from your application. (A custom window definition procedure, for example, is separately compiled and linked, and then included as a resource of type `'WDEF'` in your application's resource fork.) The linker cannot resolve any offsets from the value in the A5 register, because the code segment doesn't have an A5 world.

A stand-alone code segment can solve this problem quite simply at run time, by determining the location of your application's A5 world and then copying the data it needs to access into blocks of memory that it allocates itself. In the code segment, all references to data in the A5 world are indirect: the code segment manipulates local copies of the relevant data. Using this technique, you can avoid explicit symbolic references to the A5 world, which the linker cannot resolve.

In theory, you could use this technique of copying global data into a stand-alone code segment's private storage to access any data contained in your application's A5 world. In practice, however, the A5 world can contain so much data that you wouldn't want to make local copies of it all. In addition, the precise organization of the entire A5 world is not generally determinate. Usually, a custom definition procedure or other stand-alone code segment needs to read only the QuickDraw global variables, which are of fixed size and have a well-documented organization. See the section "Using QuickDraw Global Variables in Stand-Alone Code" on page 4-18 for a complete description of how to read your application's QuickDraw global variables from within a stand-alone code segment.

Addressing Modes

The Memory Manager on the original Macintosh computers uses a 24-bit addressing mode. To the underlying hardware, only the lower 24 bits of any 32-bit address are significant. The CPU effectively ignores the upper 8 bits in a memory address by using a 24-bit address-translation mode. In this mode, the CPU (or the MMU coprocessor, if present) maps all addresses to their lower-order 24 bits whenever it reads or writes a memory location. This led both system software developers and third-party software developers to put those upper 8 bits to other uses. For example, the Memory Manager itself uses the upper 8 bits of the address in a master pointer to maintain information about the associated relocatable block. These upper 8 bits are known as **master pointer flag bits.**

When the Operating System is running in 24-bit mode, you can address at most 1 MB of the address space assigned to a NuBus expansion card. Some cards, however, can work with far more than 1 MB of memory. As a result, a device driver might need to switch the Operating System into 32-bit mode temporarily, so that it can access the entire address range of the associated device (perhaps to copy data from the device's RAM into the heap). When 32-bit address translation is enabled, the CPU or the MMU does not ignore the upper 8 bits of a memory address.

Note
Don't confuse the current address-translation mode of the Macintosh hardware with the current addressing state of the Memory Manager. The addressing state of the Memory Manager is selectable on a per-boot basis and cannot be changed by an application or driver. The address-translation mode of the underlying hardware is controlled by the CPU and MMU (if one is available) and can be changed, if necessary, at any time. ◆

The Operating System provides two utilities, `GetMMUMode` and `SwapMMUMode`, that allow you to get and set the current address-translation mode. See "Switching Addressing Modes" on page 4-20 for details.

If your device driver does in fact temporarily set the Macintosh hardware into 32-bit address-translation mode, you need to be careful when you pass addresses to the associated device. Suppose, for example, that your driver wants to transfer data to an address in the heap (which is under the control of the Memory Manager). If the 24-bit Memory Manager is in operation, you need to strip the high byte from the memory address; otherwise, the CPU would interpret the high byte of flags as part of the address and transfer the data to the wrong location.

Note
You might also need to make the block of memory in the heap immovable in physical memory, so that it is not paged out under virtual memory. See the discussion of locking memory in the chapter "Virtual Memory Manager" in this book. ◆

The Operating System provides the `StripAddress` function, which you can use to **strip** the high-order byte from a memory address. Even if you are not writing Macintosh drivers, you might still find it useful to call `StripAddress`. For example, suppose you need to compare two memory addresses (two master pointers, perhaps). If the system is running the 24-bit Memory Manager and you compare those addresses without first clearing the flag bits, you might get invalid results. You should first call `StripAddress` to convert those addresses to their correct format before comparing them.

As you can see, the operation of `StripAddress` is not dependent on the 24-bit or 32-bit address translation state of the hardware, but on the 24-bit or 32-bit addressing state of the Memory Manager. You need to call `StripAddress` only when the 24-bit Memory Manager is operating. When the 32-bit Memory Manager is operating, `StripAddress` returns unchanged any addresses passed to it, because they are already valid 32-bit addresses. See "Stripping Flag Bits From Memory Addresses" on page 4-21 for complete details on calling `StripAddress`.

Address Translation

When a driver or other software component switches the system to the 32-bit address-translation mode (perhaps to manipulate special hardware on a slot device), certain addresses normally accessible in 24-bit mode are not mapped to the same location by the Macintosh hardware. In particular, the Virtual Memory Manager uses some of the slot address space as part of the addressable RAM. In that case, the standard 24-to-32 bit translation is not valid for slot spaces that the MMU has remapped into the application address space.

You can use the `Translate24To32` function to translate 24-bit addresses that might have been remapped by the Macintosh hardware. If you intend to use 24-bit addresses when your software is executing in 32-bit mode, your code should check for the presence of that function. If it is available, you should use it to map 24-bit addresses into the 32-bit address space. For details, see "Translating Memory Addresses" on page 4-23.

Processor Caches

Some members of the Motorola MC680x0 family of microprocessors contain internal caches that can significantly improve the overall performance of software executing on those microprocessors. For example, the MC68020 microprocessor contains a 256-byte on-board **instruction cache,** an area of memory within the microprocessor that stores the most recently executed instructions. Whenever the processor needs to fetch an instruction, it first checks the instruction cache to determine whether the word required is in the cache. The operation is much faster when the information is in the cache than when it is only in RAM (which is external to the microprocessor).

Some other members of the MC680x0 family of microprocessors also contain an internal **data cache,** an area of memory that holds recently accessed data. The data cache operates much as the instruction cache does, but it caches data instead of instructions. Before reading data from RAM, the microprocessor checks the data cache to determine whether the operand required for an instruction is in the cache. Again, the overall performance of the software is greatly increased by the operation of the data cache.

Table 4-1 lists the available caches and their sizes for the various microprocessors currently used in Macintosh computers.

Table 4-1 Caches available in MC680x0 microprocessors

Microprocessor	Instruction cache?	Data cache?
MC68000	No	No
MC68020	Yes (256 bytes)	No
MC68030	Yes (256 bytes)	Yes (256 bytes)
MC68040	Yes (4 KB)	Yes (4 KB)

The operation of any available instruction and data caches is generally transparent to your application. In certain cases, however, you need to make sure that the information in the caches and the corresponding information in main memory remain consistent. When some information in RAM changes but the corresponding information in the cache does not, the cached information is said to be **stale.** The following two sections describe in detail how cached instructions and data can become stale. You can avoid using stale instructions or data by **flushing** the affected cache whenever you do something that can cause instructions or data to become stale. See "Manipulating the Processor Caches," beginning on page 4-29, for routines that you can use to maintain consistency between a cache and main memory.

Stale Instructions

Any time that you modify part of the executable code of your application or other software, you risk creating **stale instructions** in the instruction cache. Recall that the microprocessor stores the most recently executed instructions in its internal instruction cache, separately from main memory. Whenever your code modifies itself or any data in memory that contains executable code, there is a possibility that a copy of the modified instructions will be in the instruction cache (because they were executed recently). If so, attempting to execute the modified instructions actually results in the execution of the cached instructions, which are stale.

You can avoid using stale instructions by flushing the instruction cache every time you modify executable instructions in memory. Flushing the cache invalidates all entries in it and forces the processor to refill the cache from main memory.

IMPORTANT

Flushing the instruction cache has an adverse effect on the CPU's performance. You should flush the instruction cache only when absolutely necessary. ▲

Any code that modifies itself directly is likely to create stale instructions in the instruction cache. In addition, you can create stale instructions by modifying other parts of memory that contain executable instructions. For example, if you modify jump table entries, you'll need to flush the instruction cache to avoid using stale instructions. Similarly, if you install patches by copying code from one part of memory to another and modifying `JMP` instructions in order to execute the original routine, you'll need to flush the instruction cache. See the description of the `FlushInstructionCache` procedure on page 4-30 for details.

The system software automatically flushes the instruction cache when you call certain traps that are often used to move code from one location to another in memory. The system flushes the instruction cache whenever you call `_BlockMove`, `_Read`, `_LoadSeg`, and `_UnloadSeg`.

▲ **WARNING**

The `_BlockMove` trap is not guaranteed to flush the instruction cache for blocks that are 12 bytes or smaller. If you use `_BlockMove` to move very small blocks of code, you should flush the instruction cache yourself. ▲

Other traps may flush the instruction cache. In general, you need to worry about stale instructions only when your application moves code and not when the system software moves it.

Stale Data

A cache may contain **stale data** whenever information in RAM is changed and that information is already cached in the microprocessor's data cache. Suppose, for example, that a computer contains an expansion card capable of DMA data transfers from the card to main memory. The card typically reads commands from a buffer in RAM, executes the commands, and writes status information back to the buffer when the command completes. Before the card reads a command, the CPU sets up the command buffer and initializes the status code to 0. Figure 4-2 shows this situation on a computer with an MC68030 microprocessor.

Figure 4-2 Initializing a status code

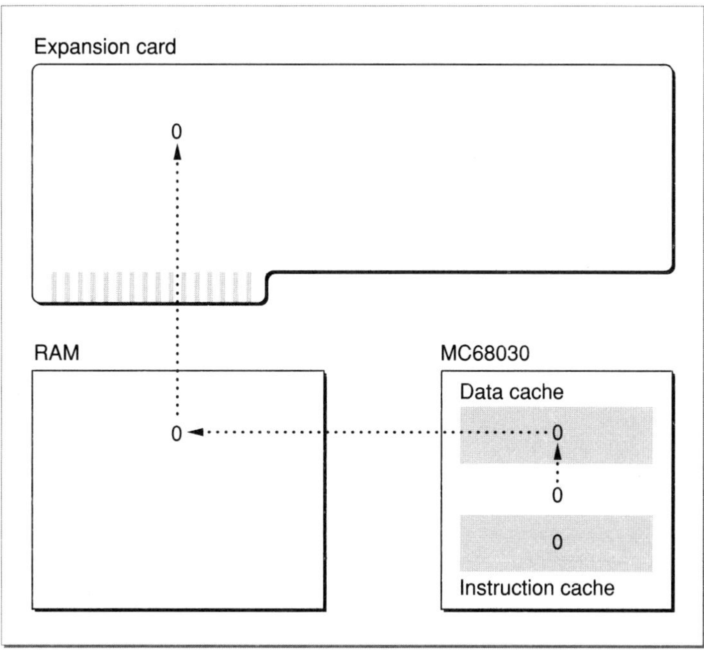

The MC68030 has a **write-through cache:** any data written to the cache is immediately written out to RAM (to avoid stale data in RAM). As a result, the cache and RAM both contain the same value (0) for the status code. Suppose next that the expansion card executes the first command and writes a nonzero status code to RAM. The card then sends an interrupt to the CPU, indicating that the operation has completed.

At this point, the microprocessor might attempt to read the status code returned by the external hardware. However, because the status code is in the microprocessor's data cache, the CPU reads the value in the cache, which is stale, instead of the value in main memory (see Figure 4-3).

Figure 4-3 Reading stale data

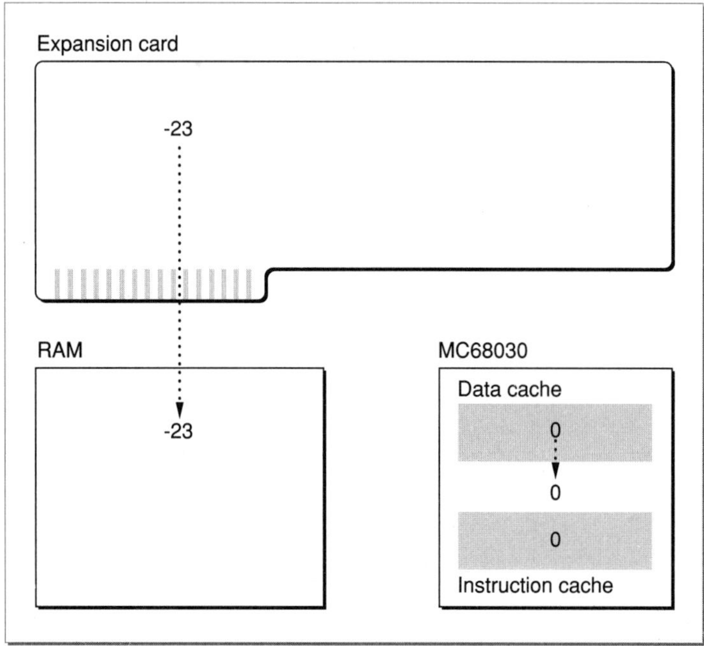

To avoid using this stale data, have your driver flush the data cache whenever you transfer data directly into main memory.

IMPORTANT
Flushing the data cache has an adverse effect on the CPU's performance. You should flush the data cache only when absolutely necessary. ▲

The MC68040 has a **copy-back cache:** any data written to the cache is written to RAM only when necessary to make room in the cache for data accessed more recently or when the cache is explicitly flushed. As you can see, a copy-back cache allows for even greater performance improvements than a write-through cache, because the data in the cache has to be written to main memory less often. This is extremely valuable for relatively small amounts of data that are needed for only a short while, such as local stack frames for C or Pascal function calls.

Because the data in a copy-back cache is written to main memory only in certain circumstances, it's possible to get stale data in RAM. If you write data that is to be read by non-CPU devices (such as an expansion card that performs DMA operations), you need to flush the data cache before instructing the alternate bus master to read that data. If you don't update the RAM, the DMA transfer from RAM will read stale data.

A copy-back data cache can also lead to the use of invalid instructions if the stale data in RAM contains executable code. When fetching instructions, the CPU looks only in the instruction cache and (if necessary) in main memory, not in the data cache. Because the instruction and data caches are separate, it's possible that the CPU will fetch invalid instructions from memory, in the following way. Suppose that you alter some jump table entries and, in doing so, write the value $A9F0 (that is, the trap number of the _LoadSeg trap) to memory. If the data cache is a copy-back cache, the data in main memory is not updated immediately, but only when necessary to make room in the cache (or when you explicitly flush the cache). As a result, the CPU might read invalid instructions from memory when attempting to execute a routine whose jump table entry you changed. Figure 4-4 illustrates this problem.

Figure 4-4 Reading invalid instructions

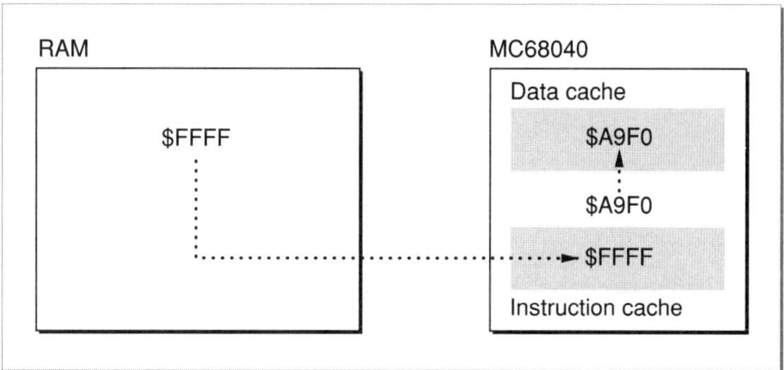

To avoid reading invalid instructions in this way, you need to flush the data cache before calling any routines whose jump table entries you've altered. More generally, whenever you need to flush the instruction cache, you also first need to flush the data cache—but only if you've changed any executable code and those changes might not have been written to main memory.

Another way to avoid using stale data is to prevent the data from being cached (and hence from becoming stale). The Virtual Memory Manager function LockMemory locks a specified range of pages in physical RAM and either disables the data cache or marks the specified pages as noncacheable (depending on what's possible and what makes the most sense). Accordingly, you need not explicitly flush the processor's data cache for data buffers located in pages that are locked in memory. See the chapter "Virtual Memory Manager" in this book for more information about locking page ranges.

Using the Memory Management Utilities

This section describes how you can

- save and restore the value of the A5 register so that you can access your application's A5 world in completion routines or other interrupt tasks
- access your application's QuickDraw global variables from within stand-alone code
- change the address-translation mode so that you can temporarily use 32-bit addresses

- strip the flag bits from a master pointer or other memory address
- convert 24-bit addresses to 32-bit addresses

Accessing the A5 World in Completion Routines

Some Toolbox and Operating System routines require you to pass the address of an application-defined **callback routine,** usually in a variable of type `ProcPtr`. After a certain condition has been met, the Toolbox executes the specified routine. The exact time at which the Toolbox executes the routine varies. The timing of execution is determined by the Toolbox routine to which you passed the routine's address and the action that must be completed before the routine is called.

Callback routines are quite common in the Macintosh system software. A grow-zone function, for instance, is an application-defined callback routine that is called every time the Memory Manager cannot find enough space in your heap to honor a memory-allocation request. Similarly, if your application plays a sound asynchronously, you can have the Sound Manager execute a **completion routine** after the sound is played. The completion routine might release the sound channel used to play the sound or perform other cleanup operations.

In general, you cannot predict what your application will be doing when an asynchronous completion or callback routine is actually executed. The routine could be called while your application is executing code of its own or executing another Toolbox or Operating System routine.

Note

The completion or callback routine might even be called when your application is in the background. Before executing a completion or callback routine belonging to your application, the Process Manager checks whether your application is in the foreground. If not, the Process Manager performs a minor switch to give your application temporary control of the CPU. ◆

Many Toolbox and Operating System routines do not need to access the calling application's global variables, QuickDraw global variables, or jump table. As a result, they sometimes use the A5 register for their own purposes. They save the current value of the register upon entry, modify the register as necessary, and then restore the original value on exit. As you can see, if one of these routines is executing when your callback routine is executed, your callback routine cannot depend on the value in the A5 register. This effectively prevents your callback routine from using any part of its A5 world.

To solve this problem, simply use the strategy that the Toolbox employs when it takes over the A5 register: save the current value in the A5 register at the start of your callback procedure, install your application's A5 value, and then restore the original value when you exit. Listing 4-1 illustrates a very simple grow-zone function that uses this technique. It uses the `SetCurrentA5` and `SetA5` utilities to manipulate the A5 register.

Listing 4-1 A sample grow-zone function

```
FUNCTION MyGrowZone (cbNeeded: Size): LongInt;
VAR
   theA5:   LongInt;           {value of A5 when function is called}
BEGIN
   theA5 := SetCurrentA5;      {remember current value of A5; install ours}
   IF (gEmergencyMemory^ <> NIL) & (gEmergencyMemory <> GZSaveHnd) THEN
      BEGIN
         EmptyHandle(gEmergencyMemory);
         MyGrowZone := kEmergencyMemorySize;
      END
   ELSE
      MyGrowZone := 0;         {no more memory to release}
   theA5 := SetA5(theA5);      {restore previous value of A5}
END;
```

The function `SetCurrentA5` does two things: it returns the current value in the A5 register, and it sets the A5 register to the value of the `CurrentA5` low-memory global variable. This global variable always contains a value that points to the boundary between the current application's parameters and its global variables. The `MyGrowZone` function defined in Listing 4-1 calls `SetCurrentA5` on entry to make sure that it can read the value of the `gEmergencyMemory` global variable.

The function `SetA5` also does two things: it returns the current value in the A5 register, and it sets the A5 register to whatever value you pass to the function. The `MyGrowZone` function calls `SetA5` with the original value of the A5 register as the parameter. In this case, the value returned by `SetA5` is ignored.

There is no way to test whether, at the time your callback routine is called, your application is executing a Toolbox routine that could change the A5 register. Therefore, to be safe, you should save and restore the A5 register in any callback routine that accesses any part of your A5 world. Such routines include

- grow-zone functions
- Sound Manager completion routines
- File Manager I/O completion routines
- control-action procedures
- TextEdit word-break and click-loop routines
- trap patches
- custom menu definition, window definition, and control definition procedures

See the section of *Inside Macintosh* describing any particular completion or callback routine for details on whether you need to save and restore the A5 register in this way.

Accessing the A5 World in Interrupt Tasks

Sometimes, an application-defined routine executes at a time when you can't reliably call `SetCurrentA5`. For example, if your application is not the current application and you call `SetCurrentA5` as illustrated in Listing 4-1, the function will not return your application's value of `CurrentA5`. The `SetCurrentA5` function always returns the value of the low-memory global variable `CurrentA5`, which always belongs to the *current* application. You'll end up reading some other application's A5 world.

In general, you cannot reliably call `SetCurrentA5` in any code that is executed in response to an interrupt, including the following:

- Time Manager tasks
- VBL tasks
- tasks installed using the Deferred Task Manager
- Notification Manager response procedures

Instead of calling `SetCurrentA5` at interrupt time, you can call it at noninterrupt time when yours is the current application. Then store the returned value where you can read it at interrupt time. For example, the Notification Manager allows you to store information in the notification record passed to `NMInstall`. When you set up a notification record, you can use the `nmRefCon` field to hold the value in the A5 register. Listing 4-2 illustrates how to save the current value in the A5 register and pass that value to a response procedure.

Listing 4-2 Passing A5 to a notification response procedure

```
VAR
   gMyNotification:  NMRec;            {a notification record}

BEGIN
   WITH gMyNotification DO
   BEGIN
      qType := ORD(nmType);            {set queue type}
      nmMark := 1;                     {put mark in Application menu}
      nmIcon := NIL;                   {no alternating icon}
      nmSound := Handle(-1);           {play system alert sound}
      nmStr := NIL;                    {no alert box}
      nmResp := @SampleResponse;       {set response procedure}
      nmRefCon := SetCurrentA5;        {pass A5 to notification task}
   END;
END;
```

The key step is to save the value of `CurrentA5` where the response procedure can find it—in this case, in the `nmRefCon` field. You must call `SetCurrentA5` at noninterrupt time; otherwise, you cannot be certain that it will return the correct value.

When the notification response procedure is executed, its first task should be to call the `SetA5` function, which sets register A5 to the value stored in the `nmRefCon` field. At the end of the routine, the notification response procedure should call the `SetA5` function again to restore the previous value of register A5. Listing 4-3 shows a simple response procedure that sets up the A5 register, modifies a global variable, and then restores the A5 register.

Listing 4-3 Setting up and restoring the A5 register at interrupt time

```
PROCEDURE SampleResponse (nmReqPtr: NMRecPtr);
VAR
   oldA5:       LongInt;         {A5 when procedure is called}
BEGIN
   oldA5 := SetA5(nmReqPtr^.nmRefCon);
                                 {set A5 to the application's A5}
   gNotifReceived := TRUE;       {set an application global }
                                 { to show alert was received}
   oldA5 := SetA5(oldA5);        {restore A5 to original value}
END;
```

Note

Many optimizing compilers (including MPW) might put the address of a global variable used by the interrupt routine into a register before the call to `SetA5`, thereby possibly generating incorrect references to global data. To avoid this problem, you can divide your completion routine into two separate routines, one to set up and restore A5 and one to do the actual completion work. Check the documentation for your development system to see if this division is necessary, or contact Macintosh Developer Technical Support. ◆

Several of the other managers that you can use to install interrupt code—including the Deferred Task Manager, the Time Manager, and the Vertical Retrace Manager—do not include a reference constant field in their task records. Therefore, if you wish to access global variables from within one of these tasks, you must use another mechanism to attach the value of the A5 register to the task record.

To do this, you can define a new record that contains the task record and your own reference constant field. You can initialize the task record as you normally would and then copy the value of your application's A5 register into the reference constant field you created. Then, when you obtain a pointer to the task record at interrupt time, you can use your knowledge of the size of the task record to compute the location of your reference constant field. See the chapters "Time Manager" and "Vertical Retrace Manager" in *Inside Macintosh: Processes* for detailed illustrations of these techniques.

Using QuickDraw Global Variables in Stand-Alone Code

If you are writing a stand-alone code segment such as a definition procedure for a window, menu, or control, you might want routines in that segment to examine the QuickDraw global variables of the current application. For example, you might want a control definition function to reference some of the QuickDraw global variables, such as `thePort`, `screenBits`, or the predefined patterns. Stand-alone segments, however, have no A5 world; if you try to link a stand-alone code segment that references your application's global variables, the linker may be unable to resolve those references.

To solve this problem, you can have the definition function find the value of the application's A5 register (by calling the `SetCurrentA5` function) and then use that information to copy all of the application's QuickDraw global variables into a record in the function's own private storage. Listing 4-4 defines a record type with the same structure as the QuickDraw global variables. Note that `randSeed` is stored lowest in memory and `thePort` is stored highest in memory.

Listing 4-4 Structure of the QuickDraw global variables

```
TYPE
   QDVarRecPtr = ^QDVarRec;
   QDVarRec =
   RECORD
      randSeed:   LongInt;        {for random-number generator}
      screenBits: BitMap;         {rectangle enclosing screen}
      arrow:      Cursor;         {standard arrow cursor}
      dkGray:     Pattern;        {75% gray pattern}
      ltGray:     Pattern;        {25% gray pattern}
      gray:       Pattern;        {50% gray pattern}
      black:      Pattern;        {all-black pattern}
      white:      Pattern;        {all-white pattern}
      thePort:    GrafPtr;        {pointer to current GrafPort}
   END;
```

The location of these variables is linker-dependent. However, the A5 register always points to the last of these global variables, `thePort`. The Operating System references all other QuickDraw global variables as negative offsets from `thePort`. Therefore, you must dereference the value in A5 (to obtain the address of `thePort`), and then subtract the combined size of the other QuickDraw global variables from that address. The difference is a pointer to the first of the QuickDraw global variables, `randSeed`. You can copy the entire record into a local variable simply by dereferencing that pointer, as illustrated in Listing 4-5.

Listing 4-5 Copying the QuickDraw global variables into a record

```
PROCEDURE GetQDVars (VAR qdVars: QDVarRec);
TYPE
   LongPtr = ^LongInt;
BEGIN
   qdVars := QDVarRecPtr(LongPtr(SetCurrentA5)^ -
                           (SizeOf(QDVarRec) - SizeOf(thePort)))^;
END;
```

Thereafter, your stand-alone code segment can read QuickDraw global variables through the structure returned by `GetQDVars`. Listing 4-6 defines a very simple draw routine for a control definition function. After reading the calling application's QuickDraw global variables, the draw routine paints a rectangle with a pattern.

Listing 4-6 A control's draw routine using the calling application's QuickDraw patterns

```
PROCEDURE DoDraw (varCode: Intcgcr; myControl: ControlHandle;
                  flag: Integer);
VAR
   cRect: Rect;
   qdVars: QDVarRec;
   origPenState: PenState;
CONST
   kDraw = 1;                          {constant to specify drawing}
BEGIN
   GetPenState(origPenState);          {get original pen state}
   cRect := myControl^^.contrlRect;    {get control's rectangle}
   IF flag = kDraw THEN
      BEGIN
         GetQDVars(qdVars);            {patterns are QD globals}
         PenPat(qdVars.gray);          {install desired pattern}
         PaintRect(cRect);             {paint the control}
      END;
   SetPenState(origPenState);          {restore original pen state}
END;
```

The `DoDraw` drawing routine defined in Listing 4-6 retrieves the calling application's QuickDraw global variables and paints the control rectangle with a light gray pattern. It also saves and restores the pen state, because the `PenPat` procedure changes that state.

Switching Addressing Modes

If you are writing a driver for a slot-card device, you can use the `SwapMMUMode` procedure to change to 32-bit address-translation mode temporarily, as follows:

```
myMode := true32b;                {specify switch to 32-bit mode}
SwapMMUMode(myMode);              {perform switch}
```

The parameter passed to `SwapMMUMode` must be a variable that is equal to the constant `false32b` or the constant `true32b`.

```
CONST
   false32b    = 0;               {24-bit addressing mode}
   true32b     = 1;               {32-bit addressing mode}
```

The `SwapMMUMode` procedure switches to the specified mode and then changes the parameter to indicate the mode previously in use. Thereafter, you can restore the previous address-translation mode by again calling

```
SwapMMUMode(myMode);
```

Note
You should switch to 32-bit mode only if the computer supports 32-bit addressing. To find out whether a system supports 32-bit mode and whether a system started up in 32-bit mode, use the `Gestalt` function, described in the chapter "Gestalt Manager" in *Inside Macintosh: Operating System Utilities*. To determine the current address-translation mode, call the `GetMMUMode` function. ◆

If you do call `SwapMMUMode`, be careful to avoid situations that can cause the system to read an invalid address from the program counter. When the system is in 24-bit mode and you load a code resource into a block of memory (for example, by calling `GetResource`), the high byte of that block's master pointer contains Memory Manager flag bits. If you try to execute that code by performing an assembly-language `JSR` instruction (typically `JSR (A0)`, with the master pointer in register A0), the entire master pointer is translated directly into the program counter. This, however, is not a valid 32-bit address. As soon as you switch to 32-bit mode, the program counter contains an invalid value. This is virtually certain to cause the system to crash.

Note
This problem can arise when you change to 32-bit mode in code loaded from a resource or placed into a block of memory that was allocated by calls to Memory Manager routines. It does not arise with standard `'CODE'` resources because the Segment Manager fixes the program counter. ◆

To avoid this problem, simply call StripAddress on the address in the program counter before you call SwapMMUMode. Listing 4-7 shows one way to do this.

Listing 4-7 Stripping the program counter

```
PROCEDURE FixPC;
   INLINE   $41FA, $000A,    {LEA *+$000C,A0}
            $2008,           {MOVE.L A0,D0}
            $A055,           {_StripAddress}
            $2040,           {MOVEA.L D0,A0}
            $4ED0;           {JMP (A0); jump to next instruction}
```

For these same reasons, you also need to call StripAddress on any address you pass to the _SetTrapAddress trap, if the address references a block in your application heap.

Stripping Flag Bits From Memory Addresses

If your code runs on a system that might have started up with the 24-bit Memory Manager, you sometimes need to **strip** the flag bits from a memory address before you use it. The Operating System provides the StripAddress function for this purpose.

The StripAddress function takes an address as a parameter and returns the value of the address's low-order 3 bytes if the computer started up in 24-bit mode. If the system started up in 32-bit mode, StripAddress returns the address unchanged (because it must already be a valid 32-bit address). Note that if a system starts up in 32-bit mode, you cannot switch it to 24-bit mode.

▲ **WARNING**
If you pass a valid 32-bit address to StripAddress and the computer started in 24-bit mode, the function still strips off the high byte of the address, thus probably rendering the address invalid. You can pass 32-bit addresses to StripAddress if the system started up in 32-bit mode, but then the function does nothing to the address. Therefore, you should ordinarily pass only 24-bit addresses to the StripAddress function. ▲

You need to use StripAddress primarily in device drivers or other software that communicates heap addresses to external hardware (such as a NuBus card). Because the external hardware might interpret the flag bits of a master pointer as part of the address, you need to call StripAddress to clear those flag bits.

There is nothing inherently dangerous about 24-bit addresses. They cause problems only when you try to use them in 32-bit mode. So, unless you are switching addressing modes (by calling SwapMMUMode), you generally don't need to call StripAddress.

You might, however, need to call `StripAddress` in these special cases, even if you are not designing a driver:

- Making ordered address comparisons. If you want to sort an array by address or do any other kind of ordered address comparison (that is, using <, >, ≥, or ≤), you need to call `StripAddress` on each address before the comparison. Even though the CPU uses only the lower 3 bytes when it determines memory addresses in 24-bit mode, it uses all 32 bits when it performs arithmetic operations.
- Comparing master pointers. If you want to perform any type of comparison on master pointers (that is, on dereferenced handles), you must first call `StripAddress` on each address. The master pointer flag bits can change at any time, so you need to clear them before making the comparison. In general, you should call `StripAddress` when comparing any two pointers, if either of them might be a dereferenced handle.
- Accessing addresses in 32-bit mode. If you switch the computer to 32-bit mode manually, you need to call `StripAddress` on all 24-bit pointers and handles that you access while in 32-bit mode. Be careful, however, not to call `StripAddress` on a valid 32-bit address.
- Fixing the program counter. You might need to use `StripAddress` to fix the value of the program counter before you switch manually to 32-bit mode. See "Switching Addressing Modes" on page 4-20 for details.
- Overcoming Resource Manager limitations. To avoid a limitation in the Resource Manager's `OpenResFile` and `OpenRFPerm` routines, you should call `StripAddress` on pointers to the filenames that you pass to those functions, but only if the strings that represent the files are hard-coded into your application's code instead of in a separate resource. When the string is embedded in a code resource, the Resource Manager calls the `RecoverHandle` function with an invalid master pointer. Here is an example of the correct way to call `OpenResFile`:

```
fileName := 'This file';
myRef := OpenResFile(StringPtr(StripAddress(@fileName))^);
```

In virtually all other cases, you don't need to call `StripAddress` before using a valid 24-bit address. In particular, you don't need to call `StripAddress` before dereferencing a pointer or handle in 24-bit mode, unless you subsequently switch to 32-bit mode by calling `SwapMMUMode`. Also, you don't need to call `StripAddress` when checking pointers and handles for equality or when performing address arithmetic.

Because you need to call `StripAddress` rarely (if ever), the additional processing time required to call `StripAddress` shouldn't adversely affect the execution of your software. In some cases, however, you might want to avoid the overhead of calling the trap dispatcher every time you need to call `StripAddress`. (A good example might be a time-critical loop in an interrupt task.) You can use the `QuickStrip` function defined in Listing 4-8 in place of `StripAddress` when speed is a real concern.

Listing 4-8 Stripping addresses in time-critical code

```
FUNCTION QuickStrip (thePtr: Ptr): Ptr;
BEGIN
   QuickStrip := Ptr(BAND(LongInt(thePtr), gStripAddressMask));
END;
```

The `QuickStrip` function defined in Listing 4-8 simply masks the address it is passed with the same mask `StripAddress` uses. You can calculate that mask by executing the lines of code in Listing 4-9 early in the execution of your software:

Listing 4-9 Calculating the `StripAddress` mask

```
VAR
   gStripAddressMask:    LongInt;     {global mask variable}

   gStripAddressMask := $FFFFFFFF;
   gStripAddressMask :=
                  LongInt(StripAddress(Ptr(gStripAddressMask)));
```

Unless you are calling `StripAddress` repeatedly at interrupt time, you probably don't need to use this technique.

Translating Memory Addresses

As explained earlier in "Address Translation" on page 4-8, you sometimes need to override the Operating System's standard translation of 24-bit addresses into their 32-bit equivalents. This is necessary because the Virtual Memory Manager might have programmed the MMU to map unused NuBus slot addresses into the address space reserved for RAM. If you try to use a 24-bit address when the system switches to 32-bit mode, the standard translation might result in a 32-bit address that points to the space reserved for expansion cards. In that case, you are virtually guaranteed to obtain invalid results.

To prevent this problem, you can use the `Translate24To32` function to get the 32-bit equivalent of a 24-bit address. In general, you should test for the presence of the `_Translate24To32` trap before you use any 24-bit addresses in 32-bit mode. If it is available, you should use it in place of the static translation process performed automatically by the Operating System while running in 32-bit mode.

Note
You need to use the `Translate24To32` function only when the computer is running in 32-bit mode, it was booted in 24-bit mode, and you are communicating with external hardware. Most applications do not need to use it. ◆

Listing 4-10 illustrates how to use Translate24To32. The DoRoutine procedure defined there calls the application-defined routine MyRoutine to process a block of data while in 32-bit mode. It checks whether the _Translate24To32 trap is available, and if so, makes sure that the address to be read is a valid 32-bit address.

Listing 4-10 Translating 24-bit to 32-bit addresses

```
PROCEDURE DoRoutine (oldAddr: Ptr; length: LongInt);
BEGIN
   IF TrapAvailable(_Translate24To32) THEN
      MyRoutine(Translate24To32(oldAddr), length);
   ELSE
      MyRoutine(oldAddr, length);
END;
```

Note that you don't need to call StripAddress before calling Translate24To32, because the Translate24To32 function automatically ignores the high-order byte of the 24-bit address you pass it. (For a definition of the TrapAvailable function, see the chapter "Gestalt Manager" in *Inside Macintosh: Operating System Utilities.*)

Memory Management Utilities Reference

This section describes the memory management utilities provided by the Operating System.

Routines

This section describes the routines you use to set and restore the A5 register, change the addressing mode, manipulate memory addresses, and manipulate the processor caches.

Setting and Restoring the A5 Register

Any code that runs asynchronously or as a callback routine and that accesses the calling application's A5 world must ensure that the A5 register correctly points to the boundary between the application parameters and the application global variables. To accomplish this, you can call the SetCurrentA5 function at the beginning of any asynchronous or callback code that isn't executed at interrupt time. If the code is executed at interrupt time, you must use the SetA5 function to set the value of the A5 register. (You determine this value at noninterrupt time by calling SetCurrentA5.) Then you must restore the A5 register to its previous value before the interrupt code returns.

SetCurrentA5

You can use the `SetCurrentA5` function to get the current value of the system global variable `CurrentA5`.

```
FUNCTION SetCurrentA5: LongInt;
```

DESCRIPTION

The `SetCurrentA5` function does two things: First, it gets the current value in the A5 register and returns it to your application. Second, `SetCurrentA5` sets register A5 to the value of the low-memory global variable `CurrentA5`. This variable points to the boundary between the parameters and global variables of the current application.

SPECIAL CONSIDERATIONS

You cannot reliably call `SetCurrentA5` in code that is executed at interrupt time unless you first guarantee that your application is the current process (for example, by calling the Process Manager function `GetCurrentProcess`). In general, you should call `SetCurrentA5` at noninterrupt time and then pass the returned value to the interrupt code.

ASSEMBLY-LANGUAGE INFORMATION

You can access the value of the current application's A5 register with the low-memory global variable `CurrentA5`.

SetA5

In interrupt code that accesses application global variables, use the `SetA5` function first to restore a value previously saved using `SetCurrentA5`, and then, at the end of the code, to restore the A5 register to the value it had before the first call to `SetA5`.

```
FUNCTION SetA5 (newA5: LongInt): LongInt;
```

`newA5` The value to which the A5 register is to be changed.

DESCRIPTION

The `SetA5` function performs two tasks: it returns the address in the A5 register when the function is called, and it sets the A5 register to the address specified in `newA5`.

SEE ALSO

See "The A5 Register" on page 4-5 for a discussion of when you need to call `SetA5`.

Changing the Addressing Mode

If you wish to change address-translation modes manually, you can use the `GetMMUMode` function to find out which mode is currently in use and the `SwapMMUMode` procedure to swap modes.

Note
In general, you need to alter the CPU's addressing mode manually only if you are designing device drivers or other software that communicates with NuBus expansion cards. ◆

GetMMUMode

To find out which address-translation mode (24-bit or 32-bit) is currently in use, use the `GetMMUMode` function.

```
FUNCTION GetMMUMode: SignedByte;
```

DESCRIPTION

The `GetMMUMode` function returns the address-translation mode currently in use. On exit, `GetMMUMode` returns one of the following constants:

```
CONST
   false32b    = 0;              {24-bit addressing mode}
   true32b     = 1;              {32-bit addressing mode}
```

SPECIAL CONSIDERATIONS

To find out which addressing mode was in effect at system startup, use the `Gestalt` function.

ASSEMBLY-LANGUAGE INFORMATION

To determine the current address-translation mode, you can test the contents of the global variable `MMU32Bit`. The value `TRUE` indicates that 32-bit mode is in effect.

SwapMMUMode

To change the address-translation mode from 24-bit to 32- bit or vice versa, use the `SwapMMUMode` procedure.

```
PROCEDURE SwapMMUMode (VAR mode: SignedByte);
```

`mode` On entry, the desired address-translation mode. On exit, the address translation mode previously in use.

DESCRIPTION

The `SwapMMUMode` procedure sets the address-translation mode to the value specified by the `mode` parameter. The mode in use prior to the call is returned in `mode`, and you can restore the previous mode by calling `SwapMMUMode` again. The value of `mode` should be one of the following constants on entry and will be one of the following constants on exit:

```
CONST
   false32b    = 0;              {24-bit addressing mode}
   true32b     = 1;              {32-bit addressing mode}
```

SPECIAL CONSIDERATIONS

You might cause a system crash if you switch to 32-bit addressing mode when your application is executing a code resource you loaded into memory while 24-bit mode was in effect. See "Switching Addressing Modes" on page 4-20 for a description of how this problem arises and how you can avoid it.

ASSEMBLY-LANGUAGE INFORMATION

The registers on entry and exit for `SwapMMUMode` are

Registers on entry

D0 New mode

Registers on exit

D0 Previous mode

Manipulating Memory Addresses

Sometimes you need to modify a memory address before using it. You can strip off a master pointer's flag bits, if any, by calling the `StripAddress` function. You can map 24-bit addresses into the 32-bit address space by calling the `Translate24To32` function.

StripAddress

Use the `StripAddress` function to strip the flag bits from a 24-bit memory address.

```
FUNCTION StripAddress (address: UNIV Ptr): Ptr;
```

`address` The address to strip.

DESCRIPTION

The `StripAddress` function returns a pointer that references the same address passed in the `address` parameter, but in a form that is comprehensible to the 32-bit Memory Manager.

The effect of the `StripAddress` function depends on the startup mode of the Memory Manager, not on the current mode. Thus, if the Memory Manager started up in 32-bit mode, the address passed to `StripAddress` is unchanged (because it already must be a 32-bit address). If the Memory Manager started up in 24-bit mode, the function returns the low-order 3 bytes of the address. You should not pass valid 32-bit addresses to `StripAddress` if the Memory Manager started up in 24-bit mode.

ASSEMBLY-LANGUAGE INFORMATION

The registers on entry and exit for `StripAddress` are

Registers on entry

D0 The address to strip

Registers on exit

D0 The function result

Translate24To32

You can use the `Translate24To32` function to map 24-bit addresses into the 32-bit address space.

```
FUNCTION Translate24To32 (addr24: UNIV Ptr): Ptr;
```

`addr24` An address that is meaningful to the 24-bit Memory Manager.

DESCRIPTION

The `Translate24To32` function translates the address specified by the `addr24` parameter from 24-bit into 32-bit addressing mode and returns that address. If `addr24` is already a 32-bit address, the function returns it unchanged.

Unlike the `StripAddress` function, `Translate24To32` does not necessarily return an address that can be used in 24-bit mode. Also, you cannot meaningfully call `Translate24To32` on the result of a previous translation.

SPECIAL CONSIDERATIONS

You need to call `Translate24To32` only if you use 24-bit addresses while communicating with external hardware in 32-bit mode and virtual memory is enabled. See “Translating Memory Addresses” on page 4-23 for details.

ASSEMBLY-LANGUAGE INFORMATION

The registers on entry and exit for `Translate24To32` are

Registers on entry

D0 A 24-bit addressing mode address

Registers on exit

D0 The translated address

Manipulating the Processor Caches

The system software provides routines that allow you to enable, disable, and flush the processor caches. Before you call any of the routines described in this section, be sure to check that the trap `_HWPriv` is implemented. The only exception is the `FlushCodeCache` procedure, which is available whenever the processor has a cache that can be flushed.

▲ **WARNING**
If you call these routines and `_HWPriv` isn't implemented, your application will crash. ▲

SwapInstructionCache

You can use the `SwapInstructionCache` function to enable or disable the instruction cache.

```
FUNCTION SwapInstructionCache (cacheEnable: Boolean): Boolean;
```

`cacheEnable`
The desired state of the instruction cache.

DESCRIPTION

The `SwapInstructionCache` function enables or disables the instruction cache, depending on whether the `cacheEnable` parameter is set to `TRUE` or `FALSE`. On exit, `SwapInstructionCache` returns the previous state of the instruction cache.

ASSEMBLY-LANGUAGE INFORMATION

The trap macro and routine selector for `SwapInstructionCache` are

Trap macro	Selector
`_HWPriv`	$0000

FlushInstructionCache

You can use the `FlushInstructionCache` procedure to flush the instruction cache.

```
PROCEDURE FlushInstructionCache;
```

DESCRIPTION

The `FlushInstructionCache` procedure flushes the current contents of the instruction cache. Because flushing this cache degrades performance of the CPU, you should call this routine only when absolutely necessary. See "Stale Instructions" on page 4-9 for details on when to call this procedure.

ASSEMBLY-LANGUAGE INFORMATION

The trap macro and routine selector for `FlushInstructionCache` are

Trap macro	Selector
`_HWPriv`	$0001

SPECIAL CONSIDERATIONS

On processors with a copy-back data cache, `FlushInstructionCache` also flushes the data cache before it flushes the instruction cache, to ensure that any instructions subsequently copied to the instruction cache are not copied from stale RAM.

SwapDataCache

You can use the `SwapDataCache` function to enable or disable the data cache.

```
FUNCTION SwapDataCache (cacheEnable: Boolean): Boolean;
```

`cacheEnable`
: The desired state of the data cache.

DESCRIPTION

The `SwapDataCache` function enables or disables the data cache, depending on whether the `cacheEnable` parameter is set to `TRUE` or `FALSE`. On exit, `SwapDataCache` returns the previous state of the data cache.

ASSEMBLY-LANGUAGE INFORMATION

The trap macro and routine selector for `SwapDataCache` are

Trap macro	Selector
`_HWPriv`	$0002

FlushDataCache

You can use the `FlushDataCache` procedure to flush the data cache.

```
PROCEDURE FlushDataCache;
```

DESCRIPTION

The `FlushDataCache` procedure flushes the current contents of the data cache. Because flushing this cache degrades performance of the CPU, you should call this routine only when absolutely necessary. See "Processor Caches" beginning on page 4-8 for details on when to call this procedure.

ASSEMBLY-LANGUAGE INFORMATION

The trap macro and routine selector for `FlushDataCache` are

Trap macro	Selector
`_HWPriv`	$0003

FlushCodeCache

You can use the `FlushCodeCache` procedure to flush the instruction cache.

```
PROCEDURE FlushCodeCache;
```

DESCRIPTION

The `FlushCodeCache` procedure flushes the current contents of the instruction cache. Because flushing this cache degrades performance of the CPU, you should call this routine only when absolutely necessary. See "Processor Caches" beginning on page 4-8 for details on when to call this procedure.

SPECIAL CONSIDERATIONS

On processors with a copy-back data cache, `FlushCodeCache` also flushes the data cache before it flushes the instruction cache, to ensure that any instructions subsequently copied to the instruction cache are not copied from stale RAM.

ASSEMBLY-LANGUAGE INFORMATION

The trap macro for `FlushCodeCache` is `_CacheFlush`.

FlushCodeCacheRange

You can use the `FlushCodeCacheRange` function to flush a portion of the instruction cache.

```
FUNCTION FlushCodeCacheRange (address: UNIV Ptr; count: LongInt):
                              OSErr;
```

`address`	The starting address of the range to flush.
`count`	The size, in bytes, of the range to flush.

DESCRIPTION

The `FlushCodeCacheRange` function flushes the current contents of the instruction cache. `FlushCodeCacheRange` is an optimized version of `FlushCodeCache` and is intended for use on processors such as the MC68040 that support flushing only a portion of the instruction cache. On processors that do not have this capability, `FlushCodeCacheRange` simply flushes the entire instruction cache.

The `FlushCodeCacheRange` function might flush a larger portion of the instruction cache than requested if it would be inefficient to satisfy the request exactly.

ASSEMBLY-LANGUAGE INFORMATION

The trap macro and routine selector for `FlushCodeCacheRange` are

Trap macro	Selector
`_HWPriv`	$0009

The registers on entry and exit for `FlushCodeCacheRange` are

Registers on entry

A0	Starting address of the range to flush
A1	Number of bytes to flush
D0	Routine selector

Registers on exit

D0	Result code

RESULT CODES

`noErr`	0	No error
`hwParamErr`	–502	Processor does not support flushing a range

Summary of the Memory Management Utilities

Pascal Summary

Constants

```
CONST
   {Gestalt constants}
   gestaltAddressingModeAttr   = 'addr';    {addressing mode attributes}
   gestalt32BitAddressing      = 0;         {started in 32-bit mode}
   gestalt32BitSysZone         = 1;         {32-bit compatible sys. zone}
   gestalt32BitCapable         = 2;         {machine is 32-bit capable}

   {addressing mode constants}
   false32b                    = 0;         {24-bit addressing mode}
   true32b                     = 1;         {32-bit addressing mode}
```

Routines

Setting and Restoring the A5 Register

```
FUNCTION SetCurrentA5        : LongInt;
FUNCTION SetA5               (newA5: LongInt): LongInt;
```

Changing the Addressing Mode

```
FUNCTION GetMMUMode:         SignedByte;
PROCEDURE SwapMMUMode        (VAR mode: SignedByte);
```

Manipulating Memory Addresses

```
FUNCTION StripAddress        (address: UNIV Ptr): Ptr;
FUNCTION Translate24To32     (addr24: UNIV Ptr): Ptr;
```

Manipulating the Processor Caches

```
FUNCTION SwapInstructionCache(cacheEnable: Boolean): Boolean;
PROCEDURE FlushInstructionCache;
FUNCTION SwapDataCache       (cacheEnable: Boolean): Boolean;
```

```
PROCEDURE FlushDataCache;
PROCEDURE FlushCodeCache;
FUNCTION FlushCodeCacheRange (address: UNIV Ptr; count: LongInt): OSErr;
```

C Summary

Constants

```
/*Gestalt constants*/
#define gestaltAddressingModeAttr   'addr';  /*addressing mode attributes*/
#define gestalt32BitAddressing      0;       /*started in 32-bit mode*/
#define gestalt32BitSysZone         1;       /*32-bit compatible sys. zone*/
#define gestalt32BitCapable         2;       /*machine is 32-bit capable*/

/*addressing mode constants*/
enum  {false32b     =  0};                   /*24-bit addressing mode*/
enum  {true32b      =  1};                   /*32-bit addressing mode*/
```

Routines

Setting and Restoring the A5 Register

```
long SetCurrentA5           (void);
long SetA5                  (long newA5);
```

Changing the Addressing Mode

```
pascal char GetMMUMode      (void);
pascal void SwapMMUMode     (char *mode);
```

Manipulating Memory Addresses

```
pascal Ptr StripAddress     (Ptr address);
pascal Ptr Translate24To32  (Ptr addr24);
```

Manipulating the Processor Caches

```
pascal Boolean SwapInstructionCache
                             (Boolean cacheEnable);
pascal void FlushInstructionCache
                             (void);
```

```
pascal Boolean SwapDataCache (Boolean cacheEnable);
pascal void FlushDataCache   (void);
void FlushCodeCache          (void);
OSErr FlushCodeCacheRange    (void *address, unsigned long count);
```

Assembly-Language Summary

Trap Macros

Trap Macros Requiring Routine Selectors

_HWPriv

Selector	Routine
$0000	SwapInstructionCache
$0001	FlushInstructionCache
$0002	SwapDataCache
$0003	FlushDataCache
$0009	FlushCodeCacheRange

Global Variables

CurrentA5	long	Address of the boundary between the application global variables and the application parameters of the current application.
MMU32Bit	byte	TRUE if 32-bit addressing mode is in effect.

Result Codes

noErr	0	No error
hwParamErr	–502	Processor does not support flushing a range

Glossary

0-length handle A handle whose associated relocatable block has a logical size of 0 bytes.

24-bit addressing The addressing mode in which only the low-order 24 bits of a pointer or handle are used in determining memory addresses.

32-bit addressing The ability of the Operating System to use all 32 bits of a pointer or handle in determining memory addresses.

32-bit clean Said of an application that is able to run in an environment where all 32 bits of a memory address are used for addressing.

A5 world An area of memory in an application's partition that contains the QuickDraw global variables, the application global variables, the application parameters, and the jump table—all of which are accessed through the A5 register.

address A number that specifies the location of a byte in memory.

Address Management Unit (AMU) The Apple custom integrated circuit in Macintosh II computers that performs 24-bit to 32-bit address mapping.

address map The assignment of portions of the address space of a computer to specific devices.

address mapping See **address translation.**

address space A range of accessible memory. See also **address map.**

address translation The conversion of one set of addresses into another, corresponding set. For example, software designed for the original Macintosh computers uses only 24 bits for addresses, whereas the Macintosh II and later models have a 32-bit address bus. As a result, the Macintosh II and later models convert (or map) the 24-bit addresses used by the software into the 32-bit addresses used by the hardware.

allocate To assign an area of memory for use.

AMU See **Address Management Unit.**

application global variables A set of variables stored in the application's A5 world that are global to the application.

application heap An area of memory in the application heap zone in which memory is dynamically allocated and released on demand. The heap contains the application's `'CODE'` segment 1, data structures, resources, and other code segments as needed.

application heap zone The heap zone initially provided by the Memory Manager for use by an application and the Toolbox; initially equivalent to the application heap, but may be subdivided into two or more independent heap zones.

application parameters Thirty-two bytes of memory in the application partition that are reserved for system use. The first long word is the address of the first QuickDraw global variable.

application partition A partition of memory reserved for use by an application. The application partition consists of free space along with the application's heap, stack, and A5 world.

application space Memory that's reserved for dynamic allocation by applications.

asynchronous execution A mode of invoking a routine. During the asynchronous execution of a routine, an application is free to perform other tasks.

backing-store file The file in which the Virtual Memory Manager stores the contents of unneeded pages of memory.

backing volume See **paging device.**

block See **memory block.**

block contents The area that's available for use in a memory block.

block header The internal housekeeping information maintained by the Memory Manager at the beginning of each block in a heap zone.

cache See **data cache, disk cache,** or **instruction cache.**

callback routine A routine that is executed as part of the operation of some other routine.

compact See **heap compaction.**

completion routine A routine that is executed when an asynchronous call to some other routine is completed.

concurrent driver A driver that can handle several requests at once.

copy-back cache A cache whose data is written to RAM only when necessary to make room in the cache for data accessed more recently or when the cache is explicitly flushed. See also **write-through cache.**

current heap zone The heap zone currently under attention, to which most Memory Manager operations implicitly apply.

cushion See **memory cushion.**

dangling pointer A copy of a master pointer that no longer points to the correct memory address.

data cache An area of memory internal to some microprocessors (for example, the MC68030 and MC68040 microprocessors) that holds recently accessed data. See also **instruction cache.**

dereference To refer to a block by its master pointer instead of its handle.

direct memory access (DMA) A technique for transferring data in or out of memory without using the CPU.

disk cache A part of RAM that acts as an intermediate buffer when data is read from and written to file systems on secondary storage devices.

disposed handle A handle whose associated relocatable block has been disposed of.

DMA See **direct memory access.**

double indirection The means by which the Memory Manager or an application accesses the data associated with a handle variable.

double page fault A page fault that occurs while the Virtual Memory Manager is handling another page fault. See also **page fault.**

empty handle A handle whose master pointer has the value `NIL` (possibly indicating that the underlying relocatable block has been purged).

fake handle A handle that was not created by the Memory Manager.

flush (1) To write data from a cache in memory to a volume. (2) To write data or instructions from a cache in the microprocessor to RAM.

fragmentation See **heap fragmentation.**

free block A memory block containing space available for allocation.

GB Abbreviation for gigabyte. A gigabyte is 1024 megabytes, or 1,073,741,824 bytes.

global variables See **application global variables, system global variables,** and **QuickDraw global variables.**

grow-zone function A function supplied by the application program to help the Memory Manager create free space within a heap.

handle A variable containing the address of a master pointer, used to access a relocatable block. See also **pointer.**

heap An area of memory in which space is dynamically allocated and released on demand, using the Memory Manager. See also **application heap.**

heap compaction The process of moving allocated blocks within a heap to collect the free space into a single block.

heap fragmentation The state of a heap when the available free space is scattered throughout the heap in numerous unused blocks.

heap zone An area of memory initialized by the Memory Manager for heap allocation. A heap zone consists of a **zone header,** a **heap,** and a **zone trailer.**

hold To temporarily prevent a range of physical memory from being paged out by the Virtual Memory Manager.

instruction cache An area of memory internal to some microprocessors (for example, the MC68020, MC68030, and MC68040 microprocessors) that holds recently used instructions. See also **data cache.**

jump table An area of memory in an application's A5 world that contains one entry for every externally referenced routine in every code segment of the application. The jump table is the means by which the loading and unloading of segments is implemented.

KB Abbreviation for kilobyte. A kilobyte is 1024 bytes.

lock (1) To temporarily prevent a relocatable block from being moved during heap compaction. (2) To temporarily prevent a range of physical memory from being paged out or moved by the Virtual Memory Manager.

logical address An address used by software. The logical address might be translated into a physical address by the memory management unit.

logical size The number of bytes in a memory block's contents.

low-memory system global variables See **system global variables.**

master pointer A pointer to a relocatable block, maintained by the Memory Manager and updated whenever the block is moved, purged, or reallocated. All handles to a relocatable block refer to it by double indirection through the master pointer.

master pointer block A nonrelocatable block of memory that contains master pointers. A master pointer block in your application heap contains 64 master pointers, and a master pointer block in the system heap contains 32 master pointers.

master pointer flag bits The high-order 8 bits of a master pointer. In 24-bit addressing mode, some of these bits are used to store information about the relocatable block referenced by the master pointer.

MB Abbreviation for megabyte. A megabyte is 1024 kilobytes, or 1,048,576 bytes.

memory block An area of contiguous memory within a heap.

memory-block record A data structure used by the translation parameter block to indicate the starting address and length of a given block of memory. This parameter block is defined by the `MemoryBlock` data type.

memory cushion An application-defined threshold below which the application should refuse to honor any requests to allocate memory for nonessential operations.

memory management unit (MMU) Any component that performs address mapping in a Macintosh computer. In Macintosh II computers, it is either the Address Management Unit (AMU) or the Paged Memory Management Unit (PMMU). The MMU function is built into the MC68030 and MC68040 microprocessors.

Memory Manager The part of the Operating System that dynamically allocates and releases memory space in the heap.

memory map See **address map.**

memory reservation The process of creating a free space at the bottom of the heap for a newly allocated block by moving unlocked relocatable blocks upward.

memory reserve An allocated block of memory in the application heap that is held in reserve and released only for essential operations when memory in the heap is low.

MMU See **memory management unit.**

nonrelocatable block A block whose location in the heap is fixed. This block can't be moved during heap compaction or other memory operations.

NuBus The 32-bit wide synchronous bus used for expansion cards in the Macintosh II family of computers.

NuBus expansion slot A connector attached to the NuBus in a Macintosh II computer, into which an expansion card can be installed.

original application heap zone See **application heap zone.**

page The basic unit of memory used in virtual memory.

Paged Memory Management Unit (PMMU) The Motorola MC68851 chip, used in the Macintosh II computer to perform logical-to-physical address translation and paged memory management.

page fault A special kind of bus error caused by an attempt to access data in a page of memory that is not currently resident in RAM. See also **double page fault.**

paging The process of moving data between physical memory and the backing-store file.

paging device The volume that contains the backing-store file.

partition A contiguous block of memory reserved for use by the Operating System or by an application. See also **application partition** and **system partition.**

physical address An address represented by bits on a physical address bus. The physical address may be different from the logical address, in which case the memory management unit translates the logical address into a physical address.

physical size The actual number of bytes a memory block occupies in its heap zone, including the block header and any unused bytes at the end of the block.

PMMU See **Paged Memory Management Unit.**

pointer A variable containing the address of a byte in memory. See also **handle.**

processor cache See **data cache** or **instruction cache.**

program counter A register in the CPU that contains a pointer to the memory location of the next instruction to be executed.

protected block A block of memory that should not be moved or purged by a grow-zone function.

purge To remove a relocatable block from the heap, leaving its master pointer allocated but set to `NIL`.

purgeable block A relocatable block that can be purged from the heap.

purge-warning procedure A procedure associated with a particular heap zone. The Memory Manager calls this procedure whenever a block is about to be purged from the zone.

QuickDraw global variables A set of variables stored in the application's A5 world that contain information used by QuickDraw.

RAM See **random-access memory.**

RAM disk A portion of the available RAM reserved for use as a temporary storage device. A user can configure a RAM disk or disable it altogether using controls in the Memory control panel.

random-access memory (RAM) Memory whose contents can be changed. The RAM in a Macintosh computer contains exception vectors, buffers used by hardware devices, the system and application heaps, the stack, and other information used by applications.

read-only memory (ROM) Memory whose contents are permanent. The ROM in a Macintosh computer contains routines for the Toolbox and the Operating System, and the various system traps.

reallocate To allocate new space in the heap for a purged block and to update the block's master pointer to point to its new location.

reentrant driver A driver that can be interrupted while servicing a request, service the new request, and then complete the original request.

relative handle A pointer to a block's master pointer, expressed as an offset relative to the start of the heap zone rather than as an absolute memory address. A block's relative handle is contained in its block header.

release (1) To free an allocated area of memory, making it available for reuse. (2) To allow a previously held range of pages to be movable in physical memory.

relocatable block A block that can be moved within the heap during compaction.

reservation See **memory reservation.**

reserve See **memory reserve.**

ROM See **read-only memory.**

size correction The number of unused bytes at the end of the block, beyond the end of the block's contents.

stack An area of memory in the application partition that is used to store temporary variables.

stack frame The area of the stack used by a routine for its parameters, return address, local variables, and temporary storage.

stale data Data in the microprocessor's data cache whose corresponding value in RAM has changed. You might need to flush the data cache to avoid using stale data.

stale instructions Instructions in the microprocessor's instruction cache whose corresponding value in RAM has changed. You might need to flush the instruction cache to avoid using stale instructions.

strip an address To clear the high-order byte of a 24-bit address, making it usable in 32-bit mode.

synchronous execution A mode of invoking a routine. After calling a routine synchronously, an application cannot perform other tasks until the routine is completed.

system global variables A collection of global variables stored in the system partition.

system heap An area of memory in the system partition reserved for use by the Operating System.

system heap zone The heap zone provided by the Memory Manager for use by the Operating System; equivalent to the system heap.

system partition A partition of memory reserved for use by the Operating System.

tag byte The first byte of a block header.

temporary memory Memory allocated outside an application partition that may be available for occasional short-term use.

translation table A data structure used by the `GetPhysical` function to indicate which physical blocks correspond to a given logical block. This parameter block is defined by the `LogicalToPhysicalTable` data type.

unlock (1) To allow a relocatable block to be moved during heap compaction. (2) To allow a previously locked range of pages to be paged out.

unpurgeable block A relocatable block that can't be purged from the heap.

virtual memory Addressable memory beyond the limits of the available physical RAM. The Operating System extends the logical address space by allowing unused applications and data to be stored on a secondary storage device instead of in physical RAM.

Virtual Memory Manager The part of the Operating System that provides virtual memory.

write-through cache A cache whose information is immediately written to RAM whenever that information changes. See also **copy-back cache.**

zero-length handle See **0-length handle.**

zone header An area of memory at the beginning of a heap zone that contains essential information about the heap, such as the number of bytes free in the heap and the addresses of the heap's grow-zone function and purge-warning procedure.

zone pointer A pointer to a zone record.

zone record A data structure representing a heap zone.

zone trailer A minimum-sized free block marking the end of a heap zone.

Index

Symbols

Numerals

A

B

C

D

E

F

G

H

I

J, K

L

M

N

O

P

Q

R

S

T

U

V

W, X, Y

Z

This Apple manual was written, edited, and composed on a desktop publishing system using Apple Macintosh computers and FrameMaker software. Proof pages were created on an Apple LaserWriter IINTX printer. Final page negatives were output directly from text files on an Agfa ProSet 9800 imagesetter. Line art was created using Adobe™ Illustrator. PostScript™, the page-description language for the LaserWriter, was developed by Adobe Systems Incorporated.

Text type is Palatino® and display type is Helvetica®. Bullets are ITC Zapf Dingbats®. Some elements, such as program listings, are set in Apple Courier.

LEAD WRITER
Tim Monroe

WRITERS
Tim Monroe, Michael Abramowicz

DEVELOPMENTAL EDITOR
Antonio Padial

ILLUSTRATOR
Peggy Kunz

PRODUCTION EDITOR
Teresa Lujan

PROJECT MANAGER
Patricia Eastman

COVER DESIGNER
Barbara Smyth

Special thanks to Eric Anderson, Jeff Crawford, and Brian McGhie.

Acknowledgments to Sanborn Hodgkins, Craig Prouse, Jim Reekes, Keith Rollin, and the entire *Inside Macintosh* team.

Inside Macintosh

Overview
A general introduction to *Inside Macintosh* and to programming for Macintosh computers. Describes the look and feel of Macintosh applications and describes how to implement that interface.

Imaging
How to create images, display them in black-and-white or color, and print them. Includes descriptions of QuickDraw, its associated graphics managers, and the Printing Manager.

Files
The parts of the Operating System that allow you to manage files. Shows how to handle File menu commands and perform other file-related operations.

Processes
The parts of the Operating System that allow you to control processes and tasks. Shows how to launch processes and to install interrupt-level tasks (such asTime Manager tasks and VBL tasks).

Macintosh Toolbox Essentials
How to create and manage
- menus
- windows
- dialog boxes
- alert boxes
- controls

Also, how your application interacts with the Finder.

Text
How to draw characters and lines of text in any font, size, and style. How to write applications that can format, sort, search, display, print, and accept input of text in any language supported by the Macintosh.

Memory
The parts of the Operating System that allow you to allocate, release, and otherwise manipulate memory. Shows how to use temporary memory and interact with virtual memory.

More Macintosh Toolbox
More about the Macintosh Toolbox, including how to
- provide support for copy and paste
- provide help balloons
- play and record sounds
- use resources

Operating System Utilities
The parts of the Operating System that perform various low-level utility operations. Includes descriptions of the Gestalt Manager, Queue Utilities, Date and Time Utilities, and others.

Guide to Software Localization*

Macintosh Human Interface Guidelines*

QuickTime
How to integrate time-based data (such as video and sounds) into your application and compress and decompress image sequences. Includes the Movie Toolbox and the Image Compression Manager.

Interapplication Communication
How applications can work together. How your application can
- share data
- request information or services
- allow the user to automate tasks

Devices
How to write a device driver, plus
- Device Manager
- Apple Desktop Bus
- Disk Driver
- Power Manager
- SCSI Manager
- Serial Driver
- Slot Manager

QuickTime Components
How to use and develop QuickTime components, such as image compressors, movie controllers, sequence grabbers, and video digitizers.

Designing Cards and Drivers for the Macintosh Family*

Networking
The components and organization of AppleTalk. How to select an AppleTalk protocol. Application interfaces to all AppleTalk protocols and to the LAP Manager.

Inside AppleTalk*

Communications
How to write powerful applications that communicate with remote databases. How to use the Communications Toolbox to write protocol-independent communications software and modular communications tools.

Key

Books that every Macintosh programmer needs.

Books that Macintosh programmers need for specialized tasks.

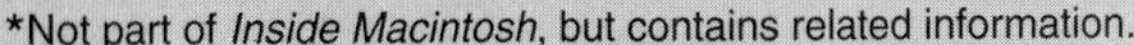

*Not part of *Inside Macintosh*, but contains related information.